Gemini: The Complete Guide

The Comprehensive Guide to Google's AI Assistant

Ken Tannenbaum

2026

Finnoybu Press

Gemini: The Complete Guide

2026 Edition

The Comprehensive Guide to Google's AI Assistant

Published by Finnoybu Press

For permissions and inquiries: press@finnoybu.org

First Edition: 2026

About the Author

Ken Tannenbaum is a technologist, entrepreneur, and AI governance researcher. He is the founder of Finnoybu Press and the founder/steward of the AEGIS Initiative, an open framework for AI safety and accountability. Learn more at aegis-initiative.com.

When he's not building governance standards for artificial intelligence, he's helping everyday people understand and use it.

Dedication

For Irene. She asked Google how to get her husband to stop talking about AI, and it suggested buying him a book deal. So technically, this is her fault. Every good thing starts and ends with her.

And for everyone who opened Gemini and thought, *"Wait, Google made something this good?"* — you're not wrong to be surprised. This book shows you how deep it goes.

The AI for Everyone Series

This book is part of the **AI for Everyone** series by Finnoybu Press, designed to help real people use AI tools effectively. Visit **press.finnoybu.org** for the latest titles and updates.

Collection One: Product Deep Dives

- *ChatGPT: The Definitive Guide (2026 Edition)*
- *ChatGPT: The Power User Guide (2026 Edition)*
- *Claude: The Definitive Guide (2026 Edition)*
- *Claude Code: The Power User Guide (2026 Edition)*
- *Gemini: The Complete Guide (2026 Edition)*
- *Gemini: The Advanced Guide (2026 Edition)*
- *Copilot: The Workplace AI Guide (2026 Edition)*
- *Copilot: The Advanced Workplace Guide (2026 Edition)*
- *Perplexity: The Research Playbook (2026 Edition)*
- *Perplexity: The Advanced Research Playbook (2026 Edition)*

Collection Two: Product Guides

- *NotebookLM: From Sources to Audio Overviews (2026 Edition)*
- *DeepSeek: Code, Math, and Reasoning (2026 Edition)*
- *Cursor: The AI Code Editor (2026 Edition)*
- *OpenClaw: Agentic AI for Everyday Work (2026 Edition)*

Collection Three: Cross-Platform Skills

- *AI Systems Playbook (2026 Edition)*
- *AI Prompt Engineering (2026 Edition)*
- *AI for Developers (2026 Edition)*
- *AI for Business (2026 Edition)*
- *AI for Students (2026 Edition)*
- *AI Governance for Practitioners (2026 Edition)*
- *Securing Agentic AI (2026 Edition)*

Table of Contents

Introduction 11

Part I: Getting Started 15

Chapter 1: What Is Gemini? 17

Chapter 2: Choosing the Right Plan 25

Chapter 3: Setting Up Your Account 35

Chapter 4: Understanding Gemini's Models 43

Chapter 5: Your First Conversations 51

Part II: Core Skills 61

Chapter 6: Writing with Gemini 63

Chapter 7: Research and Learning 73

Chapter 8: Everyday Productivity 85

Chapter 9: Work and Professional Use 95

Part III: Creative and Multimodal Tools 107

Chapter 10: Google Search Integration 109

Chapter 11: Image Understanding and Generation 117

Chapter 12: Video and Audio Understanding 127

Part IV: Power Features 137

Chapter 13: Gemini in Google Workspace 139

Chapter 14: Gems — Custom Gemini Assistants 147

Chapter 15: Extensions and Integrations 155

Chapter 16: Canvas — Collaborative Content Creation 163

Chapter 17: NotebookLM and Deep Research 171

Part V: Getting Better Results 181

Chapter 18: Prompting Fundamentals 183

Chapter 19: Working with Long and Complex Tasks 193

Chapter 20: Output Formatting and Control 203

Part VI: Gemini for Your World 213

Chapter 21: Gemini for Students and Educators 215

Chapter 22: Gemini for Business and Teams 225

Chapter 23: Gemini for Developers 235

Chapter 24: Gemini for Creators and Freelancers 247

Part VII: Safety, Ethics, and Limitations 257

Chapter 25: What Gemini Gets Wrong 259

Chapter 26: Privacy, Security, and Safe Use 269

Chapter 27: The Ethics of AI Assistance 279

Epilogue 289

Part VIII: Reference 291

Appendix A: Keyboard Shortcuts and Interface Tips 293

Appendix B: Prompt Template Library 301

Appendix C: Troubleshooting Common Issues 325

Appendix D: Glossary of AI Terms 335

Appendix E: What's New in 2025–2026 343

Appendix F: Resources and Further Reading 353

Introduction

If you have ever searched the internet, you already know Google. The company behind the world's most-used search engine, Gmail, YouTube, Android, and Chrome has been quietly — and sometimes loudly — building some of the most advanced artificial intelligence on the planet. Gemini is the result: Google's flagship AI assistant, and the subject of this book.

Gemini is not just another chatbot. It is a natively multimodal AI that reads, writes, sees, hears, and reasons across text, images, audio, and video. It is deeply integrated into the Google ecosystem you may already use every day — Gmail, Docs, Sheets, Slides, Maps, YouTube, and more. And it sits on top of one of the most powerful model families in the industry, with a context window large enough to process entire books in a single conversation.

This book is a complete guide to Gemini. If you have never used an AI assistant before, you will find everything you need to get started — from creating an account to writing your first prompts. If you already use Gemini casually and want to get more out of it, the later chapters take you deeper into Gems, Canvas, Deep Research, NotebookLM, Google Workspace integration, and the prompting techniques that separate casual users from power users. And if you are evaluating Gemini for your team or business, you will find honest comparisons, deployment guidance, and practical advice on privacy, data governance, and adoption.

This is the fifth book in the Finnoybu Press AI Guide Series. The first four cover ChatGPT and Claude — two for getting started, two for advanced use. If you have read those, you will find the same practical, no-nonsense approach here. If you have not, this book stands entirely on its own. You do not need any prior experience with AI assistants, Google products or otherwise, to follow along. A companion volume, *Gemini: The Advanced Guide*, covers advanced techniques and workflows for readers who want to go further.

The book is organized as a deliberate progression. Part I (Chapters 1 through 5) covers the fundamentals: what Gemini is, how to choose a plan, how to set up your account, how to understand the different models, and how to have your first conversations. Part II (Chapters 6 through 9) is the hands-on core: writing, research, everyday productivity, and professional use. Part III (Chapters 10 through 12) explores Gemini's multimodal and creative capabilities: Google Search integration, image understanding and generation, and video and audio. Part IV (Chapters 13 through 17) covers the power features: Google Workspace, Gems, Extensions, Canvas, NotebookLM, and Deep Research. Part V (Chapters 18 through 20) goes deeper into prompting. Part VI (Chapters 21 through 24) addresses specific audiences: students, businesses, developers, and creators. Part VII (Chapters 25 through 27) covers the hard truths: what Gemini gets wrong, privacy and security, and the ethical questions that matter. Each chapter builds on what came before, but most also work well if you skip ahead to a topic that interests you.

One more thing worth saying transparently: this book was written with the assistance of AI tools, including Gemini itself. The author used AI throughout the writing process — for drafting, research, editing, and refining arguments. This is not a secret and it is not a contradiction. A book about an AI tool should demonstrate confidence in that tool. Every word was reviewed, revised, and approved by a human author who takes responsibility for the final product. Where AI helped, it helped well. Where it needed correction, it was corrected. That is exactly how these tools are meant to be used.

Whether you are here because you are curious, because your job demands it, or because you tried Gemini once and want to understand it fully — welcome. You picked a good time to learn, and you picked the right book.

A Note About Accuracy

Gemini changes constantly. Google ships updates regularly, sometimes weekly. Features get added, interfaces get redesigned, models get upgraded. This book is accurate as of May 2026, but specific details — menu locations, exact pricing, feature availability — may have shifted by the time you read this.

The principles, techniques, and strategies in this book have a longer shelf life than the interface details. How to write effective prompts, work across modalities, and orchestrate Gemini with the Google ecosystem — those skills transfer across versions and even across different AI tools.

When something looks different from what's described here, check Google's help center at support.google.com/gemini for the latest.

Let's get started.

Part I: Getting Started

"The only way to do great work is to love what you do."

— Steve Jobs

Chapter 1: What Is Gemini?

If you have used Google Search even once, you already know the company that built Gemini. Google — the search engine that became a verb, the company behind Gmail, YouTube, Android, and Chrome — is also one of the most ambitious artificial intelligence labs on the planet. Gemini is its flagship AI assistant, and the reason you picked up this book.

But what exactly is Gemini? What does it do? And why should you care?

This chapter answers those questions. By the end, you will understand what Gemini is, where it came from, what sets it apart from the competition, and whether it deserves a place in your daily life. Spoiler: it probably does.

What Gemini Is (and Isn't)

Gemini is an AI assistant made by Google. You type or speak a question, and Gemini responds. That sounds simple — and using it is simple — but underneath sits one of the most powerful artificial intelligence systems ever built.

You can ask Gemini to explain quantum physics in plain English, draft a resignation letter, summarize a 45-minute YouTube video, analyze a photo of your leaking faucet and tell you how to fix it, plan a two-week trip to Japan, write Python code, translate a paragraph into French, or generate an image of a golden retriever wearing a space suit. It handles all of these tasks and thousands more.

What Gemini is not: it is not a search engine, though it can search Google on your behalf. It is not a human, though its conversational tone can feel remarkably natural. It is not infallible — it makes mistakes, sometimes confidently. And it is not reading your mind — the better your question, the better its answer.

Think of Gemini as a knowledgeable, fast assistant that can read, write, see, hear, and reason across an enormous range of topics. It does not get tired, it does not judge your questions, and it is available twenty-four hours a day.

Google: The Company Behind Gemini

To understand Gemini, it helps to understand who built it. Google has been investing in artificial intelligence for over a decade. In 2014, the company acquired DeepMind, a London-based AI research lab that later made headlines by building AlphaGo, the first AI system to defeat a world champion at the board game Go. Separately, Google ran its own AI research division called Google Brain, responsible for breakthroughs in machine translation, image recognition, and the foundational "transformer" architecture that powers virtually every modern AI chatbot — including Gemini, ChatGPT, and Claude.

In 2023, Google merged DeepMind and Google Brain into a single entity called Google DeepMind. That combined team built the Gemini models. When you use Gemini, you are benefiting from over a decade of AI research by some of the most accomplished scientists in the field.

It also means Gemini has something no competitor can match: the entire Google ecosystem behind it. Google Search, Google Maps, Gmail, Google Docs, YouTube, Google Flights, Android — Gemini taps into all of these. That integration is not a gimmick. It is one of the most compelling reasons to choose Gemini over the alternatives.

A Brief History: From Bard to Gemini

Gemini did not arrive fully formed. Its story has a few chapters of its own.

Bard (March 2023). When ChatGPT exploded onto the scene in late 2022, Google scrambled to respond. The result was Bard, a conversational AI assistant launched in March 2023. Bard was functional but unpolished. It ran on Google's PaLM language model and was widely seen as playing catch-up to ChatGPT. Early reviews were mixed, and a factual error in Bard's first public demo famously wiped over $100 billion from Google's stock price in a single day.

Gemini 1.0 (December 2023). Google needed something better — and delivered it. In December 2023, Google announced Gemini 1.0, a new family of AI models built from the ground up by Google DeepMind. Unlike Bard's underlying PaLM model, Gemini was designed from scratch to be "natively multimodal" — understanding text, images, audio, and video as a unified system rather than bolting those capabilities on as afterthoughts.

The Rebrand (February 2024). In February 2024, Google retired the Bard name entirely and rebranded its AI assistant as Gemini. The chat interface at bard.google.com became gemini.google.com. The message was clear: this was not Bard with a new coat of paint. It was a different product on different technology.

Gemini 1.5 (2024). The 1.5 generation brought a headline feature: a context window of up to one million tokens. In plain English, that means Gemini could process roughly 700,000 words — an entire novel, or hours of video — in a single conversation. No other publicly available AI assistant came close at the time.

Gemini 2.0 (December 2024 – Early 2025). The 2.0 generation pushed performance further, with Gemini 2.0 Flash offering a fast, capable model for everyday tasks. Improvements spanned reasoning, coding, multimodal understanding, and tool use.

Gemini 2.5 (2025). Gemini 2.5 Pro introduced Deep Think — also called "thinking mode" or extended reasoning — the ability to reason step by step through complex problems before producing an answer. Gemini 2.5 Flash brought those improvements to a faster, more efficient model.

Gemini 3 (Late 2025 – 2026). The current generation. Gemini 3 Pro launched on November 18, 2025, as Google's flagship reasoning model, followed by Gemini 3 Flash in December 2025 (which became the new default in the Gemini app). A dedicated Gemini 3 Deep Think mode shipped in February 2026, alongside a 3.1 Pro preview, and Gemini 3.1 Flash-Lite arrived March 3, 2026. Gemini 3 Pro retains the 1M+ token context window and improves on 2.5 across reasoning, coding, multimodal understanding, and tool use.

The pace has been remarkable. The Gemini you use today is dramatically more capable than the Bard of early 2023, and it will keep evolving quickly.

What Makes Gemini Different

Every major tech company now has an AI assistant. OpenAI has ChatGPT. Anthropic has Claude. Microsoft has Copilot. Apple has Apple Intelligence. So why would you choose Gemini?

Gemini has four key differentiators.

Native Multimodality

Most AI assistants started as text-only systems and added image, audio, and video capabilities later. Gemini was built from the ground up to work across all of these modalities natively. You can upload a photo and ask Gemini to describe what it sees. Paste a link to a YouTube video and ask for a summary. Upload an audio file and ask for a transcription. Upload a video clip and ask detailed questions about what happens in specific scenes.

This is not just a feature checkbox. Gemini's multimodal understanding — especially long video — is ahead of the competition as of May 2026.

Google Search Grounding

When Gemini does not know something — or when you ask about recent events — it can reach out to Google Search in real time and ground its response in current, cited sources. You will see clickable links to the pages it consulted, so you can verify the information yourself.

Other assistants have web browsing, but Gemini's integration with Google Search is seamless. It is, after all, the same company.

Massive Context Windows

Gemini's context window — the amount of information it can hold in its "working memory" during a conversation — is enormous. Gemini 3 Pro supports over one million tokens, roughly 700,000 words. You can upload entire documents, codebases, or transcripts and ask questions about them without worrying about the assistant losing track of earlier material.

Deep Google Ecosystem Integration

This is the big one. If you already use Gmail, Google Docs, Google Sheets, Google Calendar, Google Maps, YouTube, or Android, Gemini fits into your life in a way no competitor can. Gemini drafts emails in Gmail, creates documents in Google Docs, analyzes data in Google Sheets, generates presentations in Google Slides, summarizes meetings in Google Meet, searches across your Google Drive, gives you directions via Google Maps, and finds flights via Google Flights — from within the Gemini interface or directly inside those apps.

If Google's products are already part of your workflow, Gemini is not just another AI tool. It is the AI tool that speaks your ecosystem's language.

How Gemini Compares to the Competition

You have probably heard of ChatGPT, Claude, and Microsoft Copilot. Here is a quick, honest comparison.

ChatGPT (by OpenAI) is the AI assistant that started the revolution. It has the largest user base, a strong brand, and a mature ecosystem of plugins and custom bots. ChatGPT's writing tends to be polished and versatile, and its image generation (via DALL-E) is well-regarded. If you do not use Google's ecosystem heavily, ChatGPT is a formidable alternative.

Claude (by Anthropic) is known for nuanced, thoughtful writing and careful reasoning. Many users find Claude's prose more natural and less formulaic than its competitors. Claude also has a reputation for being more cautious about safety. If your primary use case is writing or analysis, Claude is worth considering.

Microsoft Copilot is Microsoft's AI assistant, integrated into Windows, Office 365, Bing, and Edge. If your life revolves around Outlook, Word, Excel, and Teams, Copilot plays the same role for Microsoft that Gemini plays for Google.

A note on **Apple Intelligence**: you may see it mentioned alongside these tools, but it is a different kind of product. Apple Intelligence is an on-device feature suite built into iPhones, iPads, and Macs — it summarizes notifications, generates text suggestions, and creates images locally on your device. It is not a standalone conversational AI assistant the way Gemini, ChatGPT, and Claude are. You cannot sit down and have an extended conversation with it or ask it to research a topic. Think of it as a set of smart features woven into Apple's operating systems rather than a direct competitor.

Where Gemini wins: Google ecosystem integration, multimodal understanding (especially video), Google Search grounding, context window size, and value for users already paying for Google One.

Where Gemini falls short: Gemini's writing, while good, has historically been less nuanced than Claude's and sometimes less polished than ChatGPT's. Gemini requires a Google account, which means handing more data to a company that already knows a great deal about you. And Gemini's image generation, while capable via Imagen 4, has had well-publicized stumbles around bias and accuracy.

The honest truth: all of these assistants are remarkably capable in 2026, and the gaps between them are smaller than a year ago. The best assistant for you is the one that fits your workflow, and for the hundreds of millions of people who live inside Google's ecosystem, that assistant is Gemini.

What Gemini Is Good At (and What It Struggles With)

No AI assistant is perfect at everything. Here is where Gemini shines and where you should be cautious.

Gemini excels at:

- Answering questions with up-to-date information (thanks to Google Search grounding)
- Summarizing long content — documents, articles, videos, podcasts
- Multimodal tasks — analyzing images, understanding video, processing audio
- Google Workspace tasks — drafting emails, building spreadsheets, creating presentations
- Research — especially with the Deep Research feature that performs multi-step web research
- Planning — trips, events, schedules, meal plans
- Coding — generating, explaining, and debugging code across many languages

Gemini struggles with:

- Creative writing that requires a distinctive voice or deep emotional nuance
- Tasks where there is no room for error (always verify critical facts)
- Specialized professional advice (legal, medical, financial — use Gemini as a starting point, not a final authority)
- Complex multi-step reasoning on certain edge cases (though the 2.5 generation's Deep Think has helped here)

- Image generation involving specific real people or politically sensitive subjects

The takeaway: Gemini is a powerful general-purpose assistant, but it works best when you treat it as a collaborator rather than an oracle. Trust but verify. We will return to this throughout the book.

The Gemini Ecosystem

Gemini is not a single product. It is a family of products and integration points.

gemini.google.com — The main web interface. Most people start here. Open a browser, sign in with your Google account, and start chatting.

Gemini for Android — On Android phones and tablets, Gemini can replace Google Assistant as your default AI helper. Ask by voice, get help with on-screen content, and reach Gemini from anywhere on your device.

Gemini for iOS — A dedicated app for iPhone and iPad brings the same conversational experience to Apple devices.

Gemini in Google Workspace — If your organization uses Google Workspace, Gemini appears as a sidebar assistant inside Gmail, Docs, Sheets, Slides, and Meet. This is where the deep integration pays off.

Gemini in Chrome — Google's browser includes Gemini integration points for summarizing pages, answering questions about on-screen content, and more.

NotebookLM — A separate but related product that lets you upload documents and have AI-powered conversations about them, complete with audio overviews that sound like a podcast. We cover NotebookLM in Chapter 17.

Google AI Studio and the Gemini API — For developers, Google provides direct access to Gemini's models through APIs. If you build software, you can integrate Gemini into your own applications. We cover this in Chapter 23.

What to Expect from This Book

This book takes you from complete beginner to confident, productive Gemini user. The next few chapters get you set up with an account, walk you through the interface, and have your first real conversations with Gemini. From there, we explore every major feature in depth — writing, research, images, video, Google Workspace integration, Gems, Canvas, NotebookLM, Deep Research, and more.

Along the way, we are honest about what works, what does not, and how to get the best results. You will find practical walkthroughs, real prompt examples, and decision frameworks for when to use Gemini and when to reach for a different tool.

Whether you are a student, a professional, a creative, a developer, or simply someone who wants to understand what the AI fuss is about, this book will meet you where you are.

Let's get started. In Chapter 2, we help you choose the right Gemini plan for your needs and budget.

Chapter 2: Choosing the Right Plan

Before you type your first message to Gemini, you need to make a decision: how much are you willing to pay? The answer might be nothing — and that is fine. Gemini's Free tier is useful and will serve many readers of this book well. But Google also offers paid plans that unlock more powerful models, higher usage limits, and deeper integration with Google Workspace.

This chapter walks you through every option, explains what you get at each tier, and helps you decide which plan makes sense for your situation. We will be straightforward about what is worth paying for and what is not.

The Free Tier

The simplest way to use Gemini costs nothing. All you need is a Google account — the same one you use for Gmail, YouTube, or Google Drive. If you do not have one, you can create it for free at accounts.google.com.

With the Free tier, you get:

- **Access to Gemini 3 Flash** — Google's fast, efficient everyday model and the default for free users. This is not a stripped-down demo. Flash handles the vast majority of everyday tasks well: answering questions, writing drafts, summarizing content, brainstorming ideas, explaining concepts, and more.
- **Text, image, and file uploads** — You can upload images for Gemini to analyze, attach documents for summarization, and share files for processing.
- **Google Search grounding** — Gemini can search Google on your behalf and provide answers grounded in current web sources with citations.
- **Extensions** — Access to Google Maps, Flights, Hotels, YouTube, and other extensions that pull real-time information into your conversations.
- **Gems** — The ability to create and use custom Gemini assistants tailored to specific tasks.
- **Image generation** — Basic image creation powered by Google's Imagen 4 model.

- **Canvas** — Gemini's collaborative content creation space for drafting and editing documents and code.

What you do not get on the Free tier:

- Access to Gemini 3 Pro, the flagship model with advanced reasoning and Deep Think capabilities
- Extended context windows beyond Flash's default limits
- Deep Research, which performs multi-step web investigations
- Priority access during high-demand periods
- Gemini integration inside Google Workspace apps (Gmail, Docs, Sheets, Slides, Meet)
- Higher usage limits for image generation and file processing
- Bundled Google One storage that comes with the paid plans

For many people — perhaps most — the Free tier is enough. If you are using Gemini for casual questions, light writing assistance, trip planning, or everyday productivity, Flash handles these tasks capably. You do not need to spend a dollar to get real value from Gemini.

Our recommendation: Start with the Free tier. Use it for a week or two. If you find yourself consistently wishing for the Pro model or Workspace integration, consider upgrading. There is no reason to pay before you know what you need.

The Three Consumer Tiers: Plus, Pro, and Ultra

In May 2025, Google reorganized its consumer AI subscriptions at I/O and renamed Gemini Advanced to **Google AI Pro**. In the months that followed, Google added a more affordable tier below it (**Google AI Plus**) and a flagship tier above (**Google AI Ultra**). As of May 2026, the consumer ladder looks like this:

Tier	Price (USD)	Position
Google AI Plus	\$7.99–\$9.99/mo (region dependent)	Entry-level paid
Google AI Pro	\$19.99/mo	Mainstream premium (former Gemini Advanced)
Google AI Ultra	\$249.99/mo	Top-tier flagship

Each tier builds on the one below it. The right choice depends on how much AI you use, how much you want to pay, and which features matter to you.

Google AI Plus ($7.99–$9.99/month)

Google AI Plus is the entry-level paid tier. Pricing varies by region — around $7.99 per month in some markets and $9.99 in others. It is aimed at people who want more than the Free tier offers but are not ready to commit to Pro pricing.

With Google AI Plus, you get:

- **Higher usage limits** on Gemini compared to the Free tier — more messages, more image generations, more file uploads per day.
- **Access to current Pro-class models** for limited use, with priority access during peak demand.
- **Access to additional features** that roll out first to paid tiers, including expanded Deep Research.
- **A modest amount of bundled Google One storage** (more than free, less than Pro).

Plus is a solid middle ground if you bump into free-tier rate limits regularly but cannot justify $19.99 per month. It is not the right choice if you need full access to the flagship model or Workspace integration — those live in Pro and above.

Google AI Pro ($19.99/month)

Google AI Pro is what used to be called Gemini Advanced (and before that, Google One AI Premium). Same price point, same core promise — the most popular paid tier for individual Gemini users. It bundles 2 TB of Google One cloud storage, which on its own would cost around $9.99 per month, so the effective cost of the AI upgrade is closer to $10 if you already need the storage.

With Google AI Pro, you get everything in Plus and the Free tier, plus:

- **Gemini 3 Pro** — Google's flagship reasoning model. Pro outperforms Flash at complex reasoning, nuanced writing, detailed analysis, coding, and multi-step tasks. With Pro access, you can switch between the Pro and Flash models depending on the task.

- **Deep Think** — Gemini 3 Pro reasons through problems step by step before answering, showing its work. Especially valuable for math, logic, coding, and complex analysis.
- **Deep Research** — A feature that conducts multi-step web research on your behalf, synthesizing dozens of sources into a comprehensive, cited report. If you do any kind of research — academic, professional, or personal — Deep Research alone can justify the subscription.
- **Extended context windows** — Gemini 3 Pro supports over one million tokens, letting you upload and analyze massive documents, entire codebases, or hours of audio and video.
- **Gemini in Google Workspace** — A major perk. With Google AI Pro, the assistant appears inside Gmail, Google Docs, Google Sheets, Google Slides, and Google Meet. Draft emails, generate documents, create formulas, build presentations, and get meeting summaries — without leaving the apps you already use.
- **Higher usage limits** — More messages per day, more image generations, more file uploads, and priority access during peak demand.
- **NotebookLM Plus** — Enhanced features in Google's document-focused AI research tool: more notebooks, more sources per notebook, and longer audio overviews.
- **2 TB of Google One storage** — Shared across Google Drive, Gmail, and Google Photos.

Is Google AI Pro Worth It?

Here is our honest assessment.

Google AI Pro is worth it if:

- You use Google Workspace (Gmail, Docs, Sheets) daily and want AI assistance baked into those apps
- You do research regularly and would benefit from Deep Research
- You work with complex tasks that benefit from Pro's superior reasoning — coding, data analysis, detailed writing, strategic planning
- You need to process very long documents or videos
- You already pay for Google One storage, which makes the effective cost of the AI upgrade much lower

- You want the best mainstream Gemini experience available

Google AI Pro is probably not worth it if:

- You use Gemini casually for occasional questions and simple tasks
- Flash handles your needs well and you rarely feel limited
- You do not use Google Workspace apps regularly
- You already pay for ChatGPT Plus or Claude Pro and do not want another AI subscription
- Budget is tight and you can get by with the Free tier or AI Plus

At $19.99 per month, Google AI Pro sits in the same $20 tier as ChatGPT Plus and Claude Pro — the industry-standard price point for premium individual AI subscriptions. If you are paying for one AI subscription and you live in Google's ecosystem, Pro is the strongest choice because of the Workspace integration and bundled storage.

Google AI Ultra ($249.99/month)

Google AI Ultra is the new top tier, sitting well above Pro at $249.99 per month. It targets power users who push AI tools hard — advanced researchers, heavy creators, professionals doing high-volume AI work, and early adopters who want first access to Google's most capable features.

With Google AI Ultra, you get everything in Pro plus:

- **Highest usage limits** across Gemini, image generation, video generation, and Deep Research.
- **Priority access to new and experimental models** — including Deep Think variants, agentic capabilities, and frontier features as they roll out.
- **Expanded video generation** through Google's Veo models, with longer durations and higher quality than Pro.
- **Larger Google One storage allotment** (well above the 2 TB included with Pro).
- **Early access to capabilities** Google is testing, often months before they reach the Pro tier or never reach the Free tier.

Ultra is overkill for most readers. It earns its price for a small set of users — AI-heavy professionals, agencies, and power users — but for the vast majority, Pro is the better value.

Workspace Plans for Businesses

If you use Google Workspace through your employer, school, or organization, Gemini's integration into Workspace apps is controlled by your administrator and bundled into your Workspace plan rather than purchased separately. As of May 2026, Gemini features are included across the Workspace lineup:

- **Business Starter, Business Standard, Business Plus** — Workspace plans for small and growing businesses, with Gemini features included at progressively richer tiers.
- **Enterprise** — For larger organizations, with the deepest Gemini integration, longer meeting transcriptions, higher AI usage limits, and the strongest data controls.

Pricing varies and is typically negotiated directly with Google or through a reseller.

Key point for business users: If your organization provides Gemini through Workspace, you may already have access to many features in this book without needing a personal Google AI Pro subscription. Check with your IT department or Workspace administrator.

The Workspace versions come with important data protections. Google states that data processed by Gemini in Workspace Business and Enterprise environments is not used to train Google's AI models — a meaningful distinction for companies handling sensitive information. We discuss data privacy in Chapter 26.

Family Plans

Google AI Pro can be shared with up to five additional family members through a Google One family plan. Each member gets their own Pro access and a share of the storage pool.

The family plan costs $32.99 per month for up to six people — about $5.50 per person, a significant discount over $19.99 individual subscriptions. If multiple people in your household want Pro, the family plan is an excellent value. (Google has indicated family options for AI Plus and AI Ultra as well; check current pricing on the Google One site.)

Each family member keeps a separate Google account, conversations, Gems, and preferences. The storage pool is the only thing actually shared — your Gemini conversations remain private.

Comparing Gemini Plans at a Glance

Here is a quick reference table for the consumer tiers.

Feature	Free	AI Plus	AI Pro	AI Ultra
Price/mo	—	$7.99–$9.99	$19.99	$249.99
Gemini 3 Flash	Yes	Yes	Yes	Yes
Gemini 3 Pro	No	Limited	Yes	Yes
Deep Think	No	Limited	Yes	Yes (priority)
Deep Research	No	Expanded	Yes	Highest limits
Google Search grounding	Yes	Yes	Yes	Yes
Image generation (Imagen 4)	Basic	Enhanced	Full	Highest limits
Video generation (Veo)	No	Limited	Yes	Expanded
Extensions	Yes	Yes	Yes	Yes
Gems	Yes	Yes	Yes	Yes
Canvas	Yes	Yes	Yes	Yes
Gemini in Workspace	No	No	Yes	Yes
Context window	Standard	Standard	Extended (1M+ tokens)	Extended (1M+ tokens)
NotebookLM	Basic	Basic	Plus	Plus
Google One storage	None	Modest	2 TB	Larger allotment

Feature	Free	AI Plus	AI Pro	AI Ultra
Family sharing	N/A	N/A	$32.99/mo	Available
Early access to new models	No	No	Some	Priority

Which Plan Is Right for You?

A few quick scenarios.

You are curious about AI and want to try Gemini. Start with the Free tier. You will have a fully functional AI assistant that handles most everyday tasks. Upgrade later if you want more.

You are a student. The Free tier is a great starting point. If you find yourself doing heavy research or working with long documents, consider Google AI Pro for Deep Research and the extended context window. Check whether your school provides Google Workspace with Gemini — many do.

You bump into free-tier limits but cannot justify $20. Google AI Plus at $7.99–$9.99 per month is built for you.

You are a professional who uses Google Workspace daily. Google AI Pro is likely worth it. Having Gemini assist you directly inside Gmail, Docs, Sheets, and Slides saves time every day. The bundled 2 TB of storage is a bonus.

You and your family want AI access. The Pro family plan at $32.99 per month for up to six people is hard to beat on value.

You are a power user who pushes AI tools hard. Google AI Ultra at $249.99 per month is the right call — highest limits, priority access, and earliest features. Most people do not need this. The people who do, know who they are.

You already pay for ChatGPT Plus or Claude Pro. This is the trickiest scenario. If you are embedded in Google's ecosystem, Google AI Pro may be worth adding or switching to for the Workspace integration. If you are not a heavy Google user, your existing subscription may serve you just as well. We do not recommend paying for all three unless you have a specific professional need — the overlap in capabilities is too significant.

You are a developer. The Gemini API has its own pricing, separate from the consumer plans. You can experiment for free through Google AI Studio with generous rate limits. For production use, pricing is based on token usage through Google Cloud's Vertex AI platform. We cover this in Chapter 23.

A Note on Pricing

AI subscription pricing has evolved since the early ChatGPT-era $20 tier. Google now offers a three-tier consumer ladder (Plus, Pro, Ultra) plus a Free tier, a structure most major providers have adopted in some form. Prices and bundles can change. Google may adjust pricing, add tiers, or restructure what is included.

We have verified all pricing in this chapter as of May 2026, but check gemini.google.com or one.google.com for the latest before subscribing.

What Comes Next

Now that you know your options, it is time to set up your account and start using Gemini. In Chapter 3, we walk through account creation, app installation, and the settings you should configure before your first conversation. Whether you choose free, Plus, Pro, or Ultra, setup takes a few minutes — and then you will be ready to talk to one of the most capable AI assistants on the planet.

Chapter 3: Setting Up Your Account

You have decided to give Gemini a try. Getting started takes less time than making a cup of coffee. In this chapter, we walk through setting up Gemini — on the web, on your phone, and inside Google Workspace — and cover the settings and privacy controls you should configure before you start chatting. Think of this as the five-minute investment that makes everything else in the book possible.

What You Need Before You Start

You need one thing: a Google account.

If you use Gmail, YouTube, Google Drive, or an Android phone, you already have one. Your Google account is the email address you sign in with — something like yourname@gmail.com.

If you do not have one, go to accounts.google.com and create it for free. You will provide a name, choose an email address (or use an existing non-Gmail email), and set a password. The process takes about two minutes.

One note: Gemini is available in most countries, but not all. As of May 2026, Google has rolled Gemini out broadly across North America, Europe, Asia-Pacific, and most of Latin America and Africa. If you are in a region where Gemini is not yet available, you will see a message when you try to access it.

You must be at least 13 in most countries (with a minimum of 18 in the European Economic Area, Switzerland, and the United Kingdom). Children under 13 can be granted access by a parent through Google Family Link. Google Workspace accounts managed by schools may have different age requirements set by administrators, and students aged 13 and over can access Gemini through Workspace for Education accounts.

Getting Started on the Web

The fastest way to start using Gemini is through your web browser.

Step 1: Go to gemini.google.com. Open any modern web browser — Chrome, Firefox, Safari, Edge — and navigate to gemini.google.com.

Step 2: Sign in. If you are not already signed into your Google account, you will be prompted to sign in. Enter your email and password. If you have two-factor authentication enabled (which we recommend), complete that step as well.

Step 3: Accept the terms. The first time you visit, Google will present its terms of service for Gemini. Read them — they cover how Google handles your conversations, what data is stored, and your rights. You need to accept to proceed. We discuss the privacy implications later in this chapter and in Chapter 26.

Step 4: You are in. That is it. You will see Gemini's chat interface — a clean text box with a prompt like "Ask Gemini" at the bottom of the screen. You are ready to start typing.

A few key elements of the web interface:

- **The chat input box** at the bottom is where you type. Click the microphone icon to speak your message, the image icon to upload an image, or the attachment icon to upload files.
- **The sidebar** on the left shows your conversation history. Each conversation is saved automatically, and you can return to previous chats anytime. Start a new conversation by clicking "New chat."
- **The model selector** at the top of a new conversation lets you choose which Gemini model to use (if you have Google AI Pro). Free users default to Gemini 3 Flash.
- **The Gems section** in the sidebar gives you access to pre-built and custom Gems — specialized assistants for specific tasks.

Gemini on Android

If you have an Android phone or tablet, Gemini can become your primary AI assistant, replacing or supplementing Google Assistant.

Installing Gemini on Android:

Step 1: Open the Google Play Store and search for "Gemini." Download and install the Google Gemini app. On many newer Android devices, Gemini comes pre-installed.

Step 2: Open the app and sign in with your Google account.

Step 3: Optionally, set Gemini as your default assistant. Android will ask if you want Gemini to replace Google Assistant. If you say yes, long-pressing the home button, saying "Hey Google," or swiping from the corner will open Gemini instead.

You do not have to replace Google Assistant. You can always open the Gemini app directly from your app drawer. But for most users, setting Gemini as the default makes sense — it is more capable for conversational tasks, and it still handles the basics like timers, calls, and smart home devices.

What Gemini on Android can do that the web version cannot:

- **Overlay mode.** Gemini can appear as an overlay on top of whatever app you are using. Ask about content on your screen — a webpage, a message, a photo — without switching apps.
- **Voice conversations.** The Android app is optimized for natural, back-and-forth spoken conversations. Talk to Gemini as you would to a person.
- **Quick access.** With Gemini set as your default assistant, it is always one gesture away.

Gemini on iOS

iPhone and iPad users get a dedicated Gemini app as well.

Step 1: Open the App Store and search for "Google Gemini." Download and install it.

Step 2: Open the app and sign in with your Google account.

Step 3: Start chatting.

The iOS experience mirrors the web and Android versions: same chat interface, file uploads, image analysis, and access to conversation history. The main difference is that Gemini cannot replace Siri as the default assistant on iOS — that is an Apple restriction, not a Google one. You will need to open the Gemini app directly each time.

One tip: add the Gemini app to your iPhone's home screen dock for quick access. If you reach for it often, this small change saves you from hunting through app screens.

Gemini in Google Workspace

If you have Google AI Pro (or your organization provides Gemini through a Workspace plan), Gemini appears directly inside Google's productivity apps. This is one of the most powerful parts of the paid experience.

Here is where Gemini lives in each app:

Gmail. When composing an email, look for the "Help me write" button or the Gemini sparkle icon. Gemini drafts replies, composes new messages, adjusts tone, and shortens or expands your text. In your inbox, Gemini summarizes long email threads.

Google Docs. Open any document and look for the Gemini icon in the side panel or the "Help me write" option in the toolbar. Gemini drafts new content, rewrites existing text, summarizes documents, and answers questions about a document's content.

Google Sheets. Gemini helps you create formulas, organize data, generate charts, and analyze patterns. Look for the Gemini side panel or the "Help me organize" option.

Google Slides. Gemini generates entire presentation drafts from a prompt, creates individual slides, suggests layouts, and generates images. Access it from the Gemini icon in the toolbar.

Google Meet. During or after a meeting, Gemini provides real-time captions, takes notes, summarizes the discussion, and lists action items. The meeting organizer must have Gemini features enabled.

Google Drive. Gemini searches across your Drive files and answers questions based on the content of your documents, spreadsheets, and presentations — useful when you need information but cannot remember which file it is in.

We cover each of these integrations in depth in Chapter 13. For now, if you have Google AI Pro, keep an eye out for the Gemini sparkle icon throughout Google Workspace — it is your entry point to AI assistance in each app.

Gemini in Chrome

Google Chrome includes Gemini integration in several forms.

The address bar. In newer versions of Chrome, you can type your question directly into the address bar and get a Gemini-powered answer alongside traditional search results.

Tab summaries. Right-click a tab and look for options to summarize the page using Gemini.

Side panel. Chrome's side panel can host a Gemini chat alongside any webpage, letting you ask questions about what you are reading without leaving the page.

These features roll out progressively and may vary by Chrome version and region. If you do not see them yet, update Chrome to the latest version.

Settings Walkthrough

Before you dive into your first real conversation, take five minutes to review Gemini's settings. You will find them by clicking your profile picture or the settings gear icon.

Response Settings

Response style. Set a default preference for how Gemini responds — shorter and more concise, or longer and more detailed. This is a default, not a hard rule. You can override it in any conversation by asking Gemini to be more or less detailed.

Real-time responses. By default, Gemini streams its response word by word as it generates. Some people prefer to wait for the complete response. Toggle this in settings.

Extensions

Extensions allow Gemini to connect to other Google services and pull real-time information. By default, several extensions are enabled:

- **Google Workspace** — Access to your Gmail, Docs, and Drive (requires Google AI Pro or Workspace plan)
- **Google Maps** — Real-time directions, business information, and place recommendations
- **Google Flights** — Current flight prices and schedules

- **Google Hotels** — Hotel availability and pricing
- **YouTube** — Video search and information

You can enable or disable each extension individually. If you are uncomfortable with Gemini accessing your Gmail, for example, turn off the Workspace extension. We recommend leaving most extensions enabled — they significantly expand what Gemini can do — but the choice is yours.

Connected Apps

If you use third-party apps that integrate with Gemini, manage those connections here. Review this section periodically to confirm you are comfortable with what is connected.

Privacy: What Google Stores and How to Control It

This is the section that matters most for many readers. When you use Gemini, what happens to your conversations?

By default, Google stores your Gemini conversations. This data can be used to improve Google's products and services, including training future AI models. Your conversations are tied to your Google account and appear in your Gemini Apps Activity.

Here is how to control it:

Step 1: Go to your Gemini Apps Activity. Reach it from Gemini's settings or directly at myactivity.google.com/product/gemini.

Step 2: Review your activity. You will see a log of your past conversations. Review, search, and delete individual conversations or all of them.

Step 3: Turn off Gemini Apps Activity. If you prefer Google not store your conversations, toggle Gemini Apps Activity off. When it is off:

- Your conversations are not saved to your account history
- Your conversations are not used to train AI models
- Google still processes your conversations to generate responses, but the data is deleted after up to 72 hours

- You lose access to your conversation history — you cannot return to previous chats

The trade-off: privacy versus convenience. With activity on, you get a searchable history of every conversation and Google may use your data for model improvement. With activity off, your data is more private but you lose conversation history.

Our recommendation: If you plan to discuss sensitive material — personal matters, business strategy, confidential information — turn off Gemini Apps Activity, or at minimum be selective about what you share. For casual, non-sensitive use, leaving it on gives you searchable conversation history.

Google Workspace exception: If you use Gemini through a paid Google Workspace business or enterprise account, your administrator controls data retention policies, and Google states that Workspace data is not used to train AI models. This matters for business users.

We cover privacy and security in depth in Chapter 26. For now, the takeaway: check your Gemini Apps Activity settings and make a deliberate choice.

A Quick Tour of the Interface

A quick visual tour so you know where everything is.

Top of the screen: The model selector (if you have Google AI Pro), a button to start a new chat, and your account settings.

Left sidebar: Your conversation history, organized by date. Recent chats appear at the top. Below that, your Gems — custom assistants you have created or starred. Collapse the sidebar for a cleaner view.

Center of the screen: The conversation area, where your messages and Gemini's responses appear. Responses can include text, images, code blocks, tables, and interactive elements.

Bottom of the screen: The input area. The text box where you type or paste messages. Flanking it are icons for voice input, image upload, file attachment, and other input options. On the right is the send button.

Within Gemini's responses: Each response includes options to copy the text, give a thumbs up or down (which helps Google improve Gemini), share, modify, or see alternative drafts. If Gemini used Google Search, you will see a "Sources" section with links you can click to verify the information.

Checklist: Ready to Go

Before you move on, confirm that you have:

1. A Google account you can sign into
2. Access to Gemini through at least one platform (web, Android, or iOS)
3. Reviewed your Gemini Apps Activity settings and made a privacy choice
4. Looked at your extension settings and enabled or disabled them to taste
5. Optionally, set up Gemini in your Google Workspace apps (if you have Google AI Pro or Workspace access)

You are set up. Your account is ready, your settings are configured, and you know your way around the interface. In Chapter 4, we look at the different Gemini models — what they are, how they differ, and how to choose the right one for any given task.

Chapter 4: Understanding Gemini's Models

When you open Gemini, you are not just talking to "Gemini." You are talking to a specific model — a particular version of the AI with its own strengths, speed, and capabilities. Understanding the differences is one of the most practical things you can learn early on, because choosing the right model can mean the difference between a mediocre answer and an excellent one.

This chapter explains what models are, walks through each current Gemini model, and gives you a framework for deciding which to use and when.

What Is a Model, Exactly?

When AI researchers build a system like Gemini, they do not write traditional software with if-then rules for every possible question. Instead, they train a "model" — a massive mathematical system that learns patterns from enormous amounts of text, images, code, audio, and video. The model does not store facts like a database. It learns the relationships between words, concepts, and ideas, and uses those patterns to generate responses.

Think of it this way: the model is the brain, and the Gemini app is the body. The app provides the interface you see — the text box, the buttons, the sidebar. The intelligence behind the responses comes from the model running on Google's servers.

Google offers multiple Gemini models because no single model is perfect for every task. Some are faster. Some are smarter. Some are more efficient. By giving you a choice, Google lets you pick the right tool for the job.

On the Free tier, you do not get to choose — you use Gemini 3 Flash, an excellent everyday model. With Google AI Pro, you can switch between models at the start of each conversation.

Gemini 3 Pro: The Flagship

Gemini 3 Pro is Google's most capable model as of May 2026. It launched on November 18, 2025, and a 3.1 Pro preview shipped in February 2026. It is the one you want for your hardest, most complex, and most important tasks.

What it excels at:

- **Complex reasoning.** Multi-step math, logic puzzles, strategic analysis, and any task that requires thinking through a chain of connected ideas.
- **Coding.** Writing, debugging, and explaining code across dozens of languages. Pro outperforms Flash on large codebases and production-quality code.
- **Detailed analysis.** Summarizing and analyzing long documents, research papers, legal contracts, and financial reports with nuance and accuracy.
- **Nuanced writing.** When you need writing that captures subtlety — a persuasive argument, a sensitive email, a detailed product review — Pro produces more refined output than Flash.
- **Long context tasks.** Pro supports a context window of over one million tokens. Upload an entire book, a semester of lecture notes, hours of meeting transcripts, or a large codebase, and Pro will process and reason about all of it coherently.

What it is not great at:

- **Speed.** Pro is slower than Flash. For simple questions, you will notice the delay. There is no reason to wait for Pro on "What is the capital of France?" when Flash answers instantly.
- **Simple tasks.** Pro is overkill for basic questions, quick lookups, casual brainstorming, and everyday chitchat. Using Pro for simple tasks is like driving a Formula One car to the grocery store — it works, but you are wasting the machine.

When to use it: Reach for Pro when the task is complex, the stakes are high, the content is long, or output quality matters. Job applications, business proposals, research synthesis, complex coding projects, detailed analysis of contracts or reports — these are Pro tasks.

Deep Think: Pro's Secret Weapon

The headline feature of Gemini 3 Pro is Deep Think — sometimes called "thinking mode" or extended reasoning. When enabled, Pro does not just generate an answer. It first reasons through the problem step by step, exploring approaches and checking its own logic before presenting a final response.

Google shipped a dedicated **Gemini 3 Deep Think** mode in February 2026 that takes this further — the model spends substantially more compute reasoning through hard problems before answering. It is available on the Pro tier and above for appropriate tasks.

You can see this. When Pro uses Deep Think, the interface shows an expandable "Thinking" section above the response. Click it to read Pro's internal reasoning: what it weighed, what it tried and rejected, and the logic chain that led to its answer.

For certain tasks, Deep Think dramatically improves accuracy:

- **Math and logic.** Standard AI models often make arithmetic errors or take logical shortcuts. Deep Think forces Pro to work through calculations step by step, catching mistakes before they reach you.
- **Coding.** On complex code, Deep Think helps Pro plan the architecture, consider edge cases, and verify correctness before producing the solution.
- **Analysis.** For multi-faceted questions with no single right answer, Deep Think lets Pro weigh multiple perspectives and present a more balanced, thorough response.

Deep Think is enabled by default in Google AI Pro for appropriate tasks. Pro decides automatically when a question benefits from extended reasoning. You can also request it explicitly: "think step by step" or "reason through this carefully."

The trade-off is time. Deep Think makes responses slower — sometimes much slower on complex problems. When accuracy matters more than speed, the wait is worth it.

Gemini 3 Flash: The Everyday Workhorse

Gemini 3 Flash is the model most people will use most of the time. It launched in December 2025 and quickly became the default in the Gemini app, replacing the previous-generation 2.5 Flash. It is the default for free-tier users and the go-to for Google AI Pro subscribers who want fast, competent responses without waiting for Pro.

What it excels at:

- **Speed.** Flash is fast. Responses appear almost immediately for most questions. If you are using Gemini for frequent, quick interactions throughout the day, Flash keeps up.
- **General knowledge.** Everyday questions, explanations, recommendations, and conversational tasks.
- **Writing assistance.** Drafting emails, social posts, messages, summaries, and other routine writing.
- **Light coding.** Simple scripts, code explanations, and debugging straightforward issues.
- **Brainstorming.** Rapid-fire idea generation, list making, and creative exploration.
- **Multimodal tasks.** Image analysis, file processing, and basic video understanding.

What it is not great at:

- **Deep reasoning.** Flash can stumble on complex multi-step logic, advanced math, and nuanced analysis where Pro would succeed.
- **Very long content.** Flash's context window is generous but smaller than Pro's million-plus tokens. For truly massive documents or codebases, choose Pro.
- **High-stakes writing.** When every word matters — a keynote, a critical proposal, a cover letter for your dream job — Pro's extra care shows.

When to use it: Flash is your default for the vast majority of everyday tasks. Quick questions, routine writing, brainstorming, trip planning, recipe lookups, casual conversation, and anything where speed matters more than peak accuracy. If Flash gives you a good enough answer, there is no reason to switch.

Think of Flash as a knowledgeable colleague who gives you a solid answer quickly. Pro is the specialist you consult when the problem is hard.

Gemini 3.1 Flash-Lite: The Lightweight Option

Gemini 3.1 Flash-Lite, released March 3, 2026, is the most efficient model in the 3-era lineup — smaller and cheaper to run than 3 Flash, optimized for high-volume, latency-sensitive tasks. You will see it most often in API and embedded contexts (chatbots, content moderation, simple classification, autocomplete-style features) rather than as a default in the Gemini app.

How it compares to 3 Flash:

- A step behind on reasoning, writing nuance, and multimodal depth.
- Faster and cheaper — the right choice when you are running large volumes of simple tasks through the API.
- Smaller context window than 3 Flash.

When to use it: Rarely, as a chat user. Flash-Lite earns its keep in developer scenarios where cost and latency matter more than peak quality. If the Gemini app offers it as an option, choose 3 Flash unless you have a specific reason.

Previous-Generation Models

You may still see older models listed — Gemini 2.5 Pro, 2.5 Flash, or 2.0 Flash — in some interfaces, particularly in the API, where Google maintains older models for compatibility. These are previous generation. The 3-era models are better in almost every dimension. Google keeps the older models available as a fallback and for organizations that pinned to a specific version, but for most users, the 3-era models are the right choice. Choose 3 Pro, 3 Flash, or 3.1 Flash-Lite over their 2.x predecessors unless you have a specific reason to do otherwise.

How Model Selection Affects Your Experience

Choosing a model is not just about raw intelligence. It affects several practical aspects of your experience.

Response Quality

The most obvious difference. Pro produces more detailed, accurate, and nuanced responses than Flash, especially on complex tasks. For simple tasks, the quality gap narrows to where most users would not notice.

Response Speed

Flash responds noticeably faster than Pro. For rapid back-and-forth brainstorming or quick factual questions, Flash's speed keeps the conversation natural. Pro can take several seconds longer, and with Deep Think on a complex problem, you might wait 15 to 30 seconds or more.

Token Usage and Limits

Each model has daily usage limits. Pro's limits are lower because Pro requires more computational resources. If you hit your Pro limit for the day, switch to Flash and keep working. Another reason to use Flash as your default and save Pro for the tasks that need it.

Context Window

Pro supports over one million tokens. Flash's context window is large but smaller. For very long documents, Pro handles more content in a single conversation. For most everyday tasks, Flash's window is more than sufficient — you will not come close to its limits.

A Framework for Choosing Models

Here is a simple decision framework you can use every time you start a new conversation.

Use Flash when: - The task is straightforward (questions, simple writing, summaries, brainstorming) - Speed matters more than depth - You are doing many quick interactions throughout the day - The stakes are low to moderate

Use Pro when: - The task requires complex reasoning or careful analysis - You are working with very long documents or large amounts of data - The output needs to be high quality (important emails, proposals, reports) - You are doing math, logic, or coding that requires precision - You want Gemini to "think through" a problem before answering

When in doubt: Start with Flash. If the response is not good enough, switch to Pro. This is the most efficient approach. You save Pro's usage limits for when you need them and avoid waiting for Pro when Flash would have done the job.

The Relationship Between Models and Google's Infrastructure

A high-level look at how these models relate to Google's broader AI infrastructure.

The Gemini models run on Google's custom Tensor Processing Units (TPUs) in Google's data centers. TPUs are specialized chips built from the ground up for AI workloads — different from the GPUs most other AI companies rely on. Google's investment in custom hardware gives it control over cost and performance, which is part of why Google can offer a capable Free tier at all.

When you send a message, your text (and any uploaded files) travel to Google's servers, where the selected model processes your input and generates a response. The model does not run on your device — your phone or laptop is just the window into the system. That is why you need an internet connection and why response speed can vary with server load.

Google trains new models and updates existing ones constantly. The model you use today may be subtly better next month even if its name has not changed. Google sometimes updates models in place — better accuracy on certain tasks, fewer errors in specific categories, improved safety guardrails. You may not notice, but the changes happen regularly.

Looking Ahead: How Models Will Evolve

By the time you read this, Google may have released models beyond the 3.1 generation. The pace is rapid, and generations arrive roughly every six to twelve months. Here is what trends suggest:

- Models will keep getting smarter — better reasoning, higher accuracy, stronger instruction-following.
- Models will get faster. The gap between Flash and Pro will likely narrow.

- Context windows will keep growing. We may see 10-million-token or larger windows within a year or two.
- Multimodal capabilities will expand: better video understanding, better image generation, and potentially new modalities like real-time screen understanding.

The framework in this chapter — Flash for everyday tasks, Pro for hard tasks, upgrade as needed — holds even as model names change. Match the power of the tool to the difficulty of the task.

Key Takeaways

- Gemini offers multiple models with different strengths: Pro for complex tasks, Flash for everyday use, Flash-Lite for high-volume API workloads.
- Gemini 3 Pro is the most capable, with Deep Think capabilities (and the dedicated Gemini 3 Deep Think mode) that improve reasoning, math, and analysis.
- Gemini 3 Flash is fast, competent, and the right choice for the vast majority of everyday tasks.
- Free-tier users get Flash. Google AI Pro subscribers can choose between Pro and Flash.
- Start with Flash. Switch to Pro when the task demands it.
- Models improve continuously. The framework for choosing between them holds even as the models get better.

In Chapter 5, we put this into practice. You will have your first real conversations with Gemini, learn how to ask effective questions, and see how Gemini's massive context window changes the way you interact with an AI assistant.

Chapter 5: Your First Conversations

You have an account. You know the models. Now it is time to talk to Gemini.

This chapter is hands-on. We will walk through your first real conversations, teach you how to ask questions that get useful answers, show how follow-ups work, and help you build an intuition for Gemini as a conversational partner. By the end, you will have a practical sense of what Gemini can do — not from reading about it, but from doing it.

Open Gemini now if you can. The best way to learn this is alongside us.

How to Talk to Gemini

Talking to Gemini is exactly what it sounds like: you type a message, and Gemini responds. No special syntax, no programming language, no commands to memorize. You write in plain English (or any of dozens of supported languages), and Gemini responds in kind.

Your message is called a "prompt." The word sounds technical, but it is just the thing you type into the text box. A prompt can be a question, a request, an instruction, or even a thought you want Gemini to react to. All of these are valid:

- "What causes the northern lights?"
- "Write me a professional email declining a meeting invitation."
- "I have chicken, rice, broccoli, and soy sauce. What can I make for dinner?"
- "Explain the difference between a Roth IRA and a traditional IRA as if I were fifteen years old."
- "Here is my resume. What could I improve?"

Notice the range. Some are questions. Some are instructions. Some provide context. All work. Gemini is flexible enough to handle whatever you throw at it, and the fastest way to learn is to experiment.

One principle will serve you throughout this entire book: **the more specific your prompt, the better Gemini's response.** We will return to this again and again. For now, keep it in mind as we walk through your first conversations.

Asking Questions, Getting Answers

Start with the simplest interaction: asking a question.

Try typing this into Gemini:

> What is the tallest building in the world?

Gemini responds with the answer — the Burj Khalifa in Dubai, at 828 meters — along with some context. It might mention when it was completed, how many floors it has, or what buildings come close in height. This is Gemini at its most basic: a knowledgeable assistant answering a factual question.

Now try something more open-ended:

> Why do we dream?

This time, the response will be longer and more nuanced. There is no single definitive answer — scientists have multiple theories — and Gemini will present several. Notice the structure: it will organize the theories into clear sections, explain each in accessible language, and may note which have the most scientific support.

Now try something practical:

> I have a job interview next Tuesday for a marketing manager position at a tech startup. What should I prepare?

Here Gemini shifts into advice mode. You get a structured list of preparation steps — researching the company, preparing answers to common questions, thinking about your experience with relevant tools, preparing questions to ask the interviewer, and so on. The response is tailored to the specifics you provided: marketing manager, tech startup, next Tuesday.

That is the key lesson. The more detail you include, the more relevant Gemini's response becomes. Compare:

- Vague: "How do I prepare for an interview?"
- Specific: "I have a job interview next Tuesday for a marketing manager position at a tech startup. What should I prepare?"

Both work. But the specific one gives Gemini enough context to produce useful, tailored advice instead of generic tips you could find on any career website.

Follow-Up Questions and Refining Responses

A conversation with Gemini is not one question and done. One of the most powerful things about Gemini — and what separates it from a search engine — is its ability to maintain context across a conversation. You can ask follow-ups, and Gemini remembers what you have discussed.

Try it. Start a new conversation and type:

> What are the health benefits of walking every day?

Read the response. Now type a follow-up:

> How many minutes per day do you recommend for someone who's just starting out?

Notice that you did not need to say "minutes of walking." Gemini understood from your first question that you are talking about walking. That is conversational context: Gemini tracks everything said in the current conversation and uses it to understand your follow-ups.

You can keep building:

> What if I have bad knees? Should I do anything differently?

Again, Gemini knows you are still talking about daily walking and adjusts accordingly. You are having a conversation, not issuing isolated queries.

This is also how you refine responses that miss. If Gemini gives you an answer that is too long, too technical, too vague, or off-target, just say so:

- "Can you make that shorter?"
- "Explain that in simpler terms."
- "I meant specifically for small businesses, not large enterprises."
- "Good, but more detail on the third point."
- "That is not what I was asking. I meant..."

Gemini will adjust. This back-and-forth is one of the most effective ways to get exactly the response you need. Treat your first prompt as a rough draft and the follow-ups as fine-tuning.

Understanding Context Windows

Here is something that sets Gemini apart from most competitors: the size of its context window.

A "context window" is the amount of information Gemini can hold in its working memory during a single conversation. Everything you have said, everything Gemini has said, and any files or images you have uploaded — all of it lives in the context window. As long as something is within the window, Gemini can refer back to it.

Gemini 3 Pro has a context window of over one million tokens — roughly 700,000 words. For perspective, the entire Harry Potter series is about 1.1 million words. Gemini 3 Pro can hold most of it in a single conversation.

Why does this matter? It means you can:

- Upload a 200-page PDF and ask questions about any part of it
- Paste an entire semester's worth of lecture notes and ask Gemini to help you study
- Upload hours of meeting transcripts and ask for summaries, action items, or specific details
- Share a large codebase and ask Gemini to find bugs, explain functions, or suggest improvements
- Have a long conversation without Gemini forgetting what you discussed earlier

With a smaller context window, the AI starts "forgetting" earlier parts of the conversation as the window fills. Gemini's massive window means this rarely happens in practice.

There are still practical limits. Even with a million tokens, very long conversations can see some degradation in how precisely Gemini recalls earlier details. If Gemini seems to forget something you mentioned long ago, reference it directly or start a new conversation focused on that topic.

Gemini's Personality and Response Style

Every AI assistant has a distinct personality — a default way of communicating that shapes how its responses feel. After using Gemini for a while, you will notice its style.

Gemini tends to be helpful and thorough. It defaults to comprehensive answers. Ask a simple question and you may get a multi-paragraph response with context, examples, and related information. Usually helpful, but sometimes you just want the short answer. Say "Give me a brief answer" or "One sentence only."

Gemini is conversational but professional. Its tone strikes a balance between friendly and informative. Not stiff or robotic, but not constantly cracking jokes either. It reads like a knowledgeable colleague explaining something — approachable but focused.

Gemini likes structure. Headers, bullet points, numbered lists, bold text — Gemini reaches for these often. This usually makes responses easier to scan. If you prefer flowing prose, tell Gemini: "Write this as continuous paragraphs, not bullet points."

Gemini adjusts on request. Want it more casual? Ask. More formal? Ask. Explain something as if you are five? Ask. Respond like a cynical 1940s newspaper columnist? Ask. Gemini is flexible at adopting tones and styles when you give clear direction.

Gemini sometimes adds caveats and disclaimers. Especially on sensitive topics — health, legal, financial — Gemini will add notes like "I'm an AI and this isn't professional advice" or "Please consult a doctor." These are appropriate and responsible, if occasionally a bit much for casual questions.

When Gemini Hedges or Declines

There are times when Gemini will not give you a straight answer, or will decline to respond altogether. Understanding why helps you work with the system rather than against it.

Safety guardrails. Gemini has built-in guidelines about what it will and will not do. It will decline to generate violent content, provide instructions for illegal activities, create content that sexualizes minors, or produce content that could cause real-world harm. These boundaries are intentional and non-negotiable.

Uncertainty hedging. When Gemini is not confident, it may hedge with phrases like "I believe," "It's possible that," or "I'm not entirely sure, but." That is a good sign — Gemini is calibrating its confidence rather than presenting uncertain information as fact. When you see hedging, verify independently.

Topic sensitivity. On politically divisive topics, medical questions, and legal matters, Gemini presents multiple perspectives rather than taking a firm position. It may say "Some people believe X, while others argue Y." This is by design — Google has trained Gemini to be measured on controversial topics.

"I can't help with that." Occasionally, Gemini will decline outright. If the refusal seems unwarranted — you are asking a legitimate question that Gemini misinterpreted — rephrase with more context about why you need the information. A more detailed, clearly benign framing usually resolves it.

Walkthrough: Your First Ten Prompts

Ten prompts to try right now. Each showcases a different aspect of what Gemini can do. Try each one, read the response, then try a follow-up of your own.

Prompt 1: Factual question. > What were the three most significant scientific discoveries of 2025?

This tests Gemini's ability to provide current information via Google Search grounding. Notice whether it provides sources.

Prompt 2: Explanation. > Explain how a mortgage works to someone who has never owned a home.

See how Gemini breaks down a complex financial concept into accessible language.

Prompt 3: Creative writing. > Write a short bedtime story for a six-year-old about a brave little lighthouse.

This shows Gemini's creative capabilities. Try a follow-up: "Make it a little longer and add a friendly whale character."

Prompt 4: Practical advice. > I'm hosting a dinner party for eight people this Saturday. Three guests are vegetarian. Can you suggest a menu that works for everyone?

Notice how Gemini handles the constraint (vegetarian guests) while keeping the menu appealing for meat-eaters too.

Prompt 5: Analysis. > What are the pros and cons of working from home versus working in an office?

See how Gemini organizes a balanced analysis of a topic with multiple perspectives.

Prompt 6: Language help. > Translate "Where is the nearest pharmacy? I need cold medicine." into Spanish, French, and Japanese.

This demonstrates Gemini's multilingual capabilities.

Prompt 7: Task breakdown. > I need to organize my garage this weekend. It's a two-car garage that hasn't been cleaned in three years. Give me a step-by-step plan.

Gemini is excellent at breaking overwhelming tasks into manageable steps.

Prompt 8: Image analysis. (Upload a photo from your phone — a meal, a plant, a document, anything.) > What do you see in this image? Describe it in detail.

This tests Gemini's multimodal capabilities. Try uploading a photo of a plant and asking "What kind of plant is this and how should I care for it?"

Prompt 9: Comparison. > Compare the iPhone 17 and Samsung Galaxy S26 for someone who mainly uses their phone for photography and social media.

See how Gemini handles product comparisons with specific user needs.

Prompt 10: Personal help. > I've been putting off a difficult conversation with a coworker who keeps missing deadlines and it's affecting my work. Can you help me think through how to approach this conversation constructively?

This shows Gemini's ability to provide thoughtful interpersonal advice. Try follow-ups to roleplay the conversation.

Saved Info: Teaching Gemini About You

One of the most practical features to set up early is Gemini's Saved Info — a way to tell Gemini persistent facts about yourself so you do not repeat them in every conversation. Think of it as a brief profile Gemini references automatically.

How Saved Info Works

When you tell Gemini something about yourself — your name, job, location, preferences — you can ask it to remember. Gemini stores these facts in Saved Info, and they carry across conversations. The next time you start a new chat, Gemini already knows the basics.

For example:

- "Remember that I'm a high school teacher in Austin, Texas."
- "I'm a vegetarian — keep that in mind when suggesting recipes."
- "I prefer concise responses. Don't give me long explanations unless I ask."
- "My daughter's name is Maya and she's seven years old."

Once saved, Gemini factors these into responses without being reminded. Ask for dinner suggestions and it skips the meat. Ask for local recommendations and it defaults to Austin. Ask for activity ideas for your kid and it calibrates for a seven-year-old.

Viewing, Editing, and Deleting Saved Info

You have full control over what Gemini remembers. To manage Saved Info, go to Gemini settings and look for the Saved Info or personalization section. You will see a list of everything Gemini has stored.

Edit entries when your circumstances change — you moved, changed jobs, or your preferences shifted. Delete specific entries or clear all Saved Info if you want a fresh start.

Important: Saved Info is not conversation history. Deleting a conversation does not erase Saved Info, and clearing Saved Info does not delete past conversations. They are independent.

Practical Tips for Using Saved Info

Start with the basics. Profession, location, and communication preferences are the highest-value items. They affect the widest range of conversations.

Be specific about preferences. "I prefer bullet points over paragraphs" or "I like detailed technical explanations, not simplified overviews" shapes every future response.

Review periodically. Saved Info can go stale. If you saved your job title a year ago and have since changed roles, update it. Outdated context leads Gemini to wrong assumptions.

Do not save sensitive information. Treat Saved Info like any cloud-stored data. No passwords, financial details, or anything you would not want tied to your Google account.

Saved Info is a small feature that compounds. The more Gemini knows about you, the less setup each conversation requires.

Tips for Better Conversations

After your first ten prompts, you have a feel for how Gemini works. A few tips that will immediately improve your results.

Be specific. "Help me write an email" is vague. "Help me write a polite email to my landlord requesting a repair for a leaking kitchen faucet, noting that I reported it two weeks ago and haven't heard back" gives Gemini everything it needs.

Provide context. Gemini does not know who you are, what your situation is, or what you have already tried unless you tell it. The more relevant context, the better the response.

Tell Gemini what format you want. Want a bullet list? Say so. A table? Ask for one. Exactly 200 words? Specify it. Gemini follows formatting instructions well.

Iterate, do not restart. If the first response is close but not perfect, refine with follow-ups rather than starting over. "Good, but more concise and add a specific example" is faster than writing a new prompt from scratch.

Use the right model. As we discussed in Chapter 4, save Pro for complex tasks and use Flash for everyday questions. This keeps your experience fast and your usage limits intact.

Upload files when relevant. If you are asking about a document, do not describe it — upload it. If you are asking about an image, share it. Gemini works better with the actual content than your description of it.

What Comes Next

You now have hands-on experience with Gemini. You know how to ask questions, refine answers, maintain context, and work with Gemini's response style. These fundamentals carry through every chapter ahead.

In Part II, we dive into specific skills: writing with Gemini, using it for research and learning, everyday productivity, and professional work. Each chapter builds on the conversational foundation here, adding techniques and more sophisticated prompting strategies.

The single most important thing you can do right now is keep using Gemini. Try it on a question that comes up naturally today — a recipe, a work email, a factual curiosity, a planning challenge. The more you use it, the more intuitive it becomes, and the more you will discover what it can do for your specific life and work.

Gemini rewards curiosity. Ask it anything. See what happens. When the answer is not quite right, ask again differently. That cycle — ask, read, refine — is the core skill of working with any AI assistant, and you are already doing it.

Part II: Core Skills

"It is not the strongest of the species that survives, nor the most intelligent, but the one most responsive to change."

— Charles Darwin (attributed)

Chapter 6: Writing with Gemini

You already know how to write. You have been doing it your entire life — emails, texts, social media posts, maybe the occasional report or blog article. But knowing how to write and enjoying it are different things. Most people would rather do almost anything else than stare at a blank page hunting for the right words for a tricky email or a LinkedIn post that does not sound robotic.

That is where Gemini comes in. Not as a replacement for your voice, but as a collaborator that gets you past the blank page, tightens your drafts, and handles the routine writing that eats up hours of your week. In this chapter, you will learn how to use Gemini for every kind of writing you are likely to encounter — from quick emails to polished articles — and how to keep the results sounding like you.

Drafting Emails, Letters, and Messages

Start with the writing task you probably do most often: email. Whether it is a follow-up to a client, a complaint to your internet provider, or a thank-you note after a job interview, Gemini can produce a solid first draft in seconds.

A simple example. You type:

> Write a professional email to my landlord requesting a repair for a leaking kitchen faucet. The leak started two days ago and is getting worse. I have already placed a bucket under it. My apartment number is 4B.

Gemini returns a complete, well-structured email with a subject line, greeting, clear description of the problem, and a polite closing. It typically runs three to four paragraphs — thorough without being long-winded.

What makes Gemini effective for email is its directness. Where other AI tools pad responses with qualifiers and softening language, Gemini gets to the point. For professional correspondence, that is usually what you want.

Adjusting Tone

Gemini's default email tone leans professional and neutral. You can steer it in any direction:

- **"Write this in a friendly, casual tone"** — for messages to colleagues you know well
- **"Make this more formal"** — for executives, clients, or official correspondence
- **"Keep it brief — three sentences max"** — for quick replies where less is more
- **"Write this diplomatically — the situation is tense"** — for complaints, disagreements, or sensitive topics

You can also adjust after the fact. If a draft feels too stiff, say "Make this warmer and more conversational" and Gemini revises.

Handling Difficult Emails

Some of the most valuable email drafting happens when stakes are high and you are not sure what to say. Turning down a job offer gracefully, responding to an unhappy customer, asking for a raise, or delivering bad news — these are situations where the wrong word creates real problems.

Give Gemini the context it needs:

> I need to write an email turning down a job offer from Acme Corp. I liked the team but the salary was 15% below my minimum and they couldn't negotiate further. I want to leave the door open for future opportunities. Keep it professional and warm.

Gemini handles this kind of nuanced writing well. It expresses gratitude, briefly acknowledges the reason without sounding bitter, and closes with a forward-looking note. You may tweak a phrase or two, but the heavy lifting is done.

Blog Posts, Articles, and Social Media Content

Beyond email, Gemini is a capable drafting partner for longer content. Blog posts, newsletter articles, LinkedIn updates, social captions — all fall in its wheelhouse.

Blog Posts and Articles

For a blog post, give Gemini a clear brief:

> Write a 700-word blog post about the benefits of remote work for small businesses. Target audience is small business owners who are skeptical about remote work. Tone should be persuasive but not pushy. Include specific examples and data points where relevant.

Gemini produces a structured post with an introduction, several body sections, and a conclusion. It often includes statistics and examples, though you should verify any specific claims — more on fact-checking in Chapter 7.

A few tips for better long-form drafts:

- **Specify your audience.** "Write for small business owners" produces different output than "write for HR professionals" or "write for a general audience."
- **Give a word count.** Gemini respects length guidelines reasonably well. Without one, it defaults to moderate length.
- **Specify structure.** If you need an introduction, three main sections, and a conclusion, say so. If you want bullets or numbered lists, ask.
- **Provide your key points.** Instead of letting Gemini decide what to argue, give it your three main points and let it flesh them out.

Social Media Content

For shorter content, Gemini's concise style is an advantage. Try:

> Write five LinkedIn post ideas about AI in small business. Each should be 2-3 sentences with a hook and a call to action. Professional but not corporate.

Or:

> Write an Instagram caption for a photo of our team at a volunteer event. Upbeat, genuine, under 100 words. Include 5 relevant hashtags.

Gemini matches platform conventions. It knows LinkedIn posts differ from tweets, Instagram captions have their own rhythm, and a Facebook update for a local business sounds different from a brand's X account.

Batch Content Creation

One of Gemini's practical strengths is producing multiple variations at once. Need a week's worth of social media posts? Ask for all seven in one prompt. Need the same announcement for three different platforms? Gemini generates all three in a single response. This batch production is where AI writing saves the most time.

Editing, Proofreading, and Tone Adjustment

You do not have to start from scratch every time. Some of the best uses of Gemini involve improving writing you have already done. Paste in your draft and ask Gemini to:

- **"Proofread this for grammar and spelling errors"** — Gemini catches typos, subject-verb disagreements, comma splices, and other mechanical issues.
- **"Edit this for clarity and conciseness"** — useful when your draft rambles or buries the main point.
- **"Make this sound more professional"** — or more casual, more confident, more empathetic.
- **"Shorten this by half"** — Gemini is good at cutting without losing the core message.

When you paste existing text, be specific. "Edit this" is vague. "Edit this for conciseness, and flag any sentences that are unclear" gives Gemini a clear target.

Track-Changes Style Editing

If you want to see what Gemini changed rather than a clean revised version, ask:

> Edit this paragraph for clarity. Show me what you changed and explain your reasoning for each change.

Gemini lists the original and revised versions of each sentence it altered, with brief explanations. Useful for learning and for deciding which edits to accept.

Preserving Your Voice

A common concern with AI writing tools is that everything ends up sounding the same — generic, smooth, forgettable. To avoid this:

1. **Give Gemini a sample of your writing.** Paste a paragraph or two of your natural style and say "Match this voice and tone."
2. **Be specific about what you do not want.** Hate corporate jargon? Say so. Never use exclamation points? Mention it.
3. **Edit the output.** The best workflow is not to use Gemini's output verbatim. Treat it as a strong first draft, then add your personality on revision.

Translation

Gemini handles translation competently across a wide range of languages. For common pairs — English to Spanish, French, German, Japanese, Mandarin, and others — quality is reliable for everyday communication.

To translate, just say:

> Translate this email into Spanish: [paste your email]

Or for more nuanced needs:

> Translate this into Japanese. This is a business email to a client I have not met before, so use appropriately formal language.

That second prompt matters. Many languages have formal and informal registers, and the default translation may not match the social context you need. Telling Gemini about the relationship and setting helps it choose the right level of formality.

Gemini can also help you understand text in another language without a full translation:

> Summarize this French article in English. Focus on the main argument and key data points.

For critical translations — legal documents, medical communications, anything where a mistake has real consequences — have a human translator review the output. Gemini is good but not perfect, and subtleties in specialized language can trip up any AI.

Gemini's Writing Style Compared to ChatGPT and Claude

If you have used other AI writing tools, you will notice Gemini has its own personality on the page. Knowing the differences helps you pick the right tool — or adjust your prompts to get what you want from Gemini.

Gemini tends toward direct, clean prose. It gets to the point without excessive hedging or preamble. Its default leans slightly more concise than ChatGPT, and it is less likely to open with filler like "Absolutely!" or "Great question!" It handles structured content — lists, comparisons, step-by-step instructions — with particular clarity.

ChatGPT produces slightly more elaborate prose. It tends to be more enthusiastic in tone and more likely to add qualifiers and transitions. Some prefer this warmer, more conversational style; others find it verbose.

Claude tends toward more nuanced, thoughtful prose. It is better at capturing subtlety and complexity, and its output often feels more carefully considered. For sensitive or complex writing, Claude sometimes edges ahead.

None of these differences are absolute — all three can be prompted to write in virtually any style. But knowing the defaults helps you work more efficiently. If you want Gemini warmer, ask. More concise than its default? That works too.

Walkthrough: Writing a Professional Bio

Let us put everything together with a practical example. You need a professional bio — maybe for a conference, a company website, or a freelance profile. Here is how to approach it with Gemini.

Step 1: Give Gemini the Raw Material

Start with the facts. Do not worry about making it pretty — just dump the relevant information:

> I need a professional bio. Here are the details:

- Name: Jordan Chen

- Title: Senior Product Manager at TechFlow Inc.
- 8 years in product management, previously at two startups
- Led the launch of TechFlow's flagship analytics platform
- MBA from University of Washington
- BS in Computer Science from UC San Diego
- Speaker at ProductCon 2025
- Based in Seattle
- Passionate about making data tools accessible to non-technical users

Step 2: Specify the Format and Context

> Write this as a third-person bio, about 150 words. This is for a conference speaker page, so emphasize professional accomplishments and speaking experience. Tone should be confident but not boastful.

Gemini produces something like:

> Jordan Chen is a Senior Product Manager at TechFlow Inc., where they led the launch of the company's flagship analytics platform. With eight years of experience in product management spanning two startups and a growth-stage company, they specialize in building data tools that non-technical users actually want to use. Jordan holds an MBA from the University of Washington and a BS in Computer Science from UC San Diego. They have spoken at ProductCon 2025 and are based in Seattle.

Step 3: Request Variations

One bio rarely fits every context. Ask for alternatives:

> Now write a shorter version (50 words) for a social media profile, and a longer version (250 words) for the company website that includes more personality.

Gemini produces both. The short version distills Jordan to title, company, key accomplishment, and location. The longer version expands on career trajectory and may add a sentence about outside interests or approach to work.

Step 4: Refine

Maybe the conference bio is close but not quite right:

> In the 150-word version, mention that they were previously at two Y Combinator-backed startups. Also, make the last sentence more engaging — it feels flat.

Gemini incorporates the detail and reworks the closing. You may go back and forth a couple more times until it feels right.

Step 5: Adapt for Different Platforms

> Now adapt the 150-word bio for my LinkedIn summary. Switch to first person and make it more conversational.

Gemini handles this format-shifting effortlessly. The facts stay the same; the voice and structure change to match the platform.

Tips for Better Writing with Gemini

A few principles that will serve you across all your writing with Gemini:

1. **Start with the context, not the request.** "I'm a freelance graphic designer writing to a potential client who found me through my portfolio website. Write an introductory email..." gives Gemini much more to work with than "Write an email to a client."

2. **Use Gemini for the tedious parts.** If you enjoy writing introductions but hate conclusions, let Gemini handle the conclusions. If you are good at arguments but weak on transitions, let Gemini smooth the seams.

3. **Iterate in conversation.** Your first prompt rarely produces the final result. Treat it as a starting point and refine. Gemini remembers the full conversation, so "make the second paragraph punchier" works without re-explaining anything.

4. **Always review before sending.** Gemini will occasionally produce a phrase that is slightly off, a claim that is not quite right, or a tone that does not match. A quick read-through catches these.

5. **Save prompts that work.** When you find a formula that consistently produces good results — for weekly newsletters, client proposals, whatever your recurring writing is — save it. You will use it again.

Writing with Gemini is not about outsourcing your voice. It is about having a fast, capable collaborator that handles the blank-page problem and frees you to focus on the ideas, strategy, and final polish only you can provide. In the next chapter, we look at another area where Gemini shines — research and learning.

Chapter 7: Research and Learning

If there is one area where Gemini has a structural advantage over its competitors, it is research. Gemini is built by Google, and it has direct access to Google Search — the largest, most comprehensive index of the web ever created. When you ask Gemini a question that benefits from current information, it searches the web in real time, pulls in relevant results, and synthesizes an answer with citations pointing to actual sources.

This is not a bolt-on feature. Google Search grounding is woven into how Gemini works, and it changes the research experience. In this chapter, you will learn how to use Gemini as a research assistant, how its search integration works in practice, and how to get the most out of it for learning, studying, and exploring new topics.

Using Gemini as a Research Assistant

Think of Gemini as a research assistant who has read an enormous amount of material, can search the internet instantly, and can explain what it finds in plain language. It is not perfect — no research assistant is — but it is fast, available around the clock, and capable.

The simplest way to use Gemini for research is to ask a question:

> What are the current leading theories about why some people develop long COVID?

Gemini will synthesize an answer from its training data and, when appropriate, current web sources. For a question like this — where the science is evolving — Gemini will often trigger Google Search grounding automatically and include citations to recent studies, medical institutions, or news reports.

Simple questions are just the beginning. Where Gemini earns its keep is in more complex scenarios:

- **Comparative research.** "Compare the education systems of Finland and South Korea. What does each do well, and what are the criticisms?"
- **Trend analysis.** "What has happened to commercial real estate prices in major US cities since 2023?"

- **Background research.** "I am writing a presentation about renewable energy adoption in Southeast Asia. Give me an overview of the current state, key players, and recent policy changes."
- **Technical research.** "Explain the current state of solid-state battery technology. Who are the leading companies and what are the remaining technical challenges?"

For each of these, Gemini will combine its broad training knowledge with real-time search results to produce a comprehensive, sourced answer.

Google Search Integration: Grounded Responses with Citations

Understanding how Google Search grounding works will make you a more effective researcher.

When you ask Gemini a question, it makes a decision: can I answer this reliably from what I already know, or should I search the web? For historical facts, well-established concepts, or general knowledge, Gemini answers directly from its training data. For current events, recent developments, specific statistics, or anything where freshness matters, it triggers a Google Search.

You can tell when Gemini has used Search because the response includes small citation markers — numbered superscripts or linked source labels. At the bottom, the sources are listed with titles and URLs. Click through to verify anything Gemini has told you.

This is a significant advantage over competitors. When ChatGPT browses the web, it does so through a more limited tool that visits individual pages. Gemini draws on the full power of Google Search — the same infrastructure that handles billions of queries daily. The result is broader source coverage and more reliable citations.

When to Force a Search

Sometimes Gemini answers from its training data when you want fresh, sourced information. Push it toward search-grounded responses:

> Search the web and tell me about the latest developments in the EU AI Act enforcement.

Or:

> What are the most recent studies on intermittent fasting? I want current research, not general background.

Phrases like "search the web," "find recent sources," or "what are the latest" signal to Gemini that you want grounded, cited responses rather than general knowledge.

When Training Data Is Fine

Not everything needs a web search. For how photosynthesis works, the causes of World War I, or the basics of compound interest, training data is more than sufficient. These are stable topics where freshness does not matter. Triggering a search adds latency without improving the answer.

Summarizing Articles, Papers, and Documents

One of Gemini's most practical research skills is summarization. Feed it long documents and get concise, structured summaries in seconds.

Summarizing Web Content

If you have a URL, you can ask Gemini to summarize it:

> Summarize this article: [paste URL]

Gemini will pull the content and provide a summary covering the main argument, key evidence, and conclusions. You can also be more specific:

> Summarize this article in three bullet points, focusing on the policy recommendations.

Summarizing Uploaded Documents

With Google AI Pro, you can upload PDFs, Word documents, and other files directly into the conversation. This is powerful for research:

> [Upload a 40-page PDF report] Summarize this report. Focus on the methodology, key findings, and limitations the authors acknowledge.

Gemini handles long documents thanks to its context window — over one million tokens for Gemini 3 Pro. It can process documents that would overwhelm other AI tools, holding the entire text in memory while it works.

Academic Papers

For research papers, try more targeted prompts:

> I uploaded a research paper. Answer these questions: 1. What is the central hypothesis? 2. What methodology did they use? 3. What were the key findings? 4. What limitations do the authors acknowledge? 5. How does this relate to the broader literature on this topic?

This gives you a thorough but digestible breakdown of any paper, even in fields outside your expertise.

Explaining Complex Topics

Gemini explains difficult concepts in accessible language. That makes it valuable not just for formal research but for everyday learning.

The key to good explanations is telling Gemini your current level of understanding:

> Explain how mRNA vaccines work. I have a basic understanding of biology — I know what DNA and proteins are — but I do not have a medical background.

This produces a very different explanation than:

> Explain how mRNA vaccines work. I am a molecular biology graduate student.

Both will be accurate, but the first will use analogies and simpler language, while the second will assume technical vocabulary and go deeper into mechanism.

The Explain-It-Again Technique

If Gemini's first explanation does not click, do not give up. Ask it to try again from a different angle:

> That was helpful, but I am still confused about how the lipid nanoparticle delivers the mRNA into the cell. Can you explain that part using an analogy?

Or:

> Can you explain this concept as if you were teaching a high school class?

Gemini handles re-explanation requests well. It will rephrase and restructure, not just rearrange the same words.

Building Understanding Layer by Layer

For topics you want to understand deeply, try a layered approach:

1. Start with a broad overview: "Give me a five-sentence summary of how blockchain works."
2. Drill into a subtopic: "Now explain the consensus mechanism in more detail."
3. Ask about implications: "What problems does proof-of-stake solve that proof-of-work cannot?"
4. Request real-world context: "Which major blockchains use proof-of-stake, and how has it worked in practice?"

Each prompt builds on the last, and Gemini maintains context throughout. This is a far more effective way to learn than cramming everything into a single prompt.

Study Aids

Students at any level — high school, university, or self-directed learners — will find Gemini a powerful study companion. Here are several study techniques that work well with Gemini.

Flashcard Generation

> I am studying for a US history exam covering the period 1865-1920. Generate 20 flashcard-style question and answer pairs covering the most important events, people, and concepts.

Gemini produces targeted Q&A pairs you can transfer to your preferred flashcard app or study from directly.

Practice Questions

> I am preparing for the AP Biology exam. Create 10 multiple-choice practice questions about cellular respiration, each with four options and an explanation of the correct answer.

Gemini generates realistic practice questions and, crucially, explains why each answer is correct. Useful not just for testing yourself but for learning from your mistakes.

Concept Mapping

> I am studying macroeconomics. Map out the relationships between inflation, interest rates, unemployment, and GDP growth. Explain how a change in one affects the others.

Gemini walks through the interconnections, helping you see the big picture rather than memorize isolated facts.

Study Schedules

> I have a chemistry final in two weeks. The exam covers chapters 8-14 of my textbook: chemical bonding, molecular geometry, gases, intermolecular forces, solutions, kinetics, and equilibrium. Create a study schedule that covers all topics with heavier weight on my weak areas (gases and equilibrium).

Gemini produces a day-by-day plan with time allocations weighted toward your weak areas.

Fact-Checking with Google Search Grounding

One of Gemini's most valuable applications is fact-checking — verifying claims you have encountered elsewhere. This is where Google Search grounding shines.

Say you read an article claiming that "Sweden generates 60% of its electricity from renewable sources." Check it:

> Is it true that Sweden generates 60% of its electricity from renewable sources? Find current data.

Gemini searches for the latest statistics, reports what it finds, and cites its sources. You can click through to verify further.

This works for all kinds of claims:

- **Statistics and data.** "Is it accurate that the average American spends 7 hours per day on screens?"
- **Quotes and attributions.** "Did Einstein really say 'The definition of insanity is doing the same thing over and over and expecting different results'?"
- **Current events.** "Has the UK actually banned disposable vapes?"
- **Scientific claims.** "Is there evidence that cold showers boost your immune system?"

For each, Gemini searches current sources, reports what the evidence says, and flags any nuance or disagreement. Vastly faster than running the searches yourself, reading through multiple results, and synthesizing the answer.

The Double-Check Feature

Gemini includes a built-in "Double-check response" feature, accessible via a button below its responses. Tap it, and Gemini reviews its own answer against Google Search results, flagging which statements web sources support and which could not be verified. Well-supported statements appear in green; unconfirmed ones appear in orange.

No other major AI assistant offers this, and it is useful. Get in the habit of using it for any response where accuracy matters.

Comparing Gemini's Research Capabilities to Competitors

To put Gemini's research features in context, here is how it stacks up:

Gemini with Google Search grounding — real-time access to the full Google Search index. Citations are integrated naturally. The double-check feature adds verification. Best-in-class for research that needs current web information.

ChatGPT with web browsing — searches via Bing, but the integration is less seamless. It visits individual pages rather than drawing on a full search index. Citations are included, but source coverage is narrower.

Claude — Claude has had robust web search for some time, alongside its strengths in analysis and reasoning. It excels at working with documents you provide and produces strong cited responses to web queries, though its search experience is less tightly woven into a dedicated grounding system than Gemini's Google Search integration.

Perplexity — a dedicated AI search tool that provides cited answers. Strong at straightforward factual queries but lacks Gemini's conversational depth and follow-up.

For pure research — especially anything requiring current information, multiple sources, or fact verification — Gemini's Google Search integration gives it a meaningful edge. It is not the best tool for every task, but for research, the Google connection is a real advantage.

Walkthrough: Researching a Topic for a Presentation

Here is a realistic research scenario from start to finish. You need to prepare a 15-minute presentation on the state of electric vehicle adoption for a team meeting. You are not an EV expert — you just need to be informed enough to lead a discussion.

Step 1: Get an Overview

> I need to prepare a presentation on the current state of electric vehicle adoption globally. Give me a broad overview of where things stand as of May 2026: market share trends, leading countries, top manufacturers, and key challenges. Use current data with sources.

Gemini searches the web and produces a comprehensive overview with cited statistics: global EV sales figures, market share by country, top manufacturers, and a summary of challenges like charging infrastructure and battery supply chains.

Step 2: Dig Into the Data

Now pick the areas that matter most for your audience:

> What are the specific EV market share numbers for the US, China, and the EU for 2025? How do these compare to 2023 and 2024?

Gemini finds the comparative data and presents it clearly. Ask for a table:

> Put that comparison into a table with columns for each region and rows for each year.

Step 3: Understand the Counterarguments

Good presentations anticipate objections:

> What are the strongest arguments against the pace of EV adoption? What do skeptics point to? Include specific data points.

Gemini presents the counterarguments fairly — grid capacity concerns, rural charging deserts, battery mineral supply chains, lifecycle carbon footprint debates, and cost parity timelines. Each is grounded in current sources.

Step 4: Find Compelling Stories

Data is important, but stories make presentations memorable:

> Find two or three specific, recent examples or case studies that illustrate interesting trends in EV adoption — either successes or surprising setbacks. These should be specific enough to be engaging in a presentation.

Gemini might surface a story about Norway's near-total EV transition, a specific city's charging infrastructure rollout, or a manufacturer's unexpected pivot.

Step 5: Create Your Outline

> Based on everything we have discussed, create an outline for a 15-minute presentation with 8-10 slides. Include speaker notes for each slide summarizing the key points and data I should mention.

Gemini produces a complete outline with slide titles and talking points drawn from your earlier research. Because it has the full context of the session, the outline holds together.

Step 6: Verify Key Claims

Before you finalize, double-check the most important statistics:

> Let me verify: you mentioned that global EV sales reached [number] in 2025. Double-check this figure and give me the most reliable source for it.

Gemini re-searches and confirms or corrects the figure, pointing you to the authoritative source.

Tips for Better Research with Gemini

1. **Ask for sources explicitly.** While Gemini often includes citations automatically, adding "cite your sources" or "include links to your sources" to your prompt increases the likelihood of getting well-referenced responses.
2. **Specify recency requirements.** "What were the top programming languages in 2025?" is more useful than "What are the top programming languages?" when you need current data.
3. **Cross-reference important facts.** Even with Google Search grounding, do not treat Gemini as infallible. For critical facts, click through to the cited sources and verify.
4. **Use follow-up questions to go deeper.** Do not try to get everything in one prompt. Start broad and narrow down based on what you find interesting or relevant.

5. **Upload your existing research.** If you have already gathered some materials — PDFs, reports, articles — upload them and ask Gemini to build on what you have. Its large context window means it can hold all of your existing research while searching for new information.

6. **Ask Gemini what you are missing.** After a research session, try: "Based on our conversation, what important aspects of this topic have I not asked about?" Gemini will often surface gaps you had not considered.

Research and learning are among Gemini's strongest use cases. The combination of broad knowledge, real-time web access, large document handling, and conversational depth makes it a research tool that would have seemed like science fiction a few years ago. In the next chapter, we bring that same capability to your everyday life.

Chapter 8: Everyday Productivity

So far, we have focused on writing and research — tasks with a clear objective. But some of the most satisfying uses of Gemini are the everyday tasks that do not fit neatly into a category. Planning a vacation. Figuring out what to cook with half a fridge of random ingredients. Thinking through a home renovation. Getting a handle on your budget.

These are the tasks that fill the margins of your life — not quite important enough to hire a professional, but time-consuming enough to put off indefinitely. Gemini handles them well, and once you start using it for this kind of thing, you will wonder how you managed without it.

Planning Trips, Events, and Schedules

Travel planning is one of Gemini's most popular everyday use cases, and for good reason. It combines several things Gemini does well: organizing information, making recommendations under constraints, and pulling current web data for prices, availability, and logistics.

Trip Planning

Start with the big picture:

> I am planning a 10-day trip to Japan in October with my partner. We are interested in a mix of culture, food, and nature. Budget is moderate — not backpacking, but not luxury. We will fly into Tokyo. Help me plan an itinerary.

Gemini produces a day-by-day itinerary covering cities, neighborhoods, specific attractions, and travel logistics between locations. It typically mixes well-known highlights with less obvious picks.

What makes this useful is interactive refinement:

> We are not interested in shopping districts. Can you swap out the Harajuku time for something else? Also, we would love to spend a day in a smaller town that tourists do not usually visit.

Gemini adjusts the itinerary while keeping the overall structure intact. Go back and forth until the plan feels right.

For practical logistics:

> Should we get a Japan Rail Pass for this itinerary? Calculate the approximate cost of individual tickets vs. the 14-day pass.

Because Gemini can pull current web data through Google Search, it works from up-to-date pricing rather than potentially stale training data.

Event Planning

The same approach works for events closer to home:

> I am planning a birthday party for my daughter who is turning 7. We have about 15 kids coming. Budget is $300. We have a backyard but no pool. It is in June in Austin, Texas, so it will be hot. Suggest a theme, activities, food, and a timeline for the party.

Gemini produces a complete party plan — theme, age-appropriate activities, food menu, schedule, and usually a few creative touches you had not considered. It respects every constraint you set: budget, heat, no pool, kid count.

Schedule Organization

For more routine scheduling:

> I have the following commitments this week: dentist Monday 10am, team meeting Tuesday and Thursday 2pm, kids soccer practice Wednesday and Friday at 4pm, dinner with friends Saturday 7pm. I also need to find time to: finish a report (about 4 hours of work), go grocery shopping, exercise three times, and do laundry. Help me build a weekly schedule that makes sense.

Gemini slots everything in around your existing commitments and suggests logical times for the flexible tasks. Like an administrative assistant who never judges you for not having your life together.

Meal Planning and Recipes

Gemini is a versatile cooking companion, whether you need a week of meal plans or just want to figure out what to do with what is in the fridge.

Weekly Meal Planning

> Plan five weeknight dinners for a family of four. Two of us are vegetarian, two are not. Budget-conscious, nothing that takes more than 45 minutes. Include a shopping list organized by grocery store section.

Gemini produces five dinners for a mixed household — often a vegetarian base with a protein added for the meat-eaters. The organized shopping list saves time at the store.

Cooking with What You Have

This is one of the most practically useful prompts in Gemini's repertoire:

> I have chicken thighs, sweet potatoes, a can of coconut milk, garlic, onions, rice, and some wilting spinach. What can I make for dinner?

Gemini suggests two or three recipes from those ingredients with instructions. It works within constraints and avoids suggesting things that require a special trip to the store.

Recipe Adaptation

> I have a recipe that calls for heavy cream but I need a dairy-free alternative. The recipe is a mushroom risotto. What should I substitute and will I need to adjust anything else?

Gemini understands cooking chemistry well enough to suggest substitutions and flag adjustments to technique or proportions. It will tell you, for instance, that coconut cream works well in risotto but that you might reduce the amount slightly and add a squeeze of lemon to balance the flavor.

Dietary Requirements

If you have specific dietary needs — keto, low-sodium, gluten-free, diabetic-friendly — Gemini can plan around them:

> I was just diagnosed with Type 2 diabetes and my doctor told me to reduce my carb intake. Plan a week of low-carb meals — breakfast, lunch, and dinner. I do not like fish. Keep it simple and practical.

Gemini produces meals that respect the constraint while staying practical and varied. It typically notes the approximate carb content per meal, though you should verify specific nutritional information with a dedicated tool or your healthcare provider.

Personal Finance Questions

Gemini can help you think through financial decisions, understand concepts, and run basic calculations. It is not a financial advisor and should not replace one for major decisions, but it is useful for building understanding and preliminary analysis.

Understanding Financial Concepts

> Explain how a Roth IRA differs from a traditional IRA. I am 30 years old, making $75,000 a year. Which might be better for me?

Gemini explains both options and walks through the factors relevant to your situation — current tax bracket, expected future income, time to retirement. It lays out the reasoning without making a definitive recommendation, which is the responsible approach.

Budgeting

> I bring home $4,500 per month after taxes. My fixed expenses are: rent $1,400, car payment $350, insurance $180, phone $45, internet $60, student loan $280. Help me create a budget using the 50/30/20 rule and tell me how much I have left for savings and discretionary spending.

Gemini calculates your fixed expense total, breaks down the 50/30/20 allocation, and tells you where you stand. It will flag if your fixed expenses already exceed the recommended 50% and suggest adjustments.

Comparison Shopping

> I am deciding between buying and leasing a car. The car I want costs $35,000. The lease is $399/month for 36 months with $2,000 due at

> signing. If I buy, I will finance at 5.9% for 60 months. Help me compare the total cost of each option.

Gemini does the math and presents the comparison so the trade-offs are obvious. It typically mentions factors beyond the pure numbers — mileage limits on leases, equity at the end, and so on.

Health and Wellness

Gemini can be a helpful resource for health-related questions, with an important caveat: it is not a doctor, and it should never replace professional medical advice. Use it for general health education and preliminary research, not diagnosis or treatment decisions.

General Health Information

> What are the recommended cancer screenings for a 45-year-old woman with no family history of cancer?

Gemini provides current screening guidelines, typically citing sources like the American Cancer Society or the US Preventive Services Task Force. Useful for preparing for a doctor's visit or making sense of what your doctor recommended.

Fitness Planning

> Create a beginner strength training program for someone who has never lifted weights. Three days per week, using only dumbbells. I have 30 minutes per session.

Gemini produces practical workout plans with exercises, sets, reps, rest periods, and progression guidelines. For beginners, this is a solid starting point — though a session with a personal trainer to learn proper form is always worth the investment.

Understanding Symptoms

> I have been getting headaches almost every afternoon for the past two weeks. They are behind my eyes and feel like pressure. What are the most common causes?

Gemini lists possible causes — eyestrain, tension headaches, dehydration, sinus issues — without jumping to alarming conclusions. It consistently recommends seeing a healthcare provider if symptoms persist, which is the right advice.

A word of caution: do not use Gemini to self-diagnose serious conditions, interpret lab results, or make decisions about medication. It can help you understand medical terminology and prepare questions for your doctor, but the medical decisions should involve a licensed professional.

Home and DIY Project Assistance

Whether you are a seasoned DIYer or someone who has never held a drill, Gemini can help you plan and execute home projects.

Project Planning

> I want to build a raised garden bed in my backyard. The space is about 4 feet by 8 feet. I am a beginner at woodworking. What materials do I need, what will it cost approximately, and can you give me step-by-step instructions?

Gemini provides a materials list with approximate quantities and costs, tool requirements, and step-by-step instructions. It flags details a beginner might miss — like using untreated cedar or redwood instead of pressure-treated lumber if you are growing food.

Troubleshooting

> My bathroom faucet is dripping. It is a single-handle faucet. What are the most likely causes and can I fix it myself?

Gemini walks you through the probable causes (usually a worn cartridge or O-ring), the tools you need, and the repair steps. It gauges difficulty well and will tell you when a project is DIY-friendly versus when to call a professional.

Cost Estimation

> I am thinking about finishing my basement. The space is about 600 square feet. I want basic finishing — framing, drywall, flooring, lighting, and maybe a half bathroom. What is a realistic budget range for hiring a contractor vs. doing it myself?

Gemini gives ballpark cost estimates, and with Google Search grounding, it factors in current material prices and regional labor variations. These are estimates, not quotes — but they help you understand the scale of a project before you commit.

Walkthrough: Planning a Two-Week Trip

Here is a detailed walkthrough that puts these skills together. You are planning a two-week trip to Portugal and Spain with your family — two adults and two kids, ages 10 and 13.

Step 1: The Big Picture

> We are planning a two-week trip to Portugal and Spain in July. Two adults, two kids ages 10 and 13. Flying from Chicago. We want a mix of cities, beaches, and culture. The kids are interested in history and are adventurous eaters. Budget is mid-range — good hotels but not five-star. Help us plan a rough itinerary.

Gemini proposes a route — perhaps Lisbon, the Algarve coast, Seville, Granada, and Barcelona — with approximate time in each. It considers July weather (hot in southern Spain) and suggests adjustments: beach time on the hottest days, city sightseeing in the mornings and evenings.

Step 2: Refine the Itinerary

> I like the overall route but two weeks might be too much driving. Can we trim it to three cities instead of five and add more depth? We would rather really experience a few places than rush through many.

Gemini adjusts, perhaps focusing on Lisbon, Seville, and Barcelona with enough time in each for a relaxed pace. It revises day-by-day activities and suggests how to handle travel between cities — train vs. flight vs. rental car — with approximate costs and travel times.

Step 3: Kid-Friendly Details

> What are the best activities for kids ages 10 and 13 in Lisbon? They like hands-on experiences more than traditional museums.

Gemini suggests age-appropriate activities — the Oceanarium, a food tour in Alfama, surfing lessons in nearby Cascais, the interactive science museum, tram rides. It knows a 10-year-old and a 13-year-old have different thresholds for "boring museum" and calibrates accordingly.

Step 4: Logistics

> Help me figure out the travel logistics. We will fly into Lisbon and out of Barcelona. What is the best way to get from Lisbon to Seville and from Seville to Barcelona? Include approximate costs and travel times for each option.

Gemini compares options — direct trains, budget flights, rental cars — with current pricing from Google Search. It weighs convenience, cost, and family-friendliness for each leg.

Step 5: Budget

> Based on this itinerary, estimate our total trip budget including flights, hotels, local transportation, food, and activities. Assume mid-range hotels ($150-200/night) and eating out for most meals.

Gemini builds a structured budget with line items for each category, giving you a realistic total to plan around. This is not a guarantee of what you will spend, but it gives you a framework.

Step 6: Practical Tips

> What do we need to know about traveling in Portugal and Spain with kids in July? Any practical tips about heat, meal times, tipping, or cultural norms we should be aware of?

Gemini covers the practical realities — late dinner times in Spain, siesta culture, sunscreen and hydration in July, tipping customs, current travel requirements. Thanks to Google Search grounding, the information reflects current conditions rather than outdated guidebook advice.

Step 7: Create a Packing List

> Based on our itinerary and the July weather, create a packing list for each of us. Keep it practical — we want to pack light.

Gemini produces four lists tailored to each person, factoring in the activities, the weather, and the goal of packing light. It includes details you might forget — a lightweight daypack for excursions, a reusable water bottle for the heat.

Making Gemini Part of Your Daily Routine

The examples in this chapter cover a wide range of tasks, but they share something: they are things you do regularly but not often enough to become an expert. Nobody plans a trip every week or builds a raised garden bed every month. Gemini is valuable precisely because it brings expert-level knowledge to tasks you do occasionally.

Some ways to build Gemini into your daily routine:

- **Morning planning.** "What is on my calendar today and what should I prioritize?" (This works especially well if you use Google Workspace with Gemini extensions enabled.)
- **Quick decisions.** "Should I repair or replace a dishwasher that is 8 years old and has a broken pump?" Gemini can help you think through the decision in under a minute.
- **Learning moments.** When something comes up in conversation or the news that you do not fully understand, ask Gemini. "What is happening with the port strike?" or "How does ranked-choice voting actually work?"
- **Weekend projects.** Before starting any home project, run it by Gemini for a materials list, cost estimate, and difficulty assessment.

The goal is not to make Gemini a crutch. It is to remove friction from the tasks that slow you down, freeing up time and mental energy for the things that matter. In the next chapter, we take this same approach into the workplace.

Chapter 9: Work and Professional Use

If the previous chapter was about using Gemini to make your personal life easier, this one is about making your professional life better. Not in a vague, aspirational way — in a concrete, this-saves-me-two-hours-today way.

Gemini is well-suited to professional work for two reasons. First, its Google Workspace integration means it works inside the tools you already use at the office — Gmail, Docs, Sheets, Slides, and Meet. Chapter 13 covers that in depth. Second, its Google Search grounding means your work research is backed by current web data, not just whatever the model learned in training.

This chapter focuses on the core professional tasks Gemini handles well: meeting prep, report writing, data analysis, brainstorming, and job search. Each section includes practical prompts you can adapt to your own work.

Meeting Prep and Agendas

Meetings are the connective tissue of professional life. They are also, let us be honest, where a lot of time goes to die. Gemini helps at every stage — before, during, and after.

Building an Agenda

A good meeting starts with a clear agenda. Most people know this, and most people still walk in without one. Gemini retires the excuse "I did not have time to write an agenda":

> I have a 30-minute meeting tomorrow with my product team to discuss the Q3 roadmap. The main decision we need to make is whether to prioritize the mobile app redesign or the API integration project. Both have strong business cases. There are five people attending, including the engineering lead and the design lead. Create an agenda that keeps us focused and gets us to a decision.

Gemini produces a timed agenda — five minutes for context, ten for each option's case, five for discussion, five for decision and next steps. It suggests specific discussion questions and flags what each person should bring.

Pre-Meeting Research

When you are meeting with someone new — a potential client, a partner, a vendor — Gemini can help you prepare:

> I have a meeting tomorrow with the CEO of NovaTech Solutions. They are a B2B SaaS company in the supply chain space. Search the web and give me a briefing: company overview, recent news, funding history, and key products. Also find the CEO's background and any recent public statements or interviews.

Because of Google Search grounding, Gemini pulls current information — recent funding rounds, product launches, press coverage — rather than relying on stale training data. This is prep work that used to take 30 minutes of Googling. Gemini does it in about 15 seconds.

Post-Meeting Follow-Up

After a meeting, Gemini can help you turn notes into action:

> Here are my rough notes from today's product meeting: [paste notes]. Clean these up into a structured meeting summary with: key decisions made, action items with owners and deadlines, and open questions to address next time.

The result is a professional meeting summary you can share with your team immediately. No more "I'll send the notes later" that never happens.

Report and Proposal Drafting

Reports and proposals are high-stakes documents that often eat disproportionate amounts of time. Gemini accelerates every phase.

First Drafts

The most painful part of report writing is the first draft. Getting from blank page to something editable is where Gemini saves the most time:

> I need to write a quarterly business review report for my team's performance in Q1. Here are the key points:

- Revenue: $2.4M, up 12% from Q4

- New customers: 34 (target was 30)
- Churn: 5.2%, up from 4.8% (concerning trend)
- Product launches: shipped the analytics dashboard on time
- Key challenge: support ticket volume up 22%, causing response time delays
- Q2 priorities: hire two support reps, launch self-service help center, begin enterprise pricing project

> Write a professional report of about 1,000 words. Tone should be honest about challenges but overall positive. This goes to our VP.

Gemini produces a polished first draft that tells the Q1 story coherently — leading with wins, acknowledging concerns about churn and support load, positioning Q2 priorities as solutions. The structure is logical and the tone calibrated for an executive audience.

Proposals

Business proposals follow predictable structures, which makes them ideal for AI assistance:

> Write a proposal for implementing a company-wide mentorship program. The audience is the HR leadership team. Include: executive summary, problem statement (we are losing junior employees at 30% in their first year), proposed solution, implementation timeline, resource requirements, and expected outcomes. Budget should be under $50,000 for the pilot year.

Gemini produces a complete proposal framework. You fill in company-specific details and adjust the tone to match your organization's culture, but the structure, flow, and argumentation are solid.

Executive Summaries

If you have already written a long report, Gemini can produce the executive summary:

> [Paste your 3,000-word report] Write a 300-word executive summary for this report. Focus on the three most important findings and the

> recommended next steps. The reader is a C-suite executive who has five minutes.

This is a task where Gemini's direct style is an asset. It distills your report to its essence without the hedging and filler that creep into most executive summaries.

Data Analysis

Gemini does not have a built-in code execution environment like ChatGPT's Code Interpreter, so it cannot run Python scripts on your data directly. It is still a capable data analysis partner in several important ways.

Analyzing Data You Describe

Share key data points and Gemini can help you interpret them:

> Our website traffic data for the past six months: October: 45,000 sessions, 2.1% conversion November: 52,000 sessions, 2.3% conversion December: 68,000 sessions, 1.8% conversion January: 41,000 sessions, 2.4% conversion February: 39,000 sessions, 2.6% conversion March: 47,000 sessions, 2.5% conversion
>
> What trends do you see? What might explain the December spike with lower conversion? What should we investigate?

Gemini analyzes the patterns, hypothesizes about the December anomaly (likely holiday traffic with lower purchase intent), notes the improving conversion rate trend in Q1, and suggests specific things to investigate.

Working with Uploaded Data

With Google AI Pro, you can upload spreadsheets and CSV files for analysis:

> [Upload a CSV file] Analyze this sales data. I want to know: top-performing products, monthly revenue trends, which regions are growing fastest, and any anomalies or patterns worth investigating.

Gemini reads the data and provides a narrative analysis. It cannot create interactive charts the way Code Interpreter can, but it describes patterns clearly and suggests the visualizations you should create.

Formula Help

If you work in Google Sheets or Excel, Gemini is excellent at writing formulas:

> I have a Google Sheet with sales data. Column A is the date, Column B is the sales rep name, Column C is the deal amount, and Column D is the deal stage (Won, Lost, or Pipeline). Write a formula that calculates the total won deals for each sales rep in the last 90 days.

Gemini provides the formula with an explanation of how it works. Often faster than searching for formula syntax on Google, especially for complex formulas involving multiple functions.

Creating Analysis Frameworks

Even without running code, Gemini can help you structure your analysis:

> I need to analyze whether our pricing change last quarter affected customer retention. What data should I look at, what metrics should I track, and how should I structure the analysis to isolate the pricing effect from other variables?

Gemini outlines an analytical framework — cohort analysis comparing pre- and post-change customers, controlling variables, metrics to track, statistical approaches to validate findings. You still do the analysis, but having the framework saves significant time.

Brainstorming and Ideation

When you need ideas — for a marketing campaign, a product feature, a team event, a new initiative — Gemini is a tireless brainstorming partner. Unlike a human colleague, it never runs out of ideas, never judges your suggestions, and never derails the session with tangents.

Generating Options

> We are launching a loyalty program for our coffee shop chain. We have 12 locations in the Portland area. Brainstorm 10 creative loyalty program structures that go beyond the standard "buy 10 get 1 free" punch card.

Gemini produces ten distinct concepts, from practical (tiered membership with increasing perks) to creative (a "coffee passport" that rewards trying every location) to community-oriented (points donated to local charities). Not all will be viable, but several will spark useful thinking.

Building on Ideas

When one idea catches your eye, dig deeper:

> I like the coffee passport idea. Flesh this out. How would it work mechanistically? What would the rewards be? How would we track it? What would it cost us per customer? How would we promote it?

Gemini develops the concept into a detailed proposal. You are using it as an ideation accelerator — taking a seed and growing it into something you can evaluate seriously.

Devil's Advocate

Gemini can also help you stress-test ideas:

> We are considering switching from a monthly subscription model to an annual-only model. The theory is that annual commitments reduce churn and improve cash flow predictability. Play devil's advocate — what are all the reasons this might backfire?

Gemini systematically identifies risks: higher barrier to entry for new customers, backlash from existing monthly subscribers, competitive disadvantage if rivals keep monthly options, cash flow timing during the transition, and more. This structured critique is valuable because it forces you to address weaknesses before they become problems.

Naming and Branding

> We are launching a new project management tool designed for creative agencies. Suggest 15 name ideas. The name should feel modern, creative, and suggest collaboration. Avoid anything too corporate or generic.

Gemini generates a diverse set of options. Some will be terrible, some interesting, one or two might be exactly right. The value is in the volume — you are casting a wide net to find the name that resonates.

Job Search: Resumes, Cover Letters, and Interview Prep

Whether you are actively job hunting or just keeping your materials updated, Gemini is a practical job search tool.

Resume Review and Improvement

Paste your resume into Gemini and ask for feedback:

> Review my resume. I am applying for senior product manager roles at mid-size tech companies. Tell me: what is working well, what is weak, and what specific changes would make it stronger. Be direct — I want honest feedback, not flattery.

Gemini gives you actionable feedback — vague bullets that need quantification, skills that should be more prominent, formatting issues, missing elements hiring managers look for.

Tailoring for Specific Roles

> Here is my resume and here is the job description for a Senior Product Manager role at [Company]. Revise my resume to better align with this specific role. Emphasize relevant experience and use language from the job description where appropriate. Do not fabricate experience.

That last instruction matters. Gemini will align your experience with the job description's language and priorities, but always verify that the final resume accurately represents your background.

Cover Letters

> Write a cover letter for this role: [paste job description]. Here is my resume for context: [paste resume]. The letter should be concise — under 300 words. It should connect my analytics experience directly to their need for data-driven product decisions. Tone should be confident but not arrogant.

Gemini produces a focused cover letter that connects your experience to the role's requirements. Adjust the tone and add personal details to make it yours.

Interview Preparation

This is where Gemini can make the biggest difference in your job search. Thorough interview prep is one of the highest-return activities a candidate can do, and most people under-prepare.

> I have an interview for a Senior Product Manager role at [Company] on Thursday. The role focuses on their B2B analytics platform. Help me prepare. I need:

1. Background research on the company and their analytics product
2. Likely interview questions for a senior PM role
3. A framework for answering behavioral questions
4. Questions I should ask the interviewers

Gemini uses Google Search to pull current information about the company, then produces a comprehensive prep package. The interview questions it generates are typically well-calibrated to the role level and industry.

Mock Interviews

Take it a step further:

> Let us do a mock interview. You are the hiring manager for the Senior Product Manager role at [Company]. Ask me one behavioral question at a time, wait for my response, then give me feedback on how to improve my answer. Focus on the STAR method (Situation, Task, Action, Result).

The interactive mock interview is surprisingly effective. Gemini asks realistic questions, evaluates your responses, and coaches you on structure, specificity, and impact. Not a substitute for practicing with a real person, but excellent preparation you can do at midnight in your pajamas without bothering anyone.

Walkthrough: Preparing for a Job Interview

Here is a complete interview prep session showing how these pieces fit together.

Step 1: Research the Company

> I have a final-round interview at Meridian Health Technologies on Friday for a Director of Marketing role. Search the web and give me a comprehensive briefing: what the company does, recent news, key products, competitors, company culture (from Glassdoor or similar), and any challenges they might be facing.

Gemini searches current sources and compiles a briefing covering the company's business, market position, recent developments, and what employees say about the culture. This grounds your prep in reality rather than guesswork.

Step 2: Analyze the Role

> Here is the job description: [paste]. Based on this and what we know about the company, what are the three to five most important things they are looking for in this hire? What problems are they trying to solve by filling this role?

Gemini reads between the lines of the job description — identifying not just stated requirements but underlying business needs. Maybe "brand awareness" appears three times, suggesting a weak spot. Maybe "data-driven" repeats, signaling a shift away from intuition-based marketing.

Step 3: Prepare Your Stories

> Based on the role requirements, suggest six behavioral interview questions I am likely to get. For each, suggest which experience from my resume I should use to answer it.

Gemini maps your experience to likely questions so you prepare specific stories in advance rather than scrambling for examples in the moment.

Step 4: Practice Your Answers

> Let us practice. Ask me the first behavioral question. After I answer, give me honest feedback.

You type your answer. Gemini evaluates it:

> Your answer covered the situation and action well, but the result was vague. Instead of saying "it went really well," quantify the impact. Did

> the campaign increase leads by a specific percentage? Did it hit a revenue target? Interviewers remember numbers.

Step 5: Prepare Your Questions

> What are five thoughtful questions I should ask my interviewers that would demonstrate genuine interest in the role and strategic thinking about the company's challenges? These should not be questions I could answer by looking at the website.

Gemini suggests questions that go beyond surface research — strategic direction, team dynamics, success metrics, challenges. These show you have done your homework and are thinking seriously about the role.

Step 6: Final Review

> Based on everything we have discussed, give me a one-page cheat sheet I can review on the morning of the interview. Include: key company facts, the top three things they are looking for, my strongest examples for each, and my prepared questions.

Gemini distills the prep session into a concise reference document. Print it, review it over coffee, and walk in better prepared than most candidates.

A Note on Workplace AI Policies

Before using Gemini extensively at work, check whether your organization has an AI usage policy. Many companies now have guidelines about approved tools, what data can be shared, and how AI-generated content should be disclosed.

If your company uses Google Workspace with Gemini for Business or Enterprise, you are in good shape — those plans include data protection agreements, and your conversations are not used to train the model. If you use a personal Gemini account for work, be careful about what you share. Do not paste confidential data, proprietary code, or sensitive customer information into a personal AI tool.

Chapter 26 covers privacy and security in more detail. For now, the rule of thumb: if you would not email it to a stranger, do not paste it into a personal AI account.

Making Gemini a Professional Habit

The professionals who get the most from Gemini are not the ones using it for one big project. They are the ones who integrate it into their daily workflow for dozens of small tasks:

- **Start each day** by asking Gemini to help you prioritize your task list.
- **Before every meeting**, spend 60 seconds getting Gemini to generate an agenda or research the attendees.
- **After every meeting**, paste your notes in and get a clean summary with action items.
- **When writing anything** — an email, a report, a proposal — start with Gemini and iterate from there.
- **When stuck on a problem**, use Gemini as a brainstorming partner to generate options you had not considered.

The compound effect of these small savings is significant. If Gemini saves you 15 minutes per task and you use it for ten tasks a day, that is two and a half hours of recovered time — every day. Over a week, a month, a year, it adds up to a meaningful competitive advantage.

The first nine chapters give you a foundation. In the next part, we go deeper into Gemini's specialized tools — Google Search integration, image generation, video understanding, Workspace integration, Gems, and more.

Part III: Creative and Multimodal Tools

"The real problem is not whether machines think but whether men do."

— B. F. Skinner

Chapter 10: Google Search Integration

One of the most persistent problems with large language models has been their tendency to present plausible-sounding but fabricated information as fact. Gemini's answer is arguably its most powerful differentiator: deep, native integration with Google Search. This is not a bolt-on or an afterthought. It is the backbone of how Gemini keeps responses grounded in real, verifiable information — and it changes how you should think about using an AI assistant.

This chapter covers how Google Search grounding works under the hood, how to trigger it deliberately, how to interpret the citations, and how to use the "double-check" button to verify any response against the live web. By the end, you will understand why this integration matters more than any other single feature for day-to-day reliability.

Why Search Grounding Matters

Every large language model has a knowledge cutoff — a point in time beyond which it has no training data. Ask about something that happened last week, and it is flying blind. Worse, it may not tell you it is flying blind. It may confidently generate an authoritative-sounding answer that is pure fabrication.

Gemini addresses this with what Google calls "Search grounding." When you ask a question that benefits from current or factual information, Gemini can automatically query Google Search, retrieve relevant results, and synthesize them into its response. The key word is "automatically." You do not need a special command or toggle. Gemini decides, based on your query, whether grounding will improve accuracy.

This is fundamentally different from pasting search results into a chat window. Gemini reads, interprets, and synthesizes what it finds, weaving the information into a coherent response while maintaining citations back to the sources. You get the convenience of a conversational answer with the verifiability of a traditional search engine.

How Search Grounding Works

When you send a message, Gemini first evaluates whether your question benefits from real-time information. Current events, recent developments, specific facts, prices, schedules, or anything time-sensitive almost always triggers search grounding. Purely creative, conversational, or reasoning-based questions typically do not.

When grounding activates, here is what happens behind the scenes:

1. **Query formulation.** Gemini translates your conversational question into one or more effective search queries. This is more sophisticated than it sounds — your question might be vague or multi-part, and Gemini breaks it into the specific queries most likely to surface useful results.

2. **Search execution.** Those queries hit Google Search in real time. Gemini has access to the same index of web pages, news articles, and other content you would find searching manually.

3. **Result retrieval and analysis.** Gemini receives the results, reads the relevant pages, and extracts the information that answers your question.

4. **Synthesis and citation.** The model weaves the retrieved information into a natural-language response, attaching inline citations so you can trace every claim back to its source.

The whole process happens in seconds. You ask a question and receive an answer with little blue citation links embedded in the text.

Reading and Using Citations

When Gemini grounds a response with search results, you will see small numbered superscript links throughout the text. These are inline citations — your lifeline to the sources. Clicking any citation opens the source page in a new tab, letting you verify the information, read more context, or explore further.

Citations are not decorative. They let you distinguish information the model retrieved from the web from information it generated from training data. If a claim has a citation, you can verify it. If it does not, treat it with the same healthy skepticism you would apply to any AI-generated content.

A few practical tips for working with citations:

- **Check citations for controversial or high-stakes claims.** If Gemini tells you a specific statistic, a date, a price, or a quote, click the citation to confirm it.
- **Use citations as starting points for deeper research.** The cited pages often contain far more detail than what Gemini includes in its summary.
- **Notice when citations are absent.** If Gemini makes a factual claim without a citation, it is drawing from training data rather than live search results. That does not mean the claim is wrong, but you cannot verify it through the provided links.
- **Pay attention to source quality.** Not all citations are created equal. A citation from an official government website carries different weight than one from a user forum.

The Double-Check Button

Perhaps the most underappreciated feature in Gemini is the "double-check" button. After Gemini generates a response, you will see a small Google icon or "Double-check with Google" button at the bottom. Clicking it triggers something remarkable.

Gemini goes back through its own response sentence by sentence, running each factual claim against Google Search. It highlights the text in two colors:

- **Green highlighting** indicates Google Search found corroborating information. The claim appears supported by web sources.
- **Orange or yellow highlighting** indicates Google Search could not find strong corroboration, or found conflicting information. This does not necessarily mean the claim is wrong, but it is a signal to investigate further.

This is a built-in fact-checking layer. No other major AI assistant offers anything quite like it. Double-check lets you scan a long response and zero in on the parts that need verification, rather than checking every claim manually.

When to Use Double-Check

Develop the habit of using double-check whenever:

- You are researching factual information for work, school, or any important decision.
- The response contains specific numbers, dates, names, or statistics.
- You plan to share or publish the information Gemini provides.
- The topic is one where misinformation is common or where accuracy is critical.
- Something in the response strikes you as surprising or counterintuitive.

You do not need to double-check every casual conversation or creative writing session. But for anything where accuracy matters, that button should become second nature.

Triggering Search Grounding Deliberately

Gemini decides automatically when to use search grounding, but you can influence the decision. To make sure Gemini checks the web, frame your question to signal the need for current information:

- **Include time references.** "What is the current stock price of Alphabet?" or "What happened in the news today?" clearly signal that you need live information.
- **Ask for specific facts.** "What is the population of Tokyo as of 2026?" is more likely to trigger search grounding than "Tell me about Tokyo."
- **Request sources explicitly.** Asking "Can you find recent sources on renewable energy trends?" tells Gemini you want grounded, cited information.
- **Use the @Search syntax.** In some Gemini interfaces, you can explicitly invoke the Google Search extension by mentioning it directly, ensuring your query goes through the search pipeline.

If you want Gemini to rely purely on training data and reasoning — for creative writing or brainstorming — frame your prompts accordingly. "Write me a fictional story about a detective" is unlikely to trigger search grounding because there is nothing to search for.

Search Grounding in Practice

A few scenarios show how search grounding changes the Gemini experience.

Scenario 1: Current Events Research

You ask: "What were the key outcomes of the G20 summit this year?"

Without grounding, a language model would either refuse (if the event is past its training cutoff) or hallucinate details. With grounding, Gemini queries Google Search for recent G20 coverage, retrieves reporting from multiple outlets, and synthesizes a summary with citations to each source. You get a coherent overview plus the ability to click through to the original reporting.

Scenario 2: Fact-Checking a Claim

A colleague tells you that a particular company's revenue exceeded fifty billion dollars last quarter. You ask Gemini: "What was [Company X]'s revenue last quarter?"

Gemini searches for the latest earnings reports, finds the figure, cites the source (likely the company's investor relations page or a financial news outlet), and gives you the answer. Click the citation, confirm the number, and respond to your colleague with confidence.

Scenario 3: Product Comparison

You are shopping for a new laptop and ask: "Compare the latest MacBook Pro and Dell XPS 15 in terms of specs and price."

Gemini retrieves current product pages, review roundups, and pricing, then presents a structured comparison with citations. Because the information is grounded in live results, the specs and prices reflect what is available now, not what was accurate when the model was last trained.

Scenario 4: Medical or Legal Information

You ask about symptoms of a condition or the requirements for filing a specific legal form. These are queries where accuracy is critical and where outdated information could cause real harm. Search grounding ensures Gemini pulls from current, authoritative sources — and double-check adds another layer of verification.

Limitations of Search Grounding

Search grounding is powerful, but not infallible. Understanding its limits will help you use it more effectively.

It depends on what is indexed. If information is not on the web — or is behind a paywall, in a private database, or simply not indexed — grounding cannot find it.

It reflects the biases of search results. If the top results on a topic are skewed in one direction, Gemini's grounded response may reflect that skew. No different from the bias you would encounter doing a manual Google search, but worth keeping in mind.

It does not always activate. Gemini judges when to ground a response. Sometimes it decides a question does not require search when you think it does. Rephrase your question to signal the need for current information more clearly.

Synthesis is still AI-generated. Even when the underlying facts come from search results, the way Gemini combines and presents them is still the language model's work. Summaries may omit nuance, and the model may occasionally misinterpret a source. Click through to citations when precision matters.

Speed. Search-grounded responses take slightly longer to generate, because Gemini needs to run searches and process results before responding. The delay is usually a few seconds, but you will notice it.

Search Grounding vs. Traditional Search

Gemini's search integration and traditional Google Search serve different purposes. The distinction helps you pick the right tool.

Use Gemini with search grounding when you want a synthesized, conversational answer. Ideal when you want Gemini to read multiple sources and pull out the key information for you.

Use Google Search directly when you want to browse multiple sources yourself, access specific websites, or see the full breadth of results rather than a curated synthesis.

In practice, many people find Gemini with grounding handles eighty percent of informational queries more efficiently than traditional search. The remaining twenty percent — deep research, specific site access, image-heavy browsing — still benefits from going to Google Search directly or using Gemini's Deep Research feature, covered in Chapter 17.

Tips for Getting the Most Out of Search Integration

A few final recommendations for making search grounding work for you:

1. **Be specific.** The more specific the question, the better Gemini can formulate search queries and the more precise the results.

2. **Ask follow-ups.** If Gemini's first response does not fully answer the question, ask for more detail. Follow-ups often trigger additional searches that surface new information.

3. **Combine search with analysis.** Ask Gemini to find information *and* analyze it. "Find the latest GDP figures for these five countries and tell me which grew fastest" combines grounding with the model's analytical capabilities.

4. **Use double-check habitually.** Make it part of your workflow for any response with factual claims you plan to rely on.

5. **Cross-reference important claims.** For critical decisions, do not rely solely on Gemini's citations. Use them as a starting point and verify through other sources.

6. **Keep expectations calibrated.** Grounding dramatically improves accuracy for factual queries, but it does not make the model perfect. Treat it as a capable research assistant, not an infallible oracle.

Looking Ahead

Google Search integration is the foundation many of Gemini's other features build on. Extensions (Chapter 15) extend the concept to other Google services.

Deep Research (Chapter 17) takes grounding further, conducting multi-step research projects that would take hours to do manually.

In the next chapter, we explore another area where Gemini shines: understanding and generating images. The combination of visual intelligence and creative capability opens up new ways to work with an AI assistant.

Chapter 11: Image Understanding and Generation

Gemini is not limited to text. It can both understand and generate images, which makes it a true multimodal assistant. You can upload a photo and ask Gemini to describe what it sees, extract text from a document image, analyze a chart, or identify objects in a scene. You can also ask it to create images from scratch using Google's Imagen 4 model family. This chapter covers both sides — visual understanding and image generation — along with the practical considerations of each.

Understanding Images

Gemini's vision capabilities are built into the core model. When you upload an image, the model does not run it through a separate image-recognition tool and paste in the results. It processes the image natively, the same way it processes text, and reasons about visual content in context.

This lets you do things that would be impossible with a text-only model:

- Upload a photo of a whiteboard covered in handwritten notes and ask Gemini to transcribe and organize them.
- Share a screenshot of an error message and ask for troubleshooting help.
- Send a picture of a plant and ask Gemini to identify the species.
- Upload a complex chart or infographic and ask Gemini to explain the key takeaways.
- Share a photo of a meal and ask for a rough calorie estimate.
- Upload architectural plans, circuit diagrams, or any other technical visual and ask for analysis.

How to Upload Images

Sharing images with Gemini is straightforward. In the web interface, you will see a small image icon in the input area. Click it to select an image from your device, or drag and drop into the chat. On mobile, you can take a photo directly from within the Gemini app and send it to the conversation.

You can upload multiple images in a single message, which is useful for comparisons. Upload two versions of a design mockup and ask Gemini to describe the differences.

Getting Better Results from Image Analysis

The quality of Gemini's image analysis depends in part on how you frame your request:

Be specific. "What do you see in this image?" gets you a general description. "What species of bird is shown in this photo?" gets you a focused identification. "Read all the text in this image and format it as a bulleted list" gets you a structured extraction.

Provide context. Telling Gemini "This is a component from a 2024 Honda Civic engine bay" produces a more accurate and relevant analysis than uploading the same image with no context.

Ask follow-ups. After Gemini analyzes an image, you can ask follow-ups without re-uploading. The image stays in conversation context. Start with "Describe this chart" and follow up with "What trend does the data suggest for next quarter?"

Consider image quality. Gemini handles imperfect images well — blurry photos, poor lighting, unusual angles — but clearer images produce better results. When photographing text, get the shot as straight-on and well-lit as possible.

Practical Applications of Image Understanding

The range of tasks you can accomplish with image understanding is enormous. Some of the most useful patterns:

Document digitization. Upload photos of printed documents, handwritten notes, receipts, or business cards. Gemini extracts the text, organizes it, and can translate it if the original is in another language.

Visual troubleshooting. Share a screenshot of a software error, a photo of a malfunctioning device, or an image of a broken part. Gemini can often diagnose the issue or suggest next steps from what it sees.

Design feedback. Upload mockups, logos, website screenshots, or physical designs. Gemini offers aesthetic feedback, identifies accessibility issues, and compares alternatives.

Educational analysis. Upload diagrams from textbooks, equations, scientific figures, or maps. Gemini explains what the visual represents, works through the math, or provides context.

Accessibility. For users with visual impairments, Gemini serves as a detailed describer of visual content, providing rich descriptions of images shared in messages, on websites, or in documents.

Generating Images with Imagen 4

On the creation side, Gemini uses Google's Imagen 4 model family to generate images from text descriptions. Imagen 4 launched on May 20, 2025, and ships in three variants:

- **Imagen 4** — the standard model, the default for most prompts.
- **Imagen 4 Fast** — a lower-latency variant for rapid iteration when you want to try many prompts quickly.
- **Imagen 4 Ultra** — the highest-quality variant for prompts where every detail matters.

Imagen 4 produces images at up to 2K resolution with substantially improved text rendering, better prompt adherence, and faster generation than Imagen 3. Like its predecessor, every image carries a SynthID watermark (covered later in this chapter).

How Image Generation Works

Describe what you want. No special command or syntax — just ask:

- "Create an image of a cozy reading nook with warm lighting and floor-to-ceiling bookshelves."
- "Generate a watercolor painting of a coastal village at sunset."

- “Draw a diagram showing the water cycle for an elementary school presentation.”
- “Create a photorealistic image of a modern kitchen with marble countertops.”

Gemini interprets your description, passes it to Imagen 4, and returns one or more generated images. Typically takes a few seconds — faster still if Gemini routes your request to Imagen 4 Fast.

Writing Effective Image Prompts

Image quality depends heavily on how well you describe what you want. The key elements of an effective image prompt:

Subject. What is the main focus? “A dog” is vague. “A golden retriever puppy sitting in a field of wildflowers” is specific.

Style. Photorealistic, oil painting, watercolor, pencil sketch, flat illustration, pixel art, 3D render — specifying a style dramatically changes the output.

Composition. Close-up, wide angle, aerial view, eye level — these terms guide the framing.

Lighting and mood. “Warm golden hour lighting” produces a different feeling than “harsh fluorescent lighting” or “moody dramatic shadows.”

Color palette. State preferences if you have them. “Muted earth tones,” “vibrant neon colors,” or “black and white with a single red element” all steer the output.

Details. The more relevant details you include, the more control you have. Background elements, textures, weather, time of day — all can be specified.

A basic prompt versus an enhanced one:

Basic: “A cat in a garden.”

Enhanced: “A fluffy orange tabby cat lounging on a stone wall in an English cottage garden, surrounded by lavender and climbing roses, soft afternoon sunlight filtering through the trees, photorealistic style with shallow depth of field.”

The enhanced prompt produces a far more specific and visually compelling result.

Iterating on Generated Images

The first generated image is rarely exactly what you want. Gemini supports iteration:

- **Request variations.** "I like the composition but make the lighting warmer" or "Keep the same scene but change the style to watercolor."
- **Add or remove elements.** "Add a small fountain in the background" or "Remove the clouds from the sky."
- **Adjust the mood.** "Make it feel more dramatic" or "Make it brighter and more cheerful."
- **Be specific about what to change.** Vague feedback like "make it better" is less useful than "the proportions of the building look off — make it taller and narrower."

Each iteration builds on conversation context, so Gemini understands what you have been working toward and can make targeted adjustments.

Editing Existing Images

Gemini's image capabilities go beyond generating from scratch. Upload an existing photo and ask Gemini to modify it. This turns Gemini into a lightweight image editor that understands natural language — no Photoshop skills required.

How Image Editing Works

Upload a photo and describe the changes you want. Gemini processes the image and generates a modified version. You can ask for anything from subtle adjustments to significant transformations.

Practical examples:

- **"Remove the person in the background."** Gemini can identify and remove unwanted elements, filling in the background naturally.
- **"Change the background to a tropical beach."** Swap out the environment entirely while keeping the foreground subject intact.
- **"Make this photo look like it was taken during golden hour."** Adjust the color temperature, lighting, and atmosphere of the image.

- **"Add a frame of flowers around the edges."** Introduce decorative elements to an existing photo.
- **"Change the color of the car from red to blue."** Modify specific elements within the image while leaving everything else unchanged.
- **"Remove the text overlay from this image."** Clean up images that have watermarks, captions, or other text baked in.

Getting Good Results from Image Editing

The same principles that make text prompts effective apply here: specificity matters. "Edit this photo" gives Gemini nothing. "Remove the trash can on the left side of this photo and fill in the brick wall behind it" tells Gemini exactly what to do.

Be realistic about complexity. Simple changes — color adjustments, object removal against uncomplicated backgrounds, style filters — produce clean results. Complex edits — repositioning people, changing poses, adding objects that interact with existing lighting and perspective — are harder and may produce visible artifacts.

If the first result is not quite right, iterate. "The sky looks flat — make it more dramatic" or "The transition where you removed the object looks unnatural — smooth it out" refines the output.

When to Use Gemini vs. Dedicated Editing Tools

Gemini's image editing is best for quick, conversational modifications — the kind of thing where opening Photoshop feels like overkill. Cleaning up a photo for a social post, removing an unwanted background element, trying a different color scheme: Gemini handles these efficiently.

For professional-grade editing — precise retouching, complex compositing, print-quality output — dedicated tools like Adobe Photoshop, Lightroom, or Canva remain the better choice. Gemini's editing is a convenience feature, not a replacement for professional software.

SynthID: Invisible Watermarking

Every image generated by Gemini through the Imagen 4 family carries SynthID, Google's invisible digital watermarking technology. The feature operates entirely behind the scenes, but it is worth understanding.

SynthID embeds a watermark directly into the pixels. It is imperceptible — you cannot see it, and it does not degrade visual quality. Specialized tools can detect it, allowing anyone to verify whether an image was generated by Google's AI.

Why SynthID Matters

The proliferation of AI-generated images raises legitimate concerns about misinformation, fraud, and the erosion of trust in visual media. SynthID is Google's contribution — a technical mechanism for identifying AI-generated content, which matters for:

- **Media integrity.** News organizations and platforms can check whether an image is AI-generated before publishing it.
- **Transparency.** Researchers and regulators can trace the provenance of images that appear in public discourse.
- **Accountability.** The watermark creates a chain of attribution back to the generating system.

What SynthID Means for You

A few practical implications for Gemini users:

- Images you generate are permanently marked as AI-created. The watermark survives common transformations like resizing, cropping, and compression, though extreme modifications may degrade it.
- Be aware that images you generate and share can be identified as AI-generated by anyone using detection tools.
- This is a good thing. Transparency about AI-generated content helps maintain trust. In professional or public contexts, the SynthID watermark supports honest disclosure.

Content Policies and Restrictions

Gemini's image generation comes with content policies that restrict certain output. Google has implemented safeguards to prevent generation of:

- Photorealistic images of identifiable real people.
- Violent, graphic, or explicit content.
- Content that could be used for misinformation, such as fake news imagery.
- Images that violate copyright or intellectual property.

These restrictions are more conservative than some other image generation tools. You may occasionally find a prompt declined or modified. When that happens, Gemini will usually explain why and suggest how to rephrase.

This affects practical workflows. If you need to generate images of specific real people, create content that pushes content policies, or produce imagery for contexts where the restrictions are limiting, you may need alternative tools for those tasks.

Practical Workflows Combining Vision and Generation

The most powerful use cases combine image understanding and generation in a single workflow:

Design iteration. Upload an existing design, ask Gemini to analyze its strengths and weaknesses, then ask it to generate an improved version based on its own feedback.

Reference-based creation. Upload a photo as a reference and ask Gemini to create something inspired by it. "Generate an illustration in the style of this image, but depicting a mountain scene instead of a beach."

Visual brainstorming. Generate several different visual concepts for a project, analyze them with Gemini, and iterate on the strongest candidates.

Content creation. Write an article or presentation with Gemini's help, then generate custom illustrations to accompany the text, ensuring visual and narrative consistency.

Product visualization. Upload a photo of an existing product and ask Gemini to generate variations — different colors, materials, or configurations — to support design exploration.

Tips for Working with Images in Gemini

A few final recommendations:

1. **Combine text and images freely.** Mix uploaded images with text questions in any combination. Upload three photos and ask for a comparison. Include an image as context for a text question. The more fluid the interaction, the better.
2. **Use image generation for rapid prototyping.** Need a quick visual for a presentation, a concept illustration for a pitch, a placeholder for a design? Gemini produces these in seconds.
3. **Use image understanding to save time.** Instead of manually transcribing a document, retyping text from a photo, or describing a visual problem in words, upload the image. Faster and often more accurate.
4. **Remember the limits.** Gemini's image understanding is strong but not perfect. It may misread handwriting, misidentify obscure objects, or miss subtle details. Verify critical information extracted from images.
5. **Respect content policies.** Work within the policies rather than trying to circumvent them. The restrictions exist for good reasons, and working around them usually wastes time.
6. **Think multimodally.** The biggest unlock is not any single feature — it is fluidly combining text and visual reasoning. The more you treat Gemini as a visual thinker, not just a text generator, the more effective your use becomes.

Looking Ahead

Images are just one dimension of Gemini's multimodal intelligence. The next chapter covers an even more impressive capability: video and audio understanding. Uploading entire videos, analyzing their content, and processing audio recordings opens up workflows that were not possible with text-only AI systems.

Chapter 12: Video and Audio Understanding

If image understanding makes Gemini a capable visual thinker, video and audio understanding make it something closer to a universal media analyst. Upload a video file, paste a YouTube link, or share an audio recording, and Gemini will watch, listen, and answer questions about what it perceives. This is not a gimmick. It collapses hours of manual review into seconds of conversation.

This chapter covers how to work with video and audio in Gemini, what the model can and cannot do with these media types, and how to apply these capabilities to real-world tasks.

Video Understanding

Gemini handles video in two ways: direct file uploads and YouTube links. Both give the model access to the visual and audio tracks, letting it reason about what is shown and said.

Uploading Video Files

Upload a video file using the attachment button, just as you would an image. Gemini supports common video formats and processes both the visual and audio content.

Once uploaded, you can ask Gemini virtually anything about it:

- "Summarize what happens in this video."
- "At what timestamp does the speaker discuss the quarterly results?"
- "Describe the chart shown at around the two-minute mark."
- "What are the key points made in this presentation?"
- "Transcribe the dialogue in this video."
- "Are there any safety hazards visible in this footage?"

Gemini does not just skim. It processes video with enough fidelity to answer specific questions about particular moments, visual details, and spoken content.

Ask about a specific timestamp, and Gemini can direct you to the relevant moments.

Analyzing YouTube Videos

One of Gemini's most convenient integrations: analyzing YouTube videos directly from a URL. Paste a YouTube link into your conversation, and Gemini can access and analyze it.

This is useful for several reasons:

- **No download required.** Just paste the link.
- **Long-form content.** YouTube videos can be hours long. Gemini processes extended content and helps you navigate it efficiently.
- **Ubiquity.** An enormous amount of the world's video lives on YouTube — lectures, tutorials, presentations, interviews, documentaries, product reviews. Being able to analyze any of it through a single link is powerful.

Practical ways to use YouTube analysis:

- Paste a link to a two-hour conference keynote and ask for a ten-point summary.
- Share a cooking tutorial and ask Gemini to extract the recipe as a structured list of ingredients and steps.
- Link to a product review and ask Gemini to list the pros and cons the reviewer mentions.
- Share an educational lecture and ask Gemini to create study notes or quiz questions based on the content.
- Paste a link to a music video and ask about the visual themes, narrative, or lyrics.

What Gemini Sees in Video

When processing video, Gemini analyzes multiple dimensions at once:

Visual content. People, objects, text, graphics, scenes, actions, and changes over time. Gemini identifies visual elements, tracks what happens across scenes, and describes composition.

On-screen text. Titles, captions, slides, labels, watermarks — all readable. Useful for analyzing presentations, tutorials with code on screen, or any video with informational overlays.

Audio and speech. Gemini processes the audio track, including dialogue, narration, and sometimes music. It transcribes speech, attributes dialogue to different speakers, and answers questions about what was said.

Temporal structure. Video is sequential, and Gemini understands that. It can reference specific moments, describe event order, and distinguish what happened early versus late.

Practical Applications of Video Understanding

Applications span nearly every domain:

Meeting review. Upload a recorded meeting or paste a link to a webinar. Ask Gemini to summarize decisions, list action items, or identify topics by stage.

Educational content. Process lectures, tutorials, and educational videos to create notes, summaries, flashcards, or comprehension questions. Particularly valuable for students processing large volumes of recorded material.

Content creation. Upload your own videos for review. Ask Gemini to critique pacing, identify sections to tighten, suggest where to add transitions, or write descriptions and chapter markers.

Research and journalism. Analyze interview footage, press conferences, or documentary content. Extract quotes, fact-check claims against search, or create timelines of events discussed.

Quality control and compliance. Review footage for compliance issues, safety violations, brand consistency, or content policy adherence.

Accessibility. Generate detailed descriptions of video content for visually impaired audiences, or transcribe audio for hearing-impaired users.

Audio Understanding

Gemini's audio processing is robust and versatile. Upload audio files — meetings, interviews, podcasts, voice memos, or anything else — and Gemini will process the audio and answer questions about it.

Working with Audio Files

Upload an audio file using the attachment button. Gemini handles common formats and analyzes the full recording. Once uploaded, you can:

- **Request transcription.** "Transcribe this audio recording." Gemini produces a text transcription.
- **Ask for summaries.** "What are the main topics discussed in this recording?" Ideal for long meetings or interviews.
- **Extract specific information.** "What did the speaker say about the Q3 budget?" Gemini locates and extracts the relevant portions.
- **Identify speakers.** For multi-speaker recordings, Gemini can often distinguish voices and attribute statements accordingly.
- **Analyze tone and content.** "Does the speaker seem confident or uncertain when discussing the timeline?" Gemini observes delivery and tone, not just the literal words.

Audio Quality Considerations

Gemini's audio analysis depends on recording quality. Factors that affect results:

- **Speech clarity.** Clear, well-enunciated speech is easier than mumbling or heavily accented speech in noisy environments.
- **Background noise.** Significant noise — traffic, music, crowd chatter — makes accurate analysis harder.
- **Number of speakers.** Single-speaker recordings are easiest. Multi-speaker recordings work well, but crowded conversations with overlapping speakers can be challenging.
- **Recording quality.** Higher-quality recordings with good microphone placement produce better results.

That said, Gemini is resilient with imperfect audio. It handles real-world recordings — phone calls, voice memos, meetings captured on laptop microphones — better than you might expect.

Combining Video, Audio, and Text

The real power emerges when you combine these capabilities with text-based reasoning in a single conversation:

Research synthesis. Upload a recorded interview (video or audio), paste links to two YouTube videos on the same topic, and ask Gemini to compare and synthesize across all three sources.

Content repurposing. Upload a video of a presentation and ask Gemini to turn it into a blog post, a series of social posts, and key takeaway bullets — all from a single video.

Learning and study. Watch a YouTube lecture, then ask follow-up questions. The video stays in conversation context, so you can discuss the material in detail, ask for clarification on specific points, or have Gemini quiz you on it.

Translation and localization. Upload a video in one language and ask for a summary or transcription in another. Foreign-language content becomes accessible even if you do not speak the source language.

Incident analysis. In professional contexts, upload surveillance footage, dashcam video, or inspection recordings and ask Gemini to describe what it observes, flag specific events, or build a timeline.

Working with Long-Form Content

One of Gemini's strengths is handling long-form video and audio. Many AI systems struggle with content past a few minutes, but Gemini processes extended recordings — hour-long meetings, multi-hour lecture series, lengthy podcasts.

For long content, consider these strategies:

Start with a summary. Get a high-level summary first, then drill into specific sections. This gives you a map of the content before you ask detailed questions.

Use timestamps. Reference specific timestamps when asking about particular moments, and ask Gemini to provide timestamps in its responses. Makes it easy to navigate back to the original.

Break complex analysis into steps. Rather than asking one massive question about a two-hour video, ask a series of focused ones. "First, summarize the introduction. Now, what were the three main arguments? Finally, what was the conclusion?"

Combine with note-taking. Use Gemini's analysis as the foundation for your own notes. Have it generate a structured outline, then add your own observations.

Limitations and Considerations

Understand the boundaries:

Processing time. Longer files take longer to process. For very long content, expect a noticeable delay before Gemini responds.

Transcription accuracy. Gemini's transcription is strong but not perfect. Technical jargon, proper nouns, and unusual terminology can be misheard. Verify critical transcriptions.

Visual detail. Gemini may miss fine details in fast-moving or visually complex video. If specific details matter, ask about them directly rather than relying on a general summary.

Content policies. The same policies that apply to text and image generation apply here. Gemini may decline to analyze content that violates its safety guidelines.

File size. There are practical limits on direct uploads. For very large files, trim to the relevant sections or use YouTube links where possible.

YouTube availability. Not all YouTube videos are accessible. Private, restricted, or certain copyright-protected videos may not be fully processable.

Tips for Effective Video and Audio Analysis

1. **Be specific.** "Analyze this video" is a starting point. "List every action item mentioned in this meeting recording" gets far more useful results.

2. **Leverage the conversational format.** After initial analysis, ask follow-ups. The video or audio remains in context, so you can have an extended discussion.
3. **Use video analysis to triage.** If you have a backlog of recorded meetings, webinars, or lectures, Gemini can summarize each so you can decide which deserve your full attention.
4. **Combine capabilities.** After analyzing a video, ask Gemini to search the web for related information, generate images based on concepts discussed, or create written content inspired by it.
5. **Integrate into workflows.** Video and audio analysis fits into content creation, research, education, and professional review. Its value multiplies when integrated with other tools.

Gemini Live: Real-Time Voice Conversations

Everything covered so far involves uploading media and asking Gemini to analyze it. Gemini Live flips the script: instead of typing prompts, you talk to Gemini in real time, and it talks back. This is not voice-to-text followed by a text response read aloud. It is a back-and-forth spoken conversation with an AI, and it changes where and how you can use Gemini.

What Gemini Live Is

Gemini Live is a real-time voice conversation feature in the Gemini mobile app on Android and iOS. Start a session, and you enter a mode where you and Gemini speak naturally, much like a phone call. You talk, Gemini listens, it responds verbally, and you can interrupt, redirect, or build on the conversation just as you would with another person.

The experience feels natural. Gemini Live supports conversational flow — no beep, no button to press each time. You can interrupt mid-response if it is heading the wrong direction, and it adjusts. Latency is low enough that the conversation feels fluid rather than stilted.

How to Start a Gemini Live Session

Open the Gemini app and look for the Gemini Live icon — typically a waveform or audio symbol near the input area. Tap it to enter Live mode. A visual indicator shows Gemini is listening, and you can start talking immediately. To end the session, tap the close or stop button.

Gemini Live is available to Google AI Pro subscribers (and above). Free-tier users will not see the option.

What You Can Do with Gemini Live

The hands-free nature of Gemini Live makes it ideal for situations where typing is impractical or impossible.

Brainstorming while walking or driving. One of the most natural use cases. You are on a walk or behind the wheel, and an idea strikes. Instead of typing, you just start talking. "I am thinking about restructuring my team's weekly meeting format. What are some approaches that work for remote teams?" Gemini responds verbally, you push back or ask follow-ups, and by the time you reach your destination you have a plan.

Thinking through a problem out loud. Some people process ideas better by talking than writing. Gemini Live gives you a patient, knowledgeable partner to work through a problem, play devil's advocate, or organize your thoughts as you voice them.

Language practice. Ask Gemini Live to converse in Spanish, French, Japanese, or any supported language. It responds in that language, corrects your mistakes when asked, and adjusts vocabulary to your level. Not a replacement for immersion or a human tutor, but available at any hour and endlessly patient.

Quick questions when your hands are full. Cooking with messy hands, carrying groceries, exercising — any situation where typing is inconvenient. "How many tablespoons in a quarter cup?" "What time does the hardware store close?" "Remind me of the key points from our earlier conversation about the budget."

Interview and presentation practice. Ask Gemini Live to run a mock job interview or a Q&A after a presentation. It asks questions, you practice answering verbally, and you can request feedback on your responses.

How Gemini Live Differs from Text Chat

Gemini Live is not just the text experience with a microphone. There are meaningful differences.

First, conversation is more spontaneous. In text, you tend to compose careful, complete prompts. In voice, the exchange is messier and more natural — shorter turns, more interruptions, more back-and-forth. Gemini Live is optimized for that rhythm.

Second, Gemini Live does not currently support all text-mode features. You cannot upload files or images during a Live session, and Google Search grounding, Extensions, and Deep Think are not available in the same way. Live sessions are best for conversational tasks — brainstorming, Q&A, practice, discussion — rather than tasks requiring document analysis or visual input.

Third, Gemini Live conversations may not always appear in your conversation history the way text chats do. Check your settings for how Live sessions are stored.

Tips for Effective Gemini Live Sessions

Speak naturally. No formal prompt structure required. Talk as you would to a colleague.

Interrupt when needed. If Gemini is heading the wrong direction, just start talking. It will stop and listen.

Set context early. At the start of a Live session, explain what you want to accomplish. "I want to brainstorm marketing ideas for a new product launch" frames the entire conversation.

Use it where it shines. Gemini Live is best for conversational, generative tasks. For precision, complex formatting, or references to uploaded documents, switch to text mode.

Looking Ahead

The ability to understand video and audio, combined with the text and image capabilities already covered, makes Gemini one of the most versatile AI assistants available. We have only scratched the surface of its integrations. The next chapter explores how Gemini works inside Google Workspace — Gmail, Docs, Sheets, Slides, and more — transforming the productivity tools you already use every day.

Part IV: Power Features

"A picture is worth a thousand words. A video is worth a thousand pictures. AI understands both."

— Ken Tannenbaum

Chapter 13: Gemini in Google Workspace

If Gemini's standalone capabilities are impressive, its Google Workspace integration is where it becomes indispensable for anyone who lives in Gmail, Docs, Sheets, Slides, or Meet. Google has embedded Gemini directly into the productivity tools hundreds of millions of people use every day, turning them from static applications into AI-augmented work environments.

This chapter walks through how Gemini works in each major Workspace application, what it can do, and how to get the most from it. Whether you are drafting emails, writing documents, crunching data, building presentations, or running meetings, Gemini is there — and more capable than you might expect.

The Big Picture: Gemini as Your Workspace Assistant

Before diving into individual applications, the philosophy behind the Workspace integration is worth understanding. Google has not simply bolted a chatbot onto each app. Gemini is woven into the fabric of each one, aware of what you are working on and offering assistance relevant to the current task.

Gemini in Docs knows you are writing a document and helps with drafting, editing, and formatting. Gemini in Sheets knows you are working with data and helps with formulas, analysis, and visualization. Gemini in Slides knows you are building a presentation and helps with content, layout, and imagery. The AI adapts to each application's context.

Access to Gemini in Workspace requires a plan that includes Gemini features — typically Google AI Pro (or AI Ultra) for individuals, or a Google Workspace business or enterprise plan with Gemini bundled in. Specific features vary by plan.

Gemini in Gmail

Email remains one of the most time-consuming parts of most workdays. Gemini in Gmail helps you read, write, and manage email more efficiently.

Drafting Emails

When composing a new email or reply, click the "Help me write" button, describe what you want to say, and Gemini generates a draft. Specify tone (formal, casual, friendly, direct), length, and key points.

Example: "Reply to this email declining the meeting invitation politely, suggesting next Tuesday as an alternative, and asking them to send the agenda in advance." Gemini produces a complete, well-structured email you can send as-is or edit to taste.

Refining and Adjusting

Once Gemini drafts a reply, refine it with follow-up instructions:

- "Make this more formal."
- "Shorten this to three sentences."
- "Add a paragraph about the budget constraints."
- "Make the tone warmer."

These refinements happen in place, so you iterate quickly without starting over.

Summarizing Email Threads

Long email threads with many participants are painful to catch up on. Gemini summarizes an entire thread, highlighting key points, decisions, and action items. Especially valuable when you return from vacation or get copied into a conversation already in progress.

Smart Compose and Contextual Suggestions

Beyond "Help me write," Gemini enhances Gmail's Smart Compose with more sophisticated suggestions. As you type, the AI offers contextually aware completions — not just predicting the next word, but understanding what you are trying to communicate and suggesting how to express it.

Gemini in Google Docs

Google Docs is where many people do their most substantive writing, and Gemini's integration here is deep and versatile.

Help Me Write

The "Help me write" feature in Docs works like Gmail's, with broader scope. You can ask Gemini to:

- Draft entire sections of a document from a brief description.
- Generate a first draft of a report, proposal, or article.
- Write specific content types — executive summaries, meeting minutes, project plans, creative fiction.
- Produce content in a specific style or tone.

Invoke it by typing a prompt in the document or using the Gemini side panel. The generated text appears directly in your document, ready to edit.

Editing and Refining Existing Text

Gemini also works with text you have already written. Select a passage and ask Gemini to:

- **Rewrite** it in a different tone or style.
- **Shorten** it while preserving the key points.
- **Elaborate** on it with more detail.
- **Formalize** or **casualize** the language.
- **Fix** grammar, spelling, and punctuation.
- **Improve** clarity and readability.

This is not find-and-replace. Gemini understands the meaning of your text and makes intelligent revisions that preserve intent while improving expression.

Summarizing Documents

For long documents, Gemini generates summaries at various levels of detail. Ask for an executive summary, a bullet outline, or a one-paragraph abstract. Invaluable when reviewing documents written by others.

The Side Panel

Docs features a Gemini side panel that you can open while working. It gives you a conversational interface alongside your document, where you can ask questions, request drafts, get feedback, and discuss your content — all without leaving the editor.

The side panel is context-aware. Gemini knows which document you are working on and can reference its contents. "Summarize the third section" or "Is there anything inconsistent between the introduction and the conclusion?" are typical side-panel questions.

Gemini in Google Sheets

Spreadsheets are powerful but often intimidating. Gemini in Sheets makes data work more accessible by letting you interact with your spreadsheets in natural language.

Help Me Organize

Gemini helps you structure data. Describe the table you want, and Gemini generates headers, formatting, and sample data. "Create a project tracking spreadsheet with columns for task name, assignee, status, priority, due date, and notes" produces a ready-to-use template.

Formula Assistance

One of Gemini's most valuable Sheets features. Instead of memorizing formulas, describe what you want to calculate in plain English:

- "What formula would calculate the year-over-year percentage change between column B and column C?"
- "Write a VLOOKUP that matches the product ID in cell A2 against the table in Sheet2."
- "Create a formula that counts the number of cells in column D that contain the word 'complete' and have a date in column E that is before today."

Gemini generates the formula and can insert it directly. It also explains what the formula does, so you learn as you go.

Data Analysis

Beyond formulas, Gemini helps you analyze your data:

- "What trends do you see in this data?"
- "Which product had the highest growth rate?"
- "Are there any outliers in column F?"
- "Create a pivot table summarizing sales by region and quarter."

Gemini examines your data and provides insights, often suggesting visualizations or additional analyses you had not considered.

Chart Creation

Ask Gemini to create charts from your data in natural language. "Create a bar chart showing monthly revenue for the last twelve months" or "Make a pie chart of the market share data in columns A and B." Gemini generates the chart directly in your spreadsheet.

Gemini in Google Slides

Building presentations is a task that often takes longer than it should. Gemini in Slides accelerates the process dramatically.

Generating Presentations

Ask Gemini to generate an entire presentation from a brief description. "Create a ten-slide presentation about our Q3 marketing strategy, including an executive summary, key metrics, campaign highlights, and next steps." Gemini produces a complete deck with content, layout, and relevant imagery.

Creating Individual Slides

Building slide by slide? Describe the content you want on a slide, and Gemini generates it with appropriate formatting, bullet points, and visual elements.

Image Generation for Slides

Gemini generates custom images directly in Slides using the Imagen 4 model family. Describe what you need, and Gemini creates it without you ever leaving the editor. No more searching stock photo libraries or switching to a separate image tool.

Speaker Notes

Ask Gemini to write speaker notes. It generates talking points that expand on the slide content, provide context, and remind you of key details to mention during the presentation.

Summarizing Presentations

If you receive a deck from someone else, Gemini summarizes the entire thing, giving you a quick overview without clicking through every slide.

Gemini in Google Meet

Gemini's Google Meet integration transforms how you experience meetings, live or after the fact.

Real-Time Assistance During Meetings

During a Meet call, Gemini provides real-time assistance:

- **Live summaries.** If you join late, Gemini catches you up on what has been discussed.
- **Note-taking.** Gemini takes notes during the meeting, capturing key points, decisions, and action items automatically.
- **Translation.** For multilingual meetings, Gemini provides real-time caption translation.

Post-Meeting Summaries

After the meeting, Gemini generates a comprehensive summary covering:

- Key topics discussed.
- Decisions made.
- Action items with owners.
- Follow-up tasks.

Share the summary with participants or stakeholders who could not attend, replacing the tedious process of writing notes manually.

Meeting Recording Analysis

When meetings are recorded, Gemini analyzes the recordings (using the video and audio capabilities from Chapter 12). Ask questions about what was discussed at specific points, search for when a topic came up, or request detailed transcripts.

Gemini in Google Drive

Gemini's presence in Google Drive helps you find and understand files more efficiently.

Natural Language Search

Instead of relying on exact filenames or folder structures, search Drive in natural language. "Find the budget spreadsheet I worked on last month" or "Show me presentations about the product launch" surfaces the most relevant files.

Document Summarization

While browsing Drive, Gemini summarizes documents without you opening them. A massive time-saver when looking through a folder of reports for the one that addresses a specific topic.

Cross-Document Analysis

Gemini can analyze multiple Drive documents and draw connections. "Compare the proposals from all three vendors in my Project Bids folder" or "What are the common themes across the last four quarterly reports?" This kind of cross-document analysis would take hours to do manually.

Practical Tips for Workspace Integration

A few recommendations for getting the most from Gemini across Workspace:

1. **Start with your biggest pain points.** If email eats most of your time, master Gemini in Gmail first. If data analysis is your bottleneck, prioritize Sheets. You do not need to adopt everything at once.
2. **Use the side panel liberally.** The conversational side panel in Docs and other apps is your most flexible tool. Think of it as a knowledgeable colleague sitting beside you while you work.

3. **Iterate, do not expect perfection.** First drafts are starting points. The real value is in the speed of iteration — a draft in seconds, refined in minutes, instead of staring at a blank page for an hour.

4. **Combine applications.** The real power emerges across apps. Analyze data in Sheets, move the insights into a Docs report, and create a Slides presentation — with Gemini at each stage.

5. **Learn the access points.** Each app has its own ways to invoke Gemini. Fluency with the access points makes the interaction seamless rather than disruptive.

6. **Trust but verify.** Workspace outputs are subject to the same accuracy considerations as standalone responses. Review generated content, double-check formulas, and proofread AI-drafted text before finalizing.

Looking Ahead

Google Workspace integration gives Gemini a home in the tools where you already work. But what if you could customize Gemini itself to match how you work? The next chapter explores Gems — Gemini's system for creating custom AI assistants tailored to your specific needs and workflows.

Chapter 14: Gems — Custom Gemini Assistants

Out of the box, Gemini is a general-purpose assistant. It answers questions, writes content, analyzes data, and handles an enormous range of tasks. But general-purpose tools, by definition, are not optimized for any specific task. What if you could create a version of Gemini that already knows your writing style, understands your industry's jargon, follows your company's formatting guidelines, or behaves like a specialized expert in a particular domain?

That is what Gems are for. Gems are custom Gemini assistants you configure with specific instructions, personalities, and areas of expertise — specialized versions of Gemini designed for your recurring needs. If you know ChatGPT's Custom GPTs, Gems are Google's answer to that concept, with their own distinctive approach.

What Gems Are

A Gem is a saved set of instructions that shapes how Gemini behaves in a conversation. When you create a Gem, you define:

- **A name** that describes the Gem's purpose.
- **Custom instructions** that tell Gemini how to behave, what to focus on, what tone to use, what assumptions to make, and what rules to follow.

When you start a conversation with a Gem, those instructions are applied automatically. You do not have to re-explain your preferences or context. The Gem already knows.

Conceptually simple, but the practical impact is significant. Instead of spending the first few messages establishing context, you walk into a conversation with an assistant already configured for the task.

Creating Your First Gem

Creating a Gem is straightforward. In the Gemini interface, look for the Gem Manager — typically in the left sidebar or navigation menu. Click to create a new Gem, and a configuration screen opens.

Step 1: Name Your Gem

Choose a descriptive name that makes it easy to identify the Gem's purpose at a glance. "Marketing Copy Editor," "Python Tutor," "Meeting Notes Assistant," or "Recipe Converter" are all clear, functional names.

Step 2: Write Your Instructions

This is where the real work happens. Your instructions define the Gem's behavior. You are writing a system prompt — directions Gemini will follow in every conversation with this Gem.

Here is an example of instructions for a "Technical Blog Editor" Gem:

> You are a senior technical blog editor specializing in software development content. When I share a draft blog post with you, do the following:
>
> 1. Check for technical accuracy. Flag any claims that seem incorrect or misleading.
> 2. Improve clarity and readability. Simplify complex sentences without losing technical precision.
> 3. Ensure consistent formatting: use sentence case for headings, Oxford commas, and em dashes instead of parenthetical asides.
> 4. Suggest a more compelling title if the current one is weak.
> 5. Add a "TL;DR" section at the top if one is missing.
> 6. Flag any sections that would benefit from code examples.
>
> Tone: Professional but approachable. Avoid corporate jargon. Write for an audience of intermediate to senior developers.
>
> Always explain your suggested changes so I can learn from them.

Notice how specific these instructions are. They cover what the Gem should do, how, what style to use, who the audience is, and what additional value it should provide (explanations). The more specific your instructions, the more useful the Gem.

Step 3: Test and Refine

After creating your Gem, test it with real tasks. You will discover gaps or behaviors you want to adjust. Update the instructions, then test again. This iterative process is normal — most useful Gems go through several rounds of refinement before they work the way you want.

What Makes a Good Gem

Not every task benefits from a custom Gem. Gems are most valuable for recurring tasks with consistent requirements. Here are the characteristics of tasks well-suited to Gems:

Repetitive structure. If you find yourself giving Gemini the same instructions at the start of every conversation — "You are an expert in X, always use Y format, tone should be Z" — that is a prime candidate.

Domain-specific knowledge. If your work involves specialized terminology, industry conventions, or expertise a general assistant might not default to, encoding that context in a Gem saves time and improves accuracy.

Consistent formatting. If your outputs need to follow specific rules — a report template, citation style, naming convention, or document structure — a Gem can enforce them automatically.

Persona-based interactions. If you want Gemini to adopt a specific persona — a supportive tutor, a rigorous code reviewer, a brainstorming partner, a Socratic questioner — a Gem locks it in.

Gem Ideas and Examples

To spark ideas, here are practical Gem configurations covering a range of use cases:

The Email Drafter

Instructions: "You help me draft professional emails. Always match the formality level of the email I am replying to. Keep emails concise — no more than three short paragraphs unless I specify otherwise. Use a warm but professional tone. End with a clear call to action. Never use exclamation marks. If I provide bullet points, turn them into flowing prose."

The Code Reviewer

Instructions: "You are a senior software engineer conducting code reviews. When I share code, identify bugs, security vulnerabilities, performance issues, and style inconsistencies. Suggest specific fixes with code examples. Rate the overall code quality on a scale of 1-10. Prioritize issues by severity: critical, major, minor. Always explain why each issue matters, not just what to change."

The Fitness Planner

Instructions: "You are a certified personal trainer. Help me plan workouts based on my goals, available equipment, and time constraints. I have access to a full gym with free weights, machines, and cardio equipment. My current goals are building muscle and improving cardiovascular endurance. I work out five days a week. Always include warm-up and cool-down. Specify sets, reps, and rest periods."

The Meeting Summarizer

Instructions: "I will paste meeting transcripts or notes. Produce a structured summary with these sections: Key Decisions, Action Items (with owners and deadlines if mentioned), Open Questions, and a one-paragraph executive summary. Use bullet points throughout. Flag any action items that lack a clear owner or deadline. Keep the summary under 500 words unless the meeting was exceptionally long."

The Creative Writing Coach

Instructions: "You are a creative writing instructor with a focus on fiction. When I share my writing, provide constructive feedback focusing on: narrative voice, pacing, dialogue authenticity, character development, and show-versus-tell balance. Be encouraging but honest. When pointing out weaknesses, always suggest a specific way to improve. Ask me questions about my intentions before suggesting major structural changes."

The Language Tutor

Instructions: "You are a patient, encouraging French language tutor. Conduct conversations primarily in French, but switch to English when I am clearly struggling. Correct my grammar gently — point out the error and explain the rule, but do not interrupt the flow of conversation unnecessarily. Adjust your vocabulary and sentence complexity to my level. Introduce two to three new vocabulary words per conversation and use them repeatedly so I absorb them naturally."

Writing Effective Gem Instructions

A Gem's quality depends almost entirely on its instructions. Here are the principles for writing instructions that produce consistent results:

Be Specific, Not Vague

"Be helpful and professional" is vague. "Respond in a formal business tone, use complete sentences, avoid contractions, and structure long responses with headers and bullet points" is specific. The more specific your instructions, the more predictable the Gem's behavior.

Define What Not to Do

Negative instructions are just as important as positive ones. "Never provide medical diagnoses" or "Do not suggest solutions before I have finished describing the problem" or "Avoid using industry jargon without defining it first" help prevent unwanted behaviors.

Include Examples When Helpful

If your Gem needs to produce output in a specific format, include an example. "Format your responses like this: [Title] — [Date] — [One-sentence summary] — [Detailed analysis in 2-3 paragraphs]." Examples eliminate ambiguity better than descriptions alone.

Anticipate Edge Cases

Think about unusual situations your Gem might encounter. What should it do if the input is unclear? If it does not know the answer? If you ask it to do something outside its defined scope? Adding instructions for these edge cases — "If my request is ambiguous, ask a clarifying question before proceeding" — improves reliability.

Keep Instructions Focused

A Gem that tries to be everything will be good at nothing. If your instructions grow long and cover many different scenarios, consider creating multiple focused Gems instead of one sprawling one.

Managing Your Gems

As your Gem library grows, organization matters. A few practical considerations:

Naming conventions. Use consistent, descriptive names. A system like "[Category]: [Specific Purpose]" works well — "Writing: Blog Post Editor," "Data: CSV Analyzer," "Communication: Email Drafter."

Regular review. Periodically retire Gems you no longer use. As your needs evolve, your Gems should evolve with them.

Iteration. Update Gem instructions as you learn what works. The best Gems are living configurations that improve with use.

Sharing. Depending on your Gemini plan, you may be able to share Gems with colleagues. This is valuable in organizations where consistent AI behavior across a team matters.

Gems vs. Simply Re-Explaining Context

You might wonder whether Gems are really necessary. You could just paste your instructions at the start of every conversation. Technically, yes. But Gems offer several advantages:

Convenience. Starting a Gem conversation is one click. Pasting instructions is a multi-step process you have to remember every time.

Consistency. Gems guarantee the instructions are identical every time. When you paste manually, you might forget a detail, use slightly different wording, or skip a section, leading to inconsistent results.

Cognitive overhead. Remembering and managing sets of instructions adds friction. Gems offload that burden to the system.

Discoverability. Your Gems are organized in one place. You can scan your library and see your available specialized assistants at a glance, rather than searching old conversations or note files for the right instructions.

Limitations of Gems

Gems are powerful, but they have boundaries:

- **No persistent memory across conversations.** Each Gem conversation starts fresh. The Gem does not remember previous conversations (beyond what any conversation history features might provide).
- **They cannot access external tools or data on their own.** A Gem's capabilities are limited to what Gemini itself can do. For external services, you need Extensions, which we cover in the next chapter.
- **Instruction length has limits.** You cannot write a novel-length set of instructions. Keep them focused and concise.
- **They are not apps.** Gems customize Gemini's behavior through instructions, not new technical capabilities. They work within the same feature set as standard Gemini.

Tips for Getting the Most Out of Gems

1. **Start with your most frequent task.** Identify the one thing you use Gemini for most often, and create a Gem for it. Prove the value before building a whole library.

2. **Steal from yourself.** Review recent Gemini conversations. The ones where you spent the first several messages setting up context are your Gem candidates.

3. **Iterate based on real use.** The first version of your instructions will not be perfect. Use the Gem for real work, notice where it falls short, refine.

4. **Think about your team.** If you work with others, consider Gems that would benefit the whole team. Shared Gems enforce consistent quality and style across a group.

5. **Combine with other features.** Gems work alongside Gemini's other capabilities — search grounding, image generation, file analysis. A Gem configured as a "Research Assistant" can still use Google Search grounding to find current information.

Looking Ahead

Gems customize how Gemini behaves. But what if you want to extend what Gemini can do — connect it to external services and data sources beyond its default capabilities? That is what Extensions are for, and they are the subject of the next chapter.

Chapter 15: Extensions and Integrations

Gems customize how Gemini talks. Extensions expand what Gemini can do. If Gems are about personality and behavior, Extensions are about capability and reach. They connect Gemini to Google services and external data sources, letting it take actions and retrieve information otherwise beyond its grasp.

This chapter covers what Extensions are, how they work, which ones are available, and how to use them to turn Gemini from a conversational assistant into a tool that interacts with the real world.

What Extensions Are

Extensions are connections between Gemini and external services — primarily Google's own products. When enabled, Gemini can query that service, retrieve information, and incorporate the results into its responses. Some Extensions also let Gemini take actions on your behalf.

Think of Extensions as giving Gemini hands. Without them, Gemini can think and talk but cannot reach out and touch anything. With Extensions, it can look up flights, search for hotels, get directions, find YouTube videos, retrieve information from your Google Workspace, and more.

You enable Extensions in Gemini's settings and toggle them on or off based on your preferences and privacy considerations. When you ask Gemini something that falls within an Extension's domain, the model decides whether to invoke it, queries the service, and integrates the results.

Available Extensions

As of this writing, Gemini offers Extensions for several core Google services. Let us walk through each.

Google Flights

The Google Flights Extension connects Gemini to Google's flight search engine. When you ask about flights, Gemini can:

- Search for available flights between any two cities.
- Compare prices across dates, airlines, and cabin classes.
- Find the cheapest travel dates for a given route.
- Provide information about flight duration, layovers, and airlines.

Example interactions:

- "Find me round-trip flights from San Francisco to Tokyo in October, under fifteen hundred dollars."
- "What is the cheapest day to fly from New York to London next month?"
- "Compare business class flights from Chicago to Paris on the major airlines."

Gemini retrieves real-time flight data and presents it in a structured format, often with links straight to the booking page. It is faster than navigating Google Flights yourself, especially for queries with flexible dates or multi-city itineraries.

Google Hotels

Similar to Flights, the Hotels Extension connects Gemini to Google's hotel search. You can:

- Search for hotels in any city or near any landmark.
- Filter by price range, star rating, amenities, and guest ratings.
- Compare options and get recommendations based on your preferences.
- Find deals and availability for specific dates.

Example interactions:

- "Find hotels in downtown Barcelona for next weekend, under two hundred dollars a night, with a pool."
- "What are the best-reviewed hotels near the Eiffel Tower?"
- "Compare Marriott and Hilton options in Nashville for a three-night stay in June."

The Extension returns current availability and pricing, making Gemini a capable travel planner.

Google Maps

The Maps Extension gives Gemini access to location data, directions, and local business information. With it, Gemini can:

- Provide directions between two locations, including driving, walking, transit, and cycling options.
- Estimate travel times with current traffic conditions.
- Find nearby businesses, restaurants, attractions, or services.
- Provide information about specific places, including hours, ratings, and reviews.

Example interactions:

- "How long will it take to drive from Austin to Dallas right now?"
- "Find Italian restaurants near Union Square with at least four stars."
- "What are the public transit options from my hotel in London to the British Museum?"
- "Show me the three closest gas stations."

The Maps Extension shines on location-based queries that need real-time data, like current traffic or business hours.

YouTube

The YouTube Extension allows Gemini to search YouTube and find relevant videos. It can:

- Search for videos on any topic.
- Find specific types of content — tutorials, reviews, lectures, music, news coverage.
- Recommend videos based on your interests or questions.
- Provide links to the most relevant results.

Example interactions:

- "Find a YouTube tutorial on how to replace a kitchen faucet."
- "What are the best-reviewed videos about learning Python for beginners?"
- "Find the most popular TED talks about climate change."

This Extension is distinct from Gemini's ability to analyze YouTube videos (covered in Chapter 12). The Extension helps you find videos; the analysis capability helps you understand videos you have already found.

Google Workspace

The Workspace Extension connects Gemini to your Google Workspace data — Gmail, Docs, Drive, and other Workspace apps. This is one of the most powerful Extensions because it opens Gemini to your personal and professional data.

With the Workspace Extension enabled, Gemini can:

- Search your email for specific messages or information.
- Find documents in your Drive.
- Retrieve information from your Docs, Sheets, and Slides.
- Reference your calendar events.
- Combine information from multiple Workspace sources to answer complex questions.

Example interactions:

- "Find the email from Sarah about the project deadline."
- "What did the quarterly report in my Drive say about customer churn?"
- "Do I have any meetings scheduled for Thursday afternoon?"
- "Find the spreadsheet with the vendor comparison and tell me which vendor had the lowest price."

This Extension lets Gemini search and reason across your personal Workspace data — extraordinarily useful, and with privacy implications we will discuss later in this chapter.

Google Search

We covered Google Search grounding extensively in Chapter 10, but it is worth noting that Google Search also functions as an Extension. When explicitly invoked, it lets Gemini perform web searches and ground its responses in current information. The behavior matches the automatic search grounding described earlier, but the Extension framework keeps it consistent with the others.

How Extensions Work Together

The real power of Extensions emerges when Gemini combines several to answer a single query. Consider this request:

"I am traveling to Tokyo next month for a conference. Find me flights from San Francisco, a hotel near Shibuya for five nights under three hundred dollars, and a YouTube video that gives tips for first-time visitors to Tokyo."

Gemini handles this in a single response by invoking the Flights, Hotels, and YouTube Extensions simultaneously. You get a comprehensive travel planning answer that would have required three separate searches on three different platforms.

Or consider: "Check my email for the confirmation from the Tokyo conference, find the venue address, and give me transit directions from the hotels you recommended."

Gemini combines the Workspace Extension (to find the email), the Maps Extension (for directions), and the context from the previous Hotels results — all in one fluid interaction.

Orchestrating multiple services through natural language is what makes Extensions transformative rather than merely convenient.

Enabling and Managing Extensions

You manage Extensions through Gemini's settings. The process is straightforward:

1. Open Gemini's settings (usually accessible from the menu or profile icon).
2. Navigate to the Extensions section.
3. Toggle individual Extensions on or off.

Each Extension requires certain permissions. The Workspace Extension needs access to your Workspace data. Google Flights and Hotels need to query on your behalf. Enabling an Extension grants Gemini the permissions it needs.

Disable an Extension at any time if you decide you do not want Gemini accessing a particular service. You get granular control over what Gemini can and cannot do.

Privacy and Data Considerations

Extensions raise privacy questions, particularly the Workspace Extension. Enabling it gives Gemini access to your emails, documents, and other personal data. Things to consider:

Data access scope. Gemini accesses your Workspace data only when a query requires it. It does not continuously monitor your email or browse your Drive unprompted. Access is query-driven.

Data usage. Google states that data accessed through Extensions is used to generate your response and is subject to Google's privacy policies. Review the current privacy terms for your specific plan, since these policies evolve.

Sensitive information. Be mindful of what you ask Gemini to retrieve. If your email contains confidential business information, medical records, or financial data, asking Gemini to search through it means that data is being processed by the AI system.

Organizational policies. On a Workspace business or enterprise plan, your administrator may have policies about which Extensions are permitted. Check with IT if you are unsure.

Selective use. You do not have to enable everything. If you are comfortable with Gemini searching for flights and hotels but not reading your email, enable the travel Extensions and leave Workspace disabled.

The guiding principle is informed consent. Understand what each Extension accesses, decide deliberately, and review periodically.

Invoking Extensions Explicitly

Gemini automatically invokes Extensions when relevant, but you can also signal intent explicitly. The "@" syntax followed by the Extension name directs Gemini to use a specific one:

- "@Google Maps How long is the drive from here to the airport?"
- "@YouTube Find a tutorial on sourdough bread baking."
- "@Google Flights Search for flights to Rome in August."

Explicit invocation is useful when your query is ambiguous about which service is most relevant.

Limitations of Extensions

Extensions are powerful but not without constraints:

Limited third-party support. Extensions today are largely limited to Google's own services. Unlike platforms with broad third-party plugin ecosystems, Gemini's Extensions are focused on the Google ecosystem. This may expand.

Action limitations. Most Extensions are read-oriented — they retrieve information rather than take actions. Gemini can find flights but cannot book them. It can search your email but cannot send messages. The exceptions are within Google Workspace integration (covered in Chapter 13), where Gemini has more action-oriented capabilities.

Availability varies by plan. Not all Extensions are available on all Gemini plans. Some require premium subscriptions or specific Workspace configurations.

Quality of results. Extension results depend on the underlying service. If Google Flights has poor coverage for a route, Gemini cannot compensate. The Extension is only as good as the service it connects to.

Conversation context limits. Gemini is good at combining Extension results within a conversation, but there are limits to how much external data it can juggle at once. Very complex multi-Extension queries may produce incomplete results.

Practical Tips for Using Extensions

1. **Enable only what you need.** There is no benefit to enabling Extensions you will never use, and there is a small privacy cost. Start with the ones that match your actual workflows.

2. **Be specific in your queries.** "Find flights" is vague. "Find non-stop flights from LAX to JFK on Friday, returning Sunday, economy class" gives the Extension exactly what it needs.

3. **Combine Extensions with conversation.** After Gemini returns results, keep talking about them. "Which of these hotels is closest to the conference venue? And what are the nearby restaurant options?" builds on the results with further queries.

4. **Use Extensions for research, then act independently.** Since most Extensions are read-only, use them to gather information and make decisions, then go to the actual service (Flights, Hotels, etc.) to complete transactions.

5. **Compare with direct service use.** Occasionally check whether Gemini's Extension results match what you see querying the service directly. This calibrates your trust and surfaces cases where the Extension misses options.

6. **Watch for updates.** Google is actively expanding the Extension ecosystem. Check the Extensions settings periodically to see what is new.

Looking Ahead

Extensions let Gemini reach beyond its own knowledge and interact with external services. Combined with Gems (for customized behavior) and the core capabilities from earlier chapters, you now have a highly configurable, connected AI assistant.

In the next chapter, we explore Canvas — Gemini's collaborative content creation workspace, which changes how you work with the AI on longer creative and professional projects.

Chapter 16: Canvas — Collaborative Content Creation

Most interactions with AI assistants follow a simple pattern: you type a prompt, the AI generates a response, and you copy it somewhere else. This works for quick questions and short outputs, but it breaks down on substantial work – a long document, a piece of code, a detailed plan. The cycle of prompting, copying, pasting, editing, re-prompting, and re-copying creates friction that undermines the speed advantage AI is supposed to provide.

Canvas is Gemini's answer. It is a dedicated workspace alongside the chat interface – a persistent, editable surface where you and Gemini collaborate in real time. Instead of generating text in a chat bubble you have to extract and rework elsewhere, Canvas puts the output in a document-like environment you can refine directly.

What Canvas Is

Canvas opens as a panel next to your Gemini conversation. When Gemini generates content that belongs in a longer, structured format – a document, an article, a code file, a plan – it places that content in the Canvas panel instead of (or alongside) the chat. From there, you interact with it differently than you would a standard chat response.

In the Canvas, you can:

- **Read and review** the generated content in a clean, document-like format.
- **Edit directly.** Click into the Canvas and make changes just like you would in a text editor. Add sentences, delete paragraphs, fix typos, reorganize sections.
- **Ask Gemini to revise specific parts.** Select a section of text in the Canvas and ask Gemini to rewrite it, expand it, shorten it, change its tone, or modify it in any other way.

- **Iterate collaboratively.** Go back and forth between your own edits and Gemini's revisions, building up the content through a true collaborative process.
- **Keep the conversation separate from the content.** Your chat with Gemini continues in the chat panel, while the content you are developing lives in the Canvas. This separation prevents your work-in-progress from getting lost in a stream of chat messages.

When Canvas Activates

Canvas does not appear for every interaction. It is designed for content creation tasks where a persistent, editable workspace adds value. Gemini decides when to use Canvas based on your request, but you can expect it to activate when you:

- Ask Gemini to write a long-form document, article, report, or essay.
- Request code generation for a file or module.
- Ask for a detailed plan, outline, or structured content.
- Work on any task where the output is a substantial piece of content that you will likely want to edit and refine.

For short answers, quick questions, or conversational exchanges, Gemini responds in the regular chat. Canvas appears when there is something worth putting on a larger surface.

You can also request Canvas explicitly. Phrases like "Let's draft a document" or "Open this in Canvas" signal that you want the Canvas workflow.

The Canvas Workflow

A typical Canvas workflow shows how the pieces fit together.

Starting a Project

You open a Gemini conversation and type: "Help me write a project proposal for migrating our company's infrastructure to a cloud-based platform. The proposal should cover the business case, technical approach, timeline, budget estimate, and risk assessment."

Gemini drafts a comprehensive first version and places it in the Canvas panel. The chat shows a brief summary of what was generated; the Canvas contains the full document — five sections with headers, content, and a logical structure.

Reviewing and Providing Feedback

You read through the Canvas content. The business case section is strong, but the technical approach is too generic. You type in the chat: "The technical approach section needs to be more specific. We are migrating from on-premises VMware to Google Cloud. Include details about Migrate to Virtual Machines, network configuration, and database migration using Database Migration Service."

Gemini revises the technical approach section in the Canvas, incorporating the specific technologies and details you mentioned. The rest of the document remains unchanged.

Making Direct Edits

In the timeline section, Gemini assumed six months. Management expects four. Rather than asking Gemini to revise, you click into the Canvas and adjust the dates and milestones yourself.

Requesting Targeted Revisions

You select the budget estimate section and ask in the chat: "This section is too vague. Add specific line items for compute costs, storage, networking, and professional services. Use realistic numbers for a mid-size company migrating about two hundred virtual machines."

Gemini regenerates just that section with detailed line items and realistic cost estimates, while preserving your direct edits to the timeline section.

Finishing Up

After several rounds of revision — some driven by Gemini, some by your own edits — the proposal is ready. Copy the final content from Canvas or export it to another format.

Working with Code in Canvas

Canvas is not just for prose. It is equally effective for code. When you ask Gemini to generate code, Canvas provides a proper editing environment with syntax highlighting and a structure that makes it easy to read and modify.

Code generation. Ask Gemini to write a function, a class, a module, or an entire application skeleton. The code appears in the Canvas with proper formatting.

Code review and revision. Select a section and ask Gemini to optimize it, add error handling, improve readability, or fix a bug. Gemini modifies the selection while leaving the rest intact.

Incremental development. Build a codebase iteratively. Start with a basic structure, then ask Gemini to add features, implement methods, or refine logic piece by piece.

Documentation. After developing code in Canvas, ask Gemini to add comments, docstrings, or a README section without disrupting the code itself.

Seeing code in a proper editor, making direct changes, and asking for AI-driven revisions in the same workspace is dramatically more productive than chat-based code generation.

Canvas vs. Chat: When to Use Which

Knowing when Canvas adds value versus when standard chat is sufficient helps you work more efficiently.

Use Canvas when:

- You are creating content you will edit and refine.
- The output is long enough that it benefits from a dedicated reading and editing surface.
- You want to make direct edits alongside AI-generated revisions.
- You are working on a project over multiple iterations.
- You need to keep the content separate from the conversational back-and-forth.

Use standard chat when:

- You need a quick answer to a question.
- The output is short — a few sentences or a paragraph.
- You do not plan to edit the response.
- You are having a conversational exchange rather than creating content.
- You want the response inline with the conversation flow.

Gemini usually makes the right call about when to invoke Canvas. If it generates something in chat that belongs in Canvas, or vice versa, guide it with explicit instructions.

Collaboration Patterns

Canvas enables several distinct collaboration patterns between you and Gemini:

The Drafter-Editor Pattern

Gemini drafts, you edit. The most common pattern. It works when you want AI to handle the heavy lifting of initial content creation while you refine voice, accuracy, and nuance.

The Editor-Reviser Pattern

You write the initial content (or paste it from elsewhere), and Gemini revises. Useful when you have a draft and want AI assistance with improvement, editing, or expansion.

The Ping-Pong Pattern

You and Gemini alternate. You write a section, Gemini writes the next, you revise both, Gemini adds supplementary content. The back-and-forth creates a true collaborative dynamic.

The Instructor-Executor Pattern

You provide detailed instructions, Gemini executes. Best when you have a clear vision of the final product and want Gemini to handle the execution while you direct.

The Explorer Pattern

Start with a vague idea and use Canvas to explore it. Ask Gemini to generate an initial version, react, request variations, try different approaches, and gradually converge on something that works. Canvas keeps all the iterations visible and editable.

Tips for Effective Canvas Use

Here are some practical recommendations for getting the most out of Canvas:

1. **Start with a clear brief.** The better you describe what you want, the closer Gemini's first draft will be to your vision. Include purpose, audience, tone, length, and structure.

2. **Use targeted revisions.** Rather than "make this better," select specific sections and give specific instructions. "Make this paragraph more concise" or "Add a transition between these two sections" produces better results.

3. **Mix your edits with AI revisions.** Canvas is not purely an AI output surface. Jump in and make your own changes. The combination of human editing and AI revision produces better results than either alone.

4. **Iterate in stages.** Get the structure right first, then content quality, then polish. Trying to perfect everything in one pass is less effective.

5. **Use the chat panel strategically.** The chat panel is where you direct Gemini — instructions, feedback, questions. Keep Canvas for the actual content. The separation prevents confusion about what is a directive and what is part of the final output.

6. **Do not over-rely on AI for final polish.** Gemini is excellent at generating and revising, but the final pass — checking for your voice, verifying accuracy, ensuring the content serves your purpose — should always be yours.

7. **Save your work regularly.** Depending on the Gemini interface, Canvas content may or may not persist automatically. Copy important content to another location (Google Doc, local file, code repo) regularly.

Limitations of Canvas

Canvas is a powerful tool, but it has boundaries:

- **Not a full document editor.** Canvas handles basic editing but is not a replacement for Google Docs, Microsoft Word, or a full-featured IDE. For complex formatting, version control, or advanced editing, you will eventually move to a dedicated tool.
- **Context limits.** Very long documents may approach the limits of what Gemini can hold in its context window. For extremely long projects, work in sections.
- **Formatting constraints.** Canvas supports text formatting and code highlighting, but not the rich options of a full document editor. Complex layouts, embedded media, and advanced formatting may not be supported.
- **Single-user collaboration.** Canvas is a collaboration between you and Gemini, not a multi-user workspace like Google Docs. If others need to contribute, share the content elsewhere.

Looking Ahead

Canvas represents a shift in how we interact with AI — from question-and-answer to a genuine collaborative creative process. Combined with Gems for customized behavior, Extensions for external data, and Gemini's core capabilities, it creates a comprehensive creative and professional toolkit.

The next chapter covers two of Gemini's most powerful research tools: NotebookLM and Deep Research. They push what AI-assisted research can accomplish, turning hours of manual work into minutes of guided investigation.

Chapter 17: NotebookLM and Deep Research

This chapter covers two of the most powerful research tools in Google's AI ecosystem. NotebookLM and Deep Research take different approaches to the same problem: how do you use AI to understand large amounts of information quickly and thoroughly? NotebookLM lets you upload your own documents and have intelligent conversations about them. Deep Research sends Gemini out to conduct extensive, multi-step web research on your behalf. Together, they cover the full spectrum of research needs, from closed-source document analysis to open-ended internet investigation.

NotebookLM: Your Document Research Assistant

NotebookLM is a standalone Google product — separate from Gemini but built on the same AI foundations. It is designed for one purpose: helping you understand, analyze, and work with your own documents. You upload sources, and NotebookLM becomes an expert on those sources, answering questions, generating summaries, and creating audio discussions about the material.

What NotebookLM Is (and Is Not)

NotebookLM is not a general-purpose chatbot. It does not browse the internet, generate creative fiction, or perform tasks unrelated to the documents you provide. Its entire world is the set of sources you upload. That constraint is its greatest strength: because NotebookLM is grounded exclusively in your documents, its responses are traceable, verifiable, and directly relevant to your material.

When NotebookLM makes a claim, it cites the specific source and passage. There is no hallucination about external topics because the model is not trying to answer questions about external topics. It answers questions about your documents, period.

Getting Started with NotebookLM

Go to the NotebookLM website and create a new notebook. A notebook is a workspace centered around a set of source documents. You can upload several types:

- **PDF files.** Research papers, reports, manuals, legal documents, textbooks.
- **Google Docs.** Pull documents directly from your Google Drive.
- **Web pages.** Paste URLs to online articles, blog posts, or documentation.
- **YouTube videos.** Paste a YouTube link, and NotebookLM will process the video's content (primarily through its transcript).
- **Text files and other formats.** Various document formats are supported.

You can upload multiple sources into a single notebook, and NotebookLM treats them as a unified corpus. This is powerful for research that involves synthesizing across multiple documents.

Asking Questions About Your Documents

Once your sources are uploaded, you interact with NotebookLM through a chat interface. Ask questions, and it responds based exclusively on the content of your uploaded documents.

Example questions:

- "What are the three main arguments made in this paper?"
- "Compare the methodology used in Source A versus Source B."
- "Find every mention of 'supply chain disruption' across all my sources."
- "What evidence does the author provide for their central claim?"
- "Summarize the key findings of Chapter 4."
- "Are there any contradictions between these two reports?"

Every response includes inline citations linking back to the specific passages. Click a citation, and NotebookLM shows you exactly where the information came from. This traceability is essential for academic research, legal review, journalism, and any context where you need to verify claims against original sources.

Source Guides and Summaries

When you upload sources, NotebookLM automatically generates a source guide — a summary of each document highlighting key themes, arguments, and topics. You get a quick overview of your material before asking a single question.

You can also request various types of summaries:

- **Executive summaries** that capture the essential points in a few paragraphs.
- **Briefing documents** that organize information by theme.
- **Timelines** that arrange events chronologically.
- **FAQ documents** that anticipate common questions about the material.
- **Study guides** with key concepts, definitions, and review questions.

These outputs are grounded in your documents and cited, making them reliable starting points for your own work.

Audio Overviews

NotebookLM's most distinctive feature is Audio Overviews — podcast-style audio discussions about your uploaded documents. Two AI voices discuss the material in a conversational format, explaining key concepts, debating points, highlighting interesting findings, and making the content accessible in an entirely different medium.

Audio Overviews are remarkable for several reasons:

They make dense material accessible. A fifty-page research paper is daunting to read. A fifteen-minute audio discussion of the key points is far more approachable.

They support different learning styles. If you absorb information better through listening, Audio Overviews transform written content into a format that suits your preference.

They are great for commutes and exercise. Listen while you drive, walk, or work out. You absorb the key points of complex documents during time that would otherwise be unproductive.

They surface surprising connections. The discussion sometimes highlights connections between sources or implications of findings you might not have noticed on your own.

To generate an Audio Overview, click the Audio Overview option in your notebook. NotebookLM processes your sources and produces the audio within a few minutes. You can customize the focus by guiding what topics or themes the discussion should emphasize.

Practical Applications of NotebookLM

NotebookLM excels when you need to deeply understand a specific body of documents:

Academic research. Upload the papers you are reviewing for a literature survey. Compare methodologies, identify consensus and disagreement, highlight gaps in the research.

Legal document review. Upload contracts, case files, or regulatory documents. Ask specific questions about clauses, obligations, precedents, or compliance. Every answer cites the exact source passage.

Business analysis. Upload competitor reports, market analyses, and internal strategy documents. Synthesize insights across sources and identify patterns.

Studying and exam prep. Upload textbook chapters, lecture slides, and course notes. Generate study guides, quiz yourself, and create Audio Overviews for review sessions.

Content creation. Upload your research materials. Organize your notes, identify the strongest sources for each point, and generate outlines for articles, reports, or presentations.

Due diligence. For business transactions, upload financial statements, legal disclosures, and market reports. Ask NotebookLM to flag risks, inconsistencies, or unusual items across the set.

Deep Research: Multi-Step Web Investigation

Where NotebookLM analyzes documents you provide, Deep Research goes the other direction: it sends Gemini out into the open web to conduct extensive research on your behalf. It is a feature within Gemini that performs multi-step, multi-source web research, producing comprehensive cited reports that would take hours to compile manually.

What Deep Research Does

When you activate Deep Research, Gemini does not just run a single web search and summarize. It conducts an iterative research process:

1. **Understands your research question.** Gemini analyzes your query, identifies the key aspects to investigate, and develops a research plan.
2. **Proposes a research plan.** Before diving in, Gemini presents an outline of the topics it intends to investigate and the approach it will take. You can review the plan, suggest changes, and approve it before research begins.
3. **Conducts multi-step research.** Gemini runs dozens of web searches, reads through numerous pages, follows leads from one source to another, and builds a comprehensive understanding of the topic. This is not a single search — it is a sustained process that can take several minutes.
4. **Synthesizes findings.** When research finishes, Gemini produces a detailed report that synthesizes everything it found, structured with sections, headers, and logical flow.
5. **Provides citations.** Every claim is linked to its source. Click through to the original pages to verify information, read more context, or evaluate source credibility.

Starting a Deep Research Session

Look for the Deep Research option in the Gemini interface — typically available as an alternative to a standard response. Selecting it shifts Gemini into research mode.

Start with a clear, specific research question:

- "Research the current state of solid-state battery technology, including the leading companies, their approaches, estimated timelines to commercialization, and the main technical challenges remaining."

- "Investigate the economic impact of remote work policies adopted since 2020, focusing on productivity data, real estate market effects, and employee satisfaction studies."
- "Compile a comprehensive comparison of the top five project management tools for software development teams, including pricing, key features, integrations, and user reviews."

After you submit your query, Gemini presents the research plan. Review it carefully — this is your chance to steer before research begins. Add topics, remove irrelevant areas, or emphasize particular aspects. Once you approve, Gemini starts researching.

The Research Process

Deep Research typically takes several minutes — this is not a quick-answer feature. During that time, Gemini is conducting dozens of searches, reading numerous pages, and building its understanding of the topic. Progress indicators usually show what Gemini is currently investigating.

The extended duration is a feature, not a bug. Genuine research takes time, and the depth of the resulting report is proportional to the thoroughness of the investigation.

The Research Report

The output is a comprehensive, structured report. Depending on the topic, it might run several thousand words, organized into clear sections with headers and citations throughout.

A typical report includes:

- **An introduction** that frames the topic and outlines what the report covers.
- **Multiple thematic sections** addressing different aspects of the question.
- **Specific data, statistics, and facts** drawn from web sources, all cited.
- **Analysis and synthesis** that goes beyond listing facts — identifying patterns, comparing perspectives, drawing conclusions.
- **A conclusion or summary** capturing the key findings.

The report can be exported as a Google Doc, making it easy to save, share, and build on.

When to Use Deep Research

Deep Research is ideally suited for:

Pre-decision research. Before a major purchase, investment, career move, or strategic decision, compile a thorough overview of the landscape.

Competitive analysis. Research competitors, their products, strategies, and market positions. Deep Research compiles dozens of sources into a coherent picture.

Topic exploration. When you need to get up to speed on something you know little about, Deep Research is a comprehensive primer.

Report preparation. If you need to write a report, Deep Research handles the heavy lifting of information gathering, giving you a solid foundation.

Fact-finding. When the information you need is scattered across multiple sources, Deep Research beats manual searching.

NotebookLM vs. Deep Research: Choosing the Right Tool

NotebookLM and Deep Research serve complementary purposes. Knowing when to use each makes your research more effective.

Use NotebookLM when:

- You already have the documents you need to analyze.
- You need to work with specific, known sources (internal reports, academic papers, legal documents).
- Traceability to specific source passages is critical.
- You want to study or deeply understand a defined body of material.
- You need Audio Overviews for listening-based consumption.

Use Deep Research when:

- You need to gather information from the open web.

- You do not know which sources are relevant yet — you need Gemini to find them.
- Your question requires synthesizing information from many disparate sources.
- You want a comprehensive overview of a broad topic.
- You need current, up-to-date information that may not be in any document you possess.

Use both when:

- You want to combine open-web research with deep analysis of specific documents. For example, use Deep Research to identify the key papers and reports on a topic, then upload those documents to NotebookLM for detailed analysis and questioning.

Practical Tips for Research with Gemini

1. **Be specific in your questions.** Both tools produce better results when you ask focused questions rather than broad, vague ones.
2. **Review Deep Research plans before approving.** The plan is your steering mechanism. Take a minute to review and adjust before Gemini spends several minutes investigating the wrong angle.
3. **Upload high-quality sources to NotebookLM.** The quality of analysis depends on the quality of sources. Curate your uploads thoughtfully.
4. **Verify critical claims.** Both tools provide citations — use them. For important research, click through to the original sources and verify key claims yourself.
5. **Combine with other Gemini features.** After Deep Research produces a report, use Canvas to refine it into a polished deliverable. After NotebookLM helps you understand your sources, use Gemini to draft content based on what you learned.
6. **Use Audio Overviews strategically.** They are best for an initial grasp or for review, not for detailed technical analysis. Treat them as a complement to careful reading, not a replacement.

7. **Iterate.** If the first round does not fully answer your question, refine your query and go again. Deep Research can be run multiple times with different angles. NotebookLM supports unlimited follow-ups.

8. **Export and preserve.** Research outputs are valuable. Export Deep Research reports to Google Docs and save NotebookLM insights somewhere permanent. Do not let good research disappear into a closed browser tab.

Emerging Agentic Capabilities

Deep Research is a glimpse of something bigger: Gemini's evolving ability to act as an agent, not just an assistant. When it builds a plan, runs dozens of searches, follows leads, and synthesizes a report — all without your intervention between steps — it is exhibiting what the field calls agentic behavior. The model is not just answering a question. It is pursuing a goal across multiple steps, deciding along the way what to investigate next.

As of May 2026, Google is expanding these agentic capabilities across the Gemini ecosystem. You can see the foundations: Deep Research acts autonomously within a research task, Extensions let Gemini query external services and combine results, and Workspace integration lets Gemini draft emails and create documents on your behalf.

Where this is heading is multi-step task execution — give Gemini a complex goal and have it break the work down, take actions across multiple tools and services, and deliver a result without you managing each step. Imagine telling Gemini to "research the top three competitors for our new product, create a comparison spreadsheet in Google Sheets, draft an executive summary in Google Docs, and email the package to my team" — and having it handle the whole workflow end to end.

We are not fully there. Current agentic capabilities are bounded — Gemini acts autonomously within specific features like Deep Research, but it cannot yet chain arbitrary multi-step workflows across all of Google's services without human checkpoints. Google is iterating rapidly, and you should expect these capabilities to expand significantly in the coming months.

The practical takeaway: when you use Deep Research, you are already experiencing agentic AI. As these capabilities mature, the line between "assistant that answers questions" and "agent that accomplishes goals" will keep blurring. The skills you are building throughout this book — clear communication, judgment about when to trust and when to verify, thoughtful task decomposition — will become even more valuable as Gemini does more on its own.

The Research Workflow

Here is a workflow that leverages both tools for a comprehensive research project:

1. **Start with Deep Research** to survey the landscape. Get a broad understanding of the topic and identify the key sources, players, and themes.

2. **Collect key documents** surfaced during Deep Research — academic papers, reports, articles — and upload them to NotebookLM.

3. **Use NotebookLM to go deep.** Ask detailed questions about the documents. Compare sources. Identify the strongest evidence for each point you want to make.

4. **Generate an Audio Overview** for a fresh perspective and to catch connections you might have missed.

5. **Return to Gemini** to draft your final output — report, presentation, article, decision memo — using Canvas for collaborative editing and the insights from your research.

This workflow turns what might be days of manual research into a few hours of guided, AI-augmented investigation. That is the promise of NotebookLM and Deep Research — not to replace your judgment, but to accelerate the gathering and understanding of information so you can apply that judgment more effectively.

Part V: Getting Better Results

"The computer was born to solve problems that did not exist before."

— Bill Gates

Chapter 18: Prompting Fundamentals

You have a conversation partner that can write code, analyze documents, brainstorm ideas, and reason through problems — but only if you know how to talk to it. That is the core challenge of prompting. Gemini is extraordinarily capable, but the quality of what you get depends almost entirely on the quality of what you put in.

This chapter covers the foundational skills of writing effective prompts for Gemini. Whether you use Gemini in Google's web interface, through the API, or inside Google Workspace, these principles apply universally. Master them, and every interaction will improve.

What Is a Prompt, Really?

A prompt is the text you send to Gemini to get a response. It can be a single sentence, a multi-paragraph brief, or a structured set of instructions with examples. The prompt is your entire interface with the model — no buttons, no settings matter as much as the words you choose.

"Summarize this article" is a prompt. So is a 10,000-word document followed by detailed instructions about tone, audience, and format. The difference between these two is the difference between getting a generic response and getting exactly what you need.

Think of prompting not as "asking a question" but as "writing a brief." You are commissioning work from a skilled generalist. The more context, specificity, and clarity you provide, the better the deliverable.

The Five Elements of an Effective Prompt

Every strong prompt draws on some combination of five elements. You do not need all five every time, but knowing them gives you a toolkit.

1. Task

The action you want Gemini to perform. A clear verb: summarize, write, analyze, compare, translate, explain, generate, debug, review, list.

Weak: "This quarterly report."

Strong: "Summarize the key findings from this quarterly report in three bullet points."

The task is the one element you always need. Without a clear action, Gemini has to guess — and it may guess wrong.

2. Context

Context is the background Gemini needs to do the job well — who the audience is, what the situation involves, what has already happened, and why you need this output.

Without context: "Write an email about the project delay."

With context: "Write an email to our client, a mid-size law firm, explaining that the software migration project will be delayed by two weeks due to a vendor dependency. We have a strong relationship with this client and want to maintain their confidence."

Context turns a generic response into a relevant one. Gemini cannot read your mind — it does not know your audience, your industry norms, or your relationships unless you tell it.

3. Specifics

Specifics are the concrete details and constraints that shape the output. Word count, format, tone, language level, number of items, topics to include or exclude.

"Write a product description" could go a hundred directions. "Write a 150-word product description for a waterproof Bluetooth speaker, targeting outdoor enthusiasts, emphasizing durability and battery life, in a casual and energetic tone" gives Gemini a clear target.

4. Examples

Examples are the most powerful and underused element of prompting. Showing Gemini what good output looks like bypasses the need to describe your preferences in abstract terms.

If you want social media posts in your brand's voice, paste three posts you have written and liked. If you want data formatted a certain way, show one formatted entry before asking for the rest.

This technique is called few-shot prompting. Even a single example (one-shot) dramatically improves output consistency. We will explore it more shortly.

5. Persona or Role

Assigning Gemini a role shapes its tone, vocabulary, and approach. "You are a senior financial analyst" produces different output than "you are a friendly tutor explaining concepts to a beginner."

Persona is useful, but it is the element most often overused or leaned on as a crutch. A well-specified task with good context usually outperforms a vague prompt with an elaborate persona. Use persona when it adds something — expert-level depth, a specific communication style, a particular analytical lens.

Zero-Shot, One-Shot, and Few-Shot Prompting

These terms describe how many examples you include in your prompt.

Zero-shot means no examples. You just describe what you want:

> Classify the following customer review as positive, negative, or neutral: "The product arrived on time but the packaging was damaged."

Gemini handles zero-shot well for common tasks. Its training data includes enough examples of classification, summarization, and similar tasks that it can usually infer your intent without a demonstration.

One-shot means you provide a single example:

> Classify customer reviews as positive, negative, or neutral.
>
> Example: Review: "Absolutely love this product, best purchase I have made all year!" Classification: Positive
>
> Now classify: Review: "The product arrived on time but the packaging was damaged." Classification:

Few-shot means two or more examples. Particularly valuable when your task has nuances that are hard to describe in words — specific formatting, a particular judgment threshold, a unique style.

The more ambiguous or subjective your task, the more examples help. For straightforward factual tasks, zero-shot is fine. For style-sensitive or judgment-heavy tasks, invest in good examples.

The Art of Specificity

Vague prompts produce vague responses. This is the single most common prompting mistake, and fixing it produces the biggest improvement.

Compare these two prompts:

Vague: "Tell me about renewable energy."

Specific: "Explain the three most cost-effective renewable energy technologies for residential use in 2026, comparing their installation costs, maintenance requirements, and typical payback periods. Write this for a homeowner with no technical background."

The vague prompt produces a perfectly accurate overview of renewable energy — generic, probably covering ground you already know, organized in whatever way Gemini defaults to. The specific prompt produces something immediately useful.

A practical framework for adding specificity: after writing your initial prompt, ask yourself:

- **Who is this for?** (audience)
- **How long should it be?** (length)
- **What format should it take?** (structure)
- **What tone is appropriate?** (voice)
- **What must it include?** (requirements)
- **What should it avoid?** (constraints)

You do not need to answer all of these every time. But running through the list often reveals something you left out.

Structured Prompts for Complex Tasks

When your task has multiple parts, structure your prompt with clear sections. Gemini responds well to explicit organization.

A structured prompt might look like this:

```
### Role
You are a technical writer specializing in API documentation.

### Task
Write documentation for the following API endpoint.

### Endpoint Details
- Method: POST
- Path: /api/v2/users
- Authentication: Bearer token
- Request body: JSON with fields name (string, required), email (string, require
d), role (string, optional, defaults to "viewer")

### Requirements
- Include a description of the endpoint's purpose
- Document all parameters with types and constraints
- Provide a curl example and a Python example
- Include common error responses (400, 401, 409)
- Use a professional but approachable tone

### Format
Use standard API documentation formatting with headers, code blocks, and tables
where appropriate.
```

This level of structure looks like overkill for a simple task. But for anything you reuse or that requires precision, it pays for itself immediately. The model knows exactly what to produce, and you rarely need follow-up corrections.

Iterative Prompting: The Conversation Advantage

One of the most important prompting skills is knowing when to iterate rather than trying to nail everything in a single prompt. Gemini maintains context throughout a conversation, so you can build up to a complex result step by step.

First pass: "Draft a project proposal for migrating our customer database to a cloud-hosted solution."

Review the output, then refine: "Good structure. Expand the risk assessment section to include data sovereignty concerns, and add a timeline estimate assuming a team of three engineers."

Then refine further: "Rewrite the executive summary to lead with the cost savings rather than the technical benefits."

This iterative approach has several advantages. You course-correct early before Gemini invests effort in the wrong direction. You evaluate each section independently. You build on what works rather than starting over.

Be specific in your feedback. "Make it better" tells Gemini nothing useful. "Make the introduction more concise, reduce it from three paragraphs to one, and open with the most compelling statistic" tells it exactly what to change.

System Instructions and Custom Instructions

Gemini supports system instructions — a special section of the prompt that sets persistent behavior for an entire conversation or application. In the Gemini API, system instructions are a separate parameter. In the Gemini web app, you configure custom instructions through your settings. For reusable custom personas, create Gems (Chapter 14).

System instructions are ideal for:

- Setting a consistent persona ("You are a medical information assistant. Always remind users to consult a healthcare professional for medical decisions.")
- Defining output format defaults ("Always respond in bullet points unless asked otherwise.")
- Establishing guardrails ("Never provide specific investment advice. Instead, explain general concepts and recommend consulting a financial advisor.")
- Specifying audience ("All explanations should be suitable for a high school reading level.")

Think of system instructions as the "always on" layer. They apply to every turn, so you do not have to repeat them.

Common Prompting Mistakes and How to Fix Them

Overloading a single prompt. Ask Gemini to do seven things at once and some will get less attention. Break complex requests into sequential steps, or use numbered lists with explicit instructions to address each point thoroughly.

Being polite at the expense of clarity. "If it is not too much trouble, could you perhaps consider maybe writing a short summary?" Just say "Write a 100-word summary." Gemini has no feelings to hurt. Directness produces better results.

Assuming shared context. Gemini does not know what project you are working on, what your company does, or what happened in a previous conversation (unless it is the same session). State your context explicitly.

Asking leading questions. "Don't you think renewable energy is the best option?" invites Gemini to agree with you rather than analyze. Ask open-ended questions or request balanced analysis: "What are the strongest arguments for and against renewable energy as a primary power source for residential use?"

Neglecting to specify format. If you need a table, ask for a table. Bullet points, ask for bullet points. A specific heading structure, describe it. Gemini defaults to whatever format seems natural, which may not match what you need.

Prompting for Different Gemini Models

The fundamentals in this chapter apply across all Gemini models, but there are practical differences worth noting.

Gemini 3 Pro is the flagship model with the deepest reasoning capabilities. With Deep Think enabled, it engages in extended internal reasoning before responding. It excels at complex multi-step tasks, nuanced analysis, and problems requiring careful thought. For 3 Pro, you can pose harder questions and expect more sophisticated reasoning. Give it the full context it needs and let it work through the complexity.

Gemini 3 Flash is optimized for speed and cost-efficiency. It handles everyday prompting tasks — drafting, summarization, classification, Q&A — with impressive quality at much faster response times. With Flash, be slightly more explicit in your instructions, since the model trades some depth for speed. For the vast majority of daily tasks, Flash handles well-crafted prompts beautifully.

Both models support Gemini's massive context window of over one million tokens. You can include entire documents, codebases, or datasets directly in a prompt. When relevant material is available, including it as context almost always beats asking Gemini to work from general knowledge alone.

Building Your Prompting Instincts

Prompting improves with deliberate practice. Concrete ways to build your abilities:

Save your best prompts. When you get a result that is exactly what you wanted, save the prompt that produced it. Over time, you build a personal library of effective patterns.

Experiment with variations. Take a prompt that worked and change one element — the persona, the format, the level of specificity. See how the output changes. This builds intuition for which elements matter most.

Read the output critically. When Gemini produces something not quite right, diagnose why. Was the task unclear? Did you omit context? Was the format unspecified? Each miss is a learning opportunity.

Start simple and add complexity. You do not need a perfect structured prompt on the first try. Start with the core task, see what you get, then add specificity where the output falls short.

The prompts that feel effortless — the ones that produce great results on the first try — come from someone who has internalized these fundamentals through practice. No secret tricks. Just clarity, specificity, and context, applied consistently.

What Comes Next

This chapter gave you the foundational toolkit. In the chapters ahead, we apply these fundamentals to increasingly complex scenarios — long-form tasks that require planning, output formatting and control, and domain-specific applications across education, business, development, and creative work. Every technique builds on what you have learned here.

The single most important takeaway: be specific. When in doubt, add more detail. Gemini is remarkably good at following instructions — but only the ones you actually give it.

Chapter 19: Working with Long and Complex Tasks

Some tasks fit neatly into a single prompt and a single response. You ask Gemini to summarize a paragraph, it summarizes, you are done. But the most valuable work — the work that saves hours instead of minutes — involves tasks too large, too nuanced, or too multi-faceted to handle in one shot.

This chapter is about those tasks. Writing a 5,000-word report. Analyzing a 200-page document. Planning a project with dozens of moving parts. Turning a messy dataset into structured insights. These are the tasks where the right approach is the difference between a frustrating experience and a genuinely powerful one.

Why Long Tasks Are Different

A simple question gets a single read-and-respond cycle. Long tasks bring several complications.

First, the task may have multiple stages that depend on each other. You cannot write a good conclusion until you have written the body. You cannot analyze data until you have cleaned it. You need a sequencing strategy.

Second, longer tasks demand more context management. Gemini's context window is massive — over one million tokens — so it can hold an enormous amount in a single conversation. But large capacity and effective use are different things. You still need to organize your inputs so Gemini can find and use the right information at the right time.

Third, quality degrades when you ask for too much at once. A model tasked with writing ten sections simultaneously produces shallower work than one writing each section with full attention. Not a limitation unique to AI — that is how focus works.

The Decomposition Principle

The most important technique for long tasks is decomposition: breaking a large task into smaller, manageable pieces. This is not just a prompting technique — it is a thinking technique. If you cannot articulate the steps, you are not ready to delegate.

Say you need a competitive analysis report. Instead of "Write a competitive analysis of our three main competitors," decompose:

1. Define the evaluation criteria (pricing, features, market position, strengths, weaknesses)
2. Analyze Competitor A against those criteria
3. Analyze Competitor B
4. Analyze Competitor C
5. Create a comparison matrix
6. Write the executive summary with strategic recommendations

Each step becomes its own prompt or turn. The output from each feeds the next. You review and correct at each stage, so errors do not compound.

This approach takes more prompts but produces dramatically better results. And because you review at each stage, you catch problems early rather than discovering them in a finished document that needs rewriting.

Planning Before Prompting

For truly complex tasks, invest time in planning before writing a single prompt. You can use Gemini itself for the planning phase.

Start with a meta-prompt: "I need to create a comprehensive onboarding guide for new employees at a SaaS company. Before we write anything, help me create an outline. What sections should this guide include, and in what order? The audience is non-technical new hires in their first week."

Review the outline. Adjust it. Add sections you know are needed. Remove irrelevant ones. Then use the finalized outline as your roadmap, working through it section by section.

This step serves two purposes. It gives you a structure to follow, and it gives Gemini a clear picture of the whole project. When you reach Section 5, Gemini understands how it fits into the broader document because you established the context upfront.

Using Gemini's Million-Token Context Window

Gemini's context window is one of its biggest advantages for long tasks. Over one million tokens means you can include material that would be impossible with smaller models. A million tokens is roughly 750,000 words — multiple books, an entire codebase, or a year's worth of meeting notes.

How to use the capacity effectively:

Front-load your reference material. If you are writing a report based on source documents, paste them into the conversation first. Then ask Gemini to work with them. Source material directly in context produces far better results than working from memory or summaries.

Use explicit references. When your context includes multiple documents, label them: "Document A: Q3 Financial Report. Document B: Customer Survey Results. Document C: Product Roadmap." Then refer to them by name: "Using the data from Document B, identify the top three customer complaints."

Do not pad unnecessarily. Just because you can include a million tokens does not mean you should. Include material relevant to the task. Irrelevant context does not usually confuse Gemini, but it dilutes attention. Quality of context matters more than quantity.

Leverage long context for analysis. Some of the most powerful uses are analytical: "Here is our complete customer support log for March. Identify recurring issues, categorize them by severity, and recommend process changes to reduce ticket volume." This task was essentially impossible before million-token context windows.

Sequential Processing for Long Documents

Even with inputs that fit in the context window, processing in stages often produces better results.

For a 300-page legal contract:

Stage 1 — Overview: "Read this entire contract and provide a high-level summary of its structure, identifying the major sections and their purposes."

Stage 2 — Targeted Analysis: "Now focus on Sections 7 through 12, which cover liability and indemnification. Identify any clauses that are unusual, one-sided, or potentially problematic for the buyer."

Stage 3 — Specific Questions: "In Section 9.3, the limitation of liability clause caps damages at the total fees paid in the preceding 12 months. Is this standard for enterprise SaaS agreements? What alternatives might we negotiate for?"

Each stage narrows the focus. Start broad to understand the landscape, then zoom in on what matters. This mirrors how an expert would approach the same document.

Chain-of-Thought and Deep Think

For complex reasoning — mathematical proofs, strategic planning, multi-factor analysis — you want Gemini to think carefully rather than jump to a conclusion.

One approach is to request step-by-step reasoning explicitly: "Walk through your reasoning step by step before giving your final recommendation." This encourages the model to show its work and often produces more accurate results.

Gemini 3 Pro takes this further with Deep Think, a mode that engages extended internal reasoning before responding. With Deep Think active, the model spends more time considering the problem from multiple angles, checking its own logic, and refining its answer before presenting it. Google also ships a dedicated Gemini 3 Deep Think mode that pushes reasoning even further when accuracy matters more than speed.

Deep Think is particularly valuable for:

- Problems with multiple valid approaches where choosing the right one matters
- Tasks requiring careful logical or mathematical reasoning
- Situations where the obvious answer might be wrong
- Strategic questions with many interacting variables

When the task rewards careful thought over quick responses, Deep Think is worth the latency. For routine work where speed matters more than depth, the standard mode is the better choice.

Managing Multi-Turn Conversations

Long tasks often span many turns. Practices that keep extended conversations productive:

Summarize periodically. After a major section of work, ask Gemini to summarize what has been accomplished and what remains. This refreshes the working context and catches drift.

Restate requirements when shifting phases. Moving from data analysis to writing the report? Restate your formatting and tone requirements. Do not assume instructions from twenty turns ago are still front-of-mind.

Use conversation structure intentionally. Group related work together. If you need to analyze three datasets, do all three before moving to synthesis. Jumping between unrelated tasks creates confusion.

Start a new conversation when the task changes fundamentally. Finished a report and now working on something completely different? Start fresh. Old context from an unrelated task can influence outputs in subtle ways.

Handling Ambiguity and Making Decisions

Complex tasks often involve ambiguity — no single right answer, judgment calls required. Gemini can help, but you need to prompt deliberately.

Ask for options, not answers. Instead of "What should our pricing strategy be?" try "Present three distinct pricing strategies for our B2B SaaS product, with pros, cons, and ideal use case for each." This gives you material to evaluate rather than a single recommendation you may or may not agree with.

Request explicit assumptions. "What assumptions are you making in this analysis? List them so I can confirm or correct them." Surfaces hidden reasoning that might lead the output astray.

Use scenario planning. "Analyze this market entry decision under three scenarios: best case (rapid adoption), base case (moderate growth), worst case (regulatory challenges). What changes about the strategy in each?" Forces thorough thinking and helps you prepare for multiple outcomes.

Working with Data in Long Tasks

Data-intensive tasks have their own patterns — spreadsheets, survey results, financial models. These approaches help.

Describe your data before diving in. Before requesting analysis, have Gemini describe what it sees: "Here is a CSV of our sales data. Describe the columns, the time range, the number of records, and any obvious data quality issues before we begin analysis."

Clean before you analyze. If your data has issues — missing values, inconsistent formatting, duplicates — handle those first. "Identify and list any data quality issues in this dataset. Then describe how you recommend handling each."

Build analysis incrementally. Start with descriptive statistics, move to trends and patterns, then conclusions and recommendations. Each step validates the previous one.

Ask Gemini to show its work. For quantitative analysis, request calculations or methodology. "Calculate the year-over-year growth rate for each product line and show the formula you are using." This lets you verify the math and catch errors early.

Templates for Recurring Complex Tasks

If you regularly perform the same complex task — weekly reports, client proposals, project retrospectives — create a reusable template prompt.

A template for a weekly business review might look like:

```
### Task
Generate a weekly business review summary for the week of [DATE].

### Input Data
[Paste metrics, notes, or raw data here]

### Sections Required
```

```
1. Key metrics summary (revenue, active users, support tickets) with week-over-w
eek comparison
2. Notable wins and achievements
3. Issues and blockers requiring attention
4. Action items for the coming week
5. One strategic observation or recommendation

### Format
- Use headers for each section
- Use bullet points within sections
- Bold any metric that changed by more than 10% week-over-week
- Keep the total length under 800 words
```

Templates save time, ensure consistency, and improve quality by encoding your requirements once rather than trying to remember them weekly.

When to Use Multiple Conversations

A single conversation is not always the best approach, even for a unified task. Split into multiple conversations when:

- You need genuinely different perspectives on the same problem. A single conversation tends to maintain consistency, which is usually good but can limit divergent thinking.
- The task has independent components that do not need shared context. Writing three product descriptions is faster in parallel than in sequence.
- The conversation has grown so long that earlier context is important but far away in history. Starting fresh with a clear summary can be more effective.

When you split work across conversations, you become the integration layer. Paste outputs from one conversation into another as context, and synthesize the results yourself or use a final conversation to combine them.

Practical Example: From Raw Research to Finished Report

A complete example of a long task handled well:

Conversation Turn 1: "I am preparing a market analysis report on the electric vehicle charging infrastructure market. Here are four industry reports I want to base this on. [Paste reports.] Before we begin writing, summarize the key findings from each report in a bullet-point outline."

Turn 2: Review the summaries. Correct any misinterpretations. "Your summary of Report 3 missed the section on rural deployment challenges. Add that. Otherwise, this is accurate."

Turn 3: "Based on these summaries, create a detailed outline for a 3,000-word market analysis report targeting venture capital investors evaluating opportunities in this space."

Turn 4: Review and adjust the outline. "Move the competitive landscape section before the market sizing section. Add a section on regulatory tailwinds."

Turn 5: "Write Section 1: Executive Summary. Keep it under 400 words. Lead with the market opportunity size and growth rate."

Turns 6–10: Write each subsequent section, reviewing as you go.

Turn 11: "Now read the complete report from beginning to end. Check for consistency in data citations, tone, and logical flow. Flag any issues."

Turn 12: Address the flagged issues and finalize.

This takes more time than a single prompt, but the result is a polished, accurate report that genuinely serves its audience. The step-by-step approach gave you control at every stage and produced work that would be difficult to achieve in one shot.

The Mindset for Complex Work

The underlying principle: your role shifts as task complexity increases. For simple tasks, you are a requestor — ask and receive. For complex tasks, you are a project manager. You plan, delegate, review, iterate.

Gemini is at its best when you give it focused, well-defined work with clear context. The more complex the overall task, the more important it is that each individual prompt is clear and manageable. Decompose, sequence, review, refine. That is the formula for getting genuinely excellent work out of Gemini on the tasks that matter most.

Chapter 20: Output Formatting and Control

Getting Gemini to produce the right content is only half the challenge. The other half is getting that content in the right format. A brilliant analysis loses its value as a wall of unstructured text when you needed a table. A perfectly written email is useless buried in a ten-paragraph response when you asked for three sentences.

This chapter covers controlling how Gemini structures and formats its output — from simple formatting requests to advanced techniques like JSON mode and structured output schemas.

Why Format Matters

Format is not cosmetic. It determines how quickly you can use the output, whether it drops into another tool or workflow, and how your audience receives it. A summary in bullet points is scannable in seconds. The same summary in paragraph form takes longer to parse. Neither is inherently better — the right choice depends on the use case.

When you do not specify a format, Gemini defaults to whatever seems most natural. For explanations, that usually means paragraphs. For lists, numbered or bulleted items. For comparisons, sometimes a table. These defaults are reasonable, but not always what you need.

Taking explicit control of format — every time — is one of the simplest ways to make Gemini more useful in your workflow.

Basic Formatting Instructions

The simplest approach is to state your format requirement in the prompt. Gemini reliably follows these instructions.

Bullet points: "List the advantages and disadvantages of remote work in bullet points."

Numbered lists: "Give me a numbered list of the ten most important features to look for in project management software."

Tables: "Create a comparison table of the three cloud providers with columns for pricing, storage limits, and key differentiators."

Headings and sections: "Write this report with clear section headings using Markdown H2 formatting."

Specific length: "Summarize this in exactly three sentences." Or "Keep your response under 200 words."

Paragraph structure: "Write this in four paragraphs: introduction, two body paragraphs covering the pros and cons respectively, and a conclusion."

These instructions work because they are unambiguous. Gemini knows exactly what a bullet point is, what a table looks like, and how to count sentences. The more specific your instruction, the more precisely Gemini follows it.

Markdown Formatting

Gemini natively produces Markdown, making it an excellent tool for formatted documents. If your environment renders Markdown — Google Docs (via export), Notion, GitHub, many CMS platforms — ask Gemini to use the full range of Markdown syntax.

Useful Markdown formatting you can request:

- **Headers** (H1 through H6) for document structure
- **Bold** and *italic* for emphasis
- **Code blocks** with language-specific syntax highlighting
- **Tables** with aligned columns
- **Blockquotes** for callouts or citations
- **Ordered and unordered lists**, including nested lists
- **Horizontal rules** for section breaks
- **Links** formatted as clickable references

When you need a well-structured document, specify this explicitly: "Format this as a Markdown document with H2 section headers, bullet points for lists, and code blocks for any technical examples."

Controlling Tone and Style

Format extends beyond structure to tone and register. The same information can be formal or casual, technical or accessible, concise or expansive.

Formal business tone: "Write this in a professional, formal tone suitable for a board presentation."

Casual conversational tone: "Write this in a casual, friendly tone as if explaining to a colleague over coffee."

Technical precision: "Write this for a technical audience. Use precise terminology and assume familiarity with cloud architecture concepts."

Accessible language: "Write this at a sixth-grade reading level. Avoid jargon and explain any technical terms."

You can also control style through example. Paste a sample paragraph and say "Match the tone and style of this example." Gemini analyzes the sample's characteristics — sentence length, vocabulary level, formality, use of humor or analogy — and replicates them.

Structured Output: JSON, XML, and More

Technical and automation use cases often require output in a specific data format. This is where structured output becomes essential.

JSON Output

JSON is the most common structured format for AI outputs, especially when the output feeds another system.

Simple approach — just ask:

```
Extract the following information from this job posting and return it as JSON:
- Job title
- Company name
- Location
```

```
- Salary range
- Required skills (as an array)
- Years of experience required
```

Gemini produces well-formed JSON. For more control, provide a schema:

```
Extract information from this job posting and return it as JSON matching this ex
act schema:
{
  "title": "string",
  "company": "string",
  "location": {
    "city": "string",
    "state": "string",
    "remote": "boolean"
  },
  "salary": {
    "min": "number",
    "max": "number",
    "currency": "string"
  },
  "skills": ["string"],
  "experience_years": "number"
}
```

With a schema, Gemini matches it closely, using the right data types, nesting structure, and field names.

JSON Mode in the API

In the Gemini API, you can enable JSON mode to guarantee valid JSON output. Set `response_mime_type` to `application/json` in your generation config. With JSON mode active, Gemini constrains its output to valid, parseable JSON, eliminating the risk of malformed output breaking your downstream processing.

Go further by providing a response schema. This tells Gemini not just to produce JSON, but to match a specific structure with defined fields and types. The API validates the output against your schema, giving you reliable, predictable structure every time.

Invaluable for production. When your code expects a specific JSON shape, you do not want edge cases where the model reorganizes the data or adds explanatory text outside the JSON block.

Other Structured Formats

JSON is the most common, but Gemini produces other structured formats on request:

- **CSV:** "Format this data as CSV with headers in the first row."
- **XML:** "Return this as well-formed XML with the root element 'report'."
- **YAML:** "Output this configuration as YAML."
- **HTML:** "Generate an HTML table with this data, including inline CSS for styling."

For any format, an example of the exact structure you want is more reliable than describing it in words.

Controlling Response Length

Length control is one of the most requested formatting needs, and Gemini handles it well — with some nuance.

Word and sentence limits work reliably. "Summarize this in 50 words" or "Answer in one sentence" produces output close to the requested length. Gemini may be slightly over or under, but it lands in the right range.

Character limits are less precise. Models operate on tokens, not characters, so character-level precision is harder. For exact character counts (tweets, metadata fields, SMS), generate the output and verify yourself, or ask Gemini to count and adjust: "Write a meta description for this page in exactly 155 characters. Count the characters and confirm."

"Be concise" is vague. If you want short output, specify what short means. "Be concise" might mean "shorter than default" to one person and "telegram-style brevity" to another. "Respond in three bullet points, each under 20 words" is unambiguous.

Minimum length is harder to enforce. Ask for "at least 1,000 words" and Gemini usually complies, but the content may feel padded. It is often better to specify what the content should cover and let the length follow naturally, or specify a range: "Write 800 to 1,200 words."

Templates and Fill-in-the-Blank Formats

When you need output matching a precise structure — form letters, database entries, standardized reports — provide a template with placeholders.

```
Fill in this template based on the customer interaction transcript above:

**Customer Name:** [name]
**Date of Interaction:** [date]
**Issue Category:** [one of: billing, technical, account, other]
**Issue Summary:** [one sentence]
**Resolution Status:** [resolved / escalated / pending]
**Resolution Details:** [two to three sentences]
**Follow-up Required:** [yes/no]
**Follow-up Action:** [one sentence, or N/A if no follow-up required]
```

This gives you complete control over output structure. Gemini fills the brackets with extracted or generated content while preserving everything else exactly as written.

Constraining What Gemini Should Not Include

Sometimes the most important formatting instruction is about what to leave out.

"Do not include a preamble or introduction." Gemini often opens with a contextual lead-in ("Great question! Here is..."). To go straight to the content, say so.

"Do not add commentary or explanation." When you want raw output — just the code, just the data, just the translation — tell Gemini to skip its usual explanatory wrapper.

"Output only the JSON, nothing else." For machine-readable output, this prevents Gemini from wrapping the JSON in a code block with commentary.

"Do not use bullet points." When you want prose instead of lists, state it. Gemini sometimes defaults to lists when prose would serve better.

"Do not repeat the question." In some contexts, Gemini echoes your question before answering. If you do not want that, say so.

Negative instructions are surprisingly effective. Gemini respects "do not" constraints well, so use them when there are specific patterns to avoid.

Output in Multiple Formats Simultaneously

Gemini can present the same information in multiple formats within a single response:

"Analyze this sales data and present your findings in three formats: first, a narrative summary paragraph for the executive team; second, a detailed data table with monthly breakdowns; third, a bullet-point list of the three most actionable recommendations."

Useful when your output serves multiple audiences. The executive reads the paragraph, the analyst uses the table, the team lead grabs the action items.

Formatting for Specific Platforms

When your output is destined for a specific platform, tell Gemini:

- **"Format this for a LinkedIn post."** Gemini adjusts line length, spacing, and platform conventions.
- **"Write this as a Slack message."** Short paragraphs, casual tone, Slack-compatible formatting.
- **"Format this for a Google Slides presentation."** Bullet points, concise text, clear section breaks that map to individual slides.
- **"Write this as a GitHub issue."** Description, steps to reproduce, expected behavior, actual behavior.

Platform-specific formatting saves you from reformatting manually. Gemini knows the conventions of major platforms and follows them when asked.

Advanced: Grounding and Citations

When you need Gemini to ground its output in specific sources — important for research, journalism, or academic work — instruct it to cite explicitly.

"Summarize the key findings from these three research papers. For each claim, include an inline citation referencing which paper it comes from, using the format [Paper 1], [Paper 2], or [Paper 3]."

With Google Search grounding, Gemini also pulls from web sources and includes links. With the API and grounding enabled, Gemini provides structured citation metadata alongside its responses, making it straightforward to build applications that present sourced, verifiable information.

Putting It All Together

The most effective formatting combines several techniques. Here is a prompt that demonstrates comprehensive control:

```
### Task
Write a product comparison guide for noise-canceling headphones.

### Products
1. Sony WH-1000XM6
2. Apple AirPods Max 2
3. Bose QuietComfort Ultra

### Format Requirements
- Start with a one-paragraph executive summary (no more than 80 words)
- Follow with a comparison table covering: price, battery life, noise cancellati
on rating (1-10), comfort rating (1-10), and best use case
- Then write a detailed section for each product (150-200 words each) with H3 he
aders
- End with a "Bottom Line" section recommending each product for a specific type
 of buyer
- Use Markdown formatting throughout
- Do not include a preamble or any text before the executive summary
- Tone: authoritative but approachable, like a trusted tech reviewer
```

Every aspect of the output is specified — structure, length, tone, format, constraints. This prompt produces output that is immediately usable without reformatting.

Format control is not about being pedantic. It is about making sure Gemini's output fits directly into your workflow, your document, your application, or your audience's expectations. Invest a few extra seconds specifying format in every prompt, and you spend far less time reformatting after the fact.

Part VI: Gemini for Your World

"Give me six hours to chop down a tree and I will spend the first four sharpening the axe."

— Abraham Lincoln (attributed)

Chapter 21: Gemini for Students and Educators

AI is reshaping education faster than most institutions are prepared for. Students who learn to use tools like Gemini effectively will have a genuine advantage — not because AI thinks for them, but because it accelerates every part of the learning process. Educators who understand these tools can create richer learning experiences, reclaim hours of administrative time, and meet students where they are.

This chapter is for both sides of the classroom. If you are a student, you will learn how to use Gemini as a study partner, research assistant, and thinking tool without undermining your own learning. If you are an educator, you will learn how to integrate Gemini into your teaching, build better materials, and handle the real challenges AI brings to academic integrity.

For Students: Gemini as a Learning Accelerator

The most important thing to understand about using Gemini for learning: the goal is not to get answers. The goal is to understand. If you use Gemini to skip the thinking, you are paying tuition to learn nothing. If you use it to think more deeply, more efficiently, and more broadly, you are getting extraordinary value from a tool that did not exist a few years ago.

Concept Explanation and Tutoring

Gemini excels at explaining concepts at exactly the level you need. Unlike a textbook written for a general audience, or a lecture that moves at one pace for everyone, Gemini adapts to you.

If you are struggling with a concept, start here: "Explain [concept] as if I understand [prerequisite knowledge] but am new to [this specific topic]."

For example: "Explain how neural networks learn, assuming I understand basic algebra and what a function is, but have never studied machine learning."

This gives Gemini the calibration it needs to pitch the explanation correctly. If it is too simple, say "I understood all of that — go deeper, especially on backpropagation." If it is too complex, say "You lost me at gradient descent. Explain that part with a concrete example."

This back-and-forth is where the real learning happens. You are not passively reading — you are engaging with the material, identifying your own gaps, and filling them in real time.

The Socratic Method Approach

One of the most powerful study techniques is to ask Gemini to teach you through questions rather than answers.

"I am studying the causes of World War I. Instead of explaining them to me, ask me a series of questions that guide me to understand the main causes. Start with what I might already know and build from there. If I get something wrong, do not just correct me — ask a follow-up question that helps me see the error myself."

This Socratic approach forces active recall, one of the most effective learning strategies known to cognitive science. You are not reading about the causes — you are reconstructing them from your own knowledge, with Gemini guiding you when you get stuck.

Study Guide and Exam Preparation

Gemini can create customized study materials that are far more targeted than generic review sheets.

"I have an exam on organic chemistry covering chapters 8 through 12 of [textbook name]. Create a study guide that covers the key concepts, common reaction mechanisms, and typical exam question formats. Include five practice problems at exam difficulty, with solutions at the end."

For even better preparation: "Based on this study guide, create a practice exam with 20 questions. Include a mix of multiple choice, short answer, and one multi-step problem. Do not show me the answers until I have attempted all the questions."

After the practice exam, paste your answers and ask Gemini to grade them with detailed explanations of what you got right and wrong.

Research and Paper Writing

This is where students are most tempted to misuse AI and most likely to get caught. So let us be clear: having Gemini write your paper is plagiarism in virtually every academic context. But using Gemini as a research tool is not only acceptable — it is smart.

Finding sources and framing research: "I am writing a research paper on the economic effects of universal basic income. What are the major perspectives in this debate? What are the most frequently cited studies? What aspects of this topic are underdeveloped in the existing research?"

Gemini gives you a map of the intellectual landscape. You still need to read the actual sources, form your own arguments, and write in your own voice — but Gemini saves hours of preliminary research.

Strengthening your arguments: After writing a draft, paste it and ask: "Read this essay and identify the three weakest arguments. For each one, explain why it is weak and suggest how I could strengthen it." This is exactly what a good tutor or writing center consultant would do.

Improving your writing: "Review this paragraph for clarity, conciseness, and logical flow. Suggest specific improvements but do not rewrite it entirely." This helps you learn to write better rather than outsourcing the writing itself.

Learning to Code

Gemini is an exceptionally good coding tutor: it can explain concepts, generate examples, review your code, and debug errors — all interactively.

"I am learning Python and just covered for loops. Give me five progressively harder exercises that use for loops. Start simple and end with something that also requires conditional logic. Do not show solutions — I will attempt each one and paste my code for feedback."

When you get stuck: "Here is my code for exercise 3. It runs but gives the wrong output. Do not give me the answer — give me a hint about where my logic might be wrong."

This hint-based approach builds genuine debugging skills. If Gemini hands you the answer, you learn nothing about how to find bugs yourself.

Language Learning

Gemini supports dozens of languages and can function as a conversation partner, grammar tutor, and translation checker all at once.

"I am learning Spanish at an intermediate level. Have a conversation with me about weekend plans. Stay in Spanish but if I make a grammar or vocabulary error, gently correct me in parentheses and then continue the conversation."

This creates a low-pressure immersive practice environment available any time, with instant and patient feedback.

For Educators: Gemini as a Teaching Tool

Curriculum and Lesson Planning

Lesson plans, worksheets, and activities are time-consuming to build, and Gemini accelerates the work dramatically.

"Create a 50-minute lesson plan for a 10th-grade biology class on cellular respiration. Include a five-minute warm-up activity, 20 minutes of direct instruction with three key concepts, a 15-minute hands-on activity that can be done with basic classroom supplies, and a 10-minute formative assessment. Align to NGSS standards."

You will still need to review and customize — you know your students, your classroom, and your constraints better than any model. But starting with a solid draft beats staring at a blank page.

Differentiated Materials

Building materials at different levels for students with different needs is one of the most time-consuming parts of teaching. Gemini makes it dramatically faster.

Start with your core material, then: "Rewrite this reading passage at a fifth-grade level, preserving all the key concepts but simplifying the vocabulary and sentence structure." Or: "Create an advanced extension version of this worksheet that adds two open-ended analysis questions for students who finish early."

You can produce three versions of the same assignment in minutes — work that might take hours by hand.

Assessment Creation

"Create a 20-question assessment on the American Civil War for 8th-grade students. Include 10 multiple-choice questions, 5 short-answer questions, and 1 essay question. Provide an answer key with point values. Ensure the questions cover factual recall, cause-and-effect relationships, and historical analysis at varying difficulty levels."

For rubric creation: "Create a detailed rubric for a persuasive essay assignment. Include four criteria (thesis statement, evidence quality, organization, and writing mechanics) with four performance levels each (exceeding, meeting, approaching, and below expectations). Include specific descriptions and point values for each cell."

Feedback and Grading Assistance

Detailed feedback on student work is one of the most valuable things a teacher does — and one of the most time-consuming. Gemini can draft feedback that you then review and personalize.

"Here is a student essay on climate change. Provide detailed feedback covering: thesis clarity, evidence use, paragraph organization, and writing mechanics. Be encouraging but honest. Identify two specific strengths and three specific areas for improvement, with concrete suggestions for each."

Always review AI-generated feedback before sharing it with students. Gemini may miss context about a student's individual circumstances, growth trajectory, or the specific learning objectives you are prioritizing.

Professional Development

Teachers are perpetual learners, and Gemini can support your own professional growth.

"I want to incorporate more inquiry-based learning in my high school chemistry class, but I am not sure how to structure it without losing all classroom management. I currently use mostly lecture and worksheets. Suggest a gradual transition plan that introduces inquiry-based elements over a semester, starting with structured inquiry and moving toward guided inquiry."

"Summarize the key findings from recent research on retrieval practice and spaced repetition. How can I practically apply these techniques in a middle school math class with 45-minute periods?"

Academic Integrity in the AI Era

This is the topic that keeps educators up at night, and for good reason. AI-generated text is increasingly hard to detect, AI detectors produce both false positives and false negatives, and the line between legitimate AI use and academic dishonesty is blurry.

Establishing Clear Policies

The single most important step is an explicit, detailed AI use policy for your class. Vague policies like "do not use AI" are unenforceable and unrealistic. Instead, specify exactly what is and is not acceptable.

A clear policy might define levels of AI use:

- **Level 0 — No AI:** This assignment must be completed entirely without AI assistance. (Reserve this for assessments that specifically measure unaided skill.)
- **Level 1 — AI as research tool:** You may use AI to find sources, understand concepts, and brainstorm ideas. All writing must be your own.
- **Level 2 — AI as editor:** You may use AI for grammar checking, style suggestions, and feedback on your drafts. The content and structure must be yours.
- **Level 3 — AI as collaborator:** You may use AI to help generate content, but you must substantially revise, fact-check, and take intellectual ownership of the final product. You must submit your AI interaction log alongside your work.

Labeling each assignment with its AI level removes ambiguity and gives students clear guidelines.

Designing AI-Resilient Assessments

Rather than fighting AI use, design assessments that hold value whether or not AI is involved.

Process-based assessments: Require students to submit drafts, outlines, and revision histories. The learning is in the process, not just the final product.

Personal and experiential prompts: "Analyze this historical event through the lens of your own family's immigration experience." AI can help with structure and polish, but only the student can provide the personal content.

In-class demonstrations of knowledge: Oral exams, live presentations, and in-class writing — where students cannot access external tools — remain reliable measures of understanding.

Reflective components: "In 200 words, explain the most challenging part of this assignment and how you worked through it." Reflection requires genuine engagement with the process.

Having Honest Conversations

The best approach to AI and academic integrity is transparency. Talk with your students about why these tools exist, what they are good at, what they are bad at, and why developing their own skills still matters.

The argument that resonates with most students: AI makes skilled people more productive, but it cannot give you skills you do not have. A student who uses Gemini to avoid learning to write will graduate unable to write — and no employer will care that they can prompt an AI, because everyone can. The students who thrive are those who develop genuine expertise and then amplify it with AI.

Google Workspace for Education Integration

Gemini's integration with Google Workspace creates specific opportunities for educational use. Schools and universities on Google Workspace for Education can access Gemini features directly within the tools students and teachers already use daily.

In Google Docs, Gemini helps students brainstorm and outline — a legitimate and valuable use of the tool. In Google Slides, it helps create visual presentations, freeing time from formatting for focus on content. In Google Sheets, it helps students analyze data for science fair projects or social studies research.

For educators, Workspace integration means you do not need to teach students a new tool. They are already in Docs, Sheets, and Slides every day. The AI capabilities extend the familiar environment.

Administrators can control Gemini access through the Google Admin console, setting age-appropriate limits and usage policies at the organizational unit level. Schools can enable AI features for older students while restricting them for younger ones, or enable them only for specific educational purposes.

Practical Exercises

Here are five exercises to build your skills with Gemini in an educational context:

1. **Concept tutorial:** Pick a topic you find difficult. Ask Gemini to explain it three different ways — using an analogy, using a technical explanation, and using a step-by-step walkthrough. Note which approach helps you understand best.

2. **Study group simulation:** Paste your notes from a recent class and ask Gemini to quiz you. Attempt each question before revealing the answer. Track your accuracy.

3. **Writing feedback loop:** Write a short essay, then ask Gemini to critique it. Revise based on the feedback. Ask for a second critique. Notice how your writing improves through iteration.

4. **Lesson differentiation (for educators):** Take an existing lesson plan and ask Gemini to create three versions for different learning levels. Review how well each version preserves the core learning objectives.

5. **Assessment redesign (for educators):** Take an existing assignment that is vulnerable to AI completion. Redesign it using the AI-resilient strategies discussed in this chapter. Compare the old and new versions for learning value.

The Bigger Picture

AI is not going away, and pretending it does not exist serves neither students nor educators. The question is not whether students will use these tools — they will. The question is whether they will use them well.

Students who treat Gemini as a thinking partner — deepening understanding, accelerating research, strengthening their own work — will be genuinely better prepared for a world where AI is ubiquitous. Students who use it as a shortcut will graduate with credentials but no capabilities.

Educators who embrace these tools thoughtfully — using them to enhance teaching while maintaining academic rigor — will create learning environments that prepare students for reality rather than an idealized past.

The key, for both students and educators, is intentionality. Use AI on purpose, with clear goals, and with honest reflection about whether it is helping you learn or helping you avoid learning. That distinction makes all the difference.

Chapter 22: Gemini for Business and Teams

Every business runs on communication, analysis, and decision-making. Gemini can accelerate all three. But the difference between a company that gets real value from AI and one that just adds another tool to the stack comes down to how deliberately it is deployed. This chapter covers practical applications of Gemini in business — from individual productivity to team-wide workflows — and addresses the organizational questions that determine whether AI adoption actually sticks.

The Business Case for Gemini

Before diving into applications, let us be direct about where Gemini delivers measurable value.

Time savings on routine communication. Drafting emails, meeting summaries, status updates, and internal documentation eats a staggering percentage of knowledge worker time. Gemini does not eliminate this work, but it can cut drafting time by fifty percent or more for most professional writing.

Faster analysis. Turning raw data into insights — from spreadsheets, customer feedback, market research, or internal reports — accelerates significantly when you can paste data into Gemini and get structured analysis in seconds.

Improved consistency. When teams use shared prompts and templates for recurring tasks, output quality and format become more consistent across the organization.

Better decision support. Gemini can synthesize information from multiple sources, present options with trade-offs, and stress-test assumptions — giving decision-makers better-organized inputs.

The value is real, but it is not magic. Gemini does not replace human judgment, industry expertise, or relationship skills. It makes the people who have those things more productive.

Individual Productivity Applications

Email and Communication

Professional email is a near-perfect use case for Gemini. You know what you want to say; the friction is in finding the right words and tone.

"Draft a reply to this email from our vendor who is requesting a 15 percent price increase. Our position is that we are willing to accept a 5 percent increase but want a two-year rate lock in exchange. Tone should be firm but collaborative — we value this relationship."

Paste the original email for context, and Gemini produces a draft that captures your position with appropriate professional nuance. You review, adjust, and send. Fifteen minutes of careful wordsmithing becomes three.

For recurring communications — weekly updates, client check-ins, project status reports — create template prompts that you fill in with specifics each time.

Meeting Preparation and Follow-Up

Before a meeting: "I have a meeting with the VP of Engineering to discuss migrating our infrastructure to Google Cloud. Prepare a one-page briefing document covering the key questions I should ask, the main decision points, and potential objections she might raise."

After a meeting: Paste your raw notes (or a transcript, if you recorded the meeting) and prompt: "Turn these meeting notes into a structured summary with three sections: key decisions made, action items with owners and deadlines, and open questions for follow-up. Format as bullet points."

This workflow turns chaotic meeting notes into clean, distributable records in seconds. Done consistently, it makes meetings more accountable and improves follow-through.

Document Review and Analysis

Gemini's large context window makes it exceptionally useful for reviewing long documents.

"Review this 40-page vendor proposal. Summarize the key terms, identify anything that deviates from our standard requirements (listed below), and flag any areas where the pricing seems significantly above market rate."

"Compare these two contract versions and produce a tracked-changes-style summary showing what was added, removed, and modified between Version 1 and Version 2."

These tasks can take a human professional hours. Gemini produces a first-pass analysis in moments, letting you focus on the sections that actually need careful human judgment.

Data Analysis and Reporting

Paste a spreadsheet or dataset into Gemini and ask targeted analytical questions:

"This CSV contains our sales data for the last 12 months. Calculate the month-over-month growth rate, identify which product categories are growing fastest and slowest, and flag any months where total revenue dropped more than 10 percent from the previous month. Present the results as a table with a brief narrative summary."

For recurring reports, build a prompt template you populate with fresh data each period. This creates reporting consistency and saves hours of manual analysis.

Team-Wide Applications

Shared Prompt Libraries

One of the highest-leverage moves a team can make is to build a shared library of tested, refined prompts for common tasks. Instead of each person figuring out how to prompt for a competitive analysis or a client brief, the team develops standard prompts that produce reliable results.

A shared prompt library might include:

- Client proposal template prompt
- Meeting summary format prompt
- Weekly status report generator
- Customer feedback analysis template

- Job description writer with company tone guide
- Sales call preparation briefing

Document these in a shared location — a Google Doc, a Notion database, a wiki page. Include the prompt text, example outputs, and customization notes. Update the library as people discover improvements.

Onboarding and Training

New employees face a flood of information in their first weeks. Gemini can serve as an always-available reference.

"You are an onboarding assistant for [Company Name]. Here is our employee handbook, our product documentation, and our team directory. Answer questions about company policies, processes, and products based on these documents. If the answer is not in the provided documents, say so rather than guessing."

This does not replace human onboarding — new hires still need relationships, context, and mentorship. But it lets them get answers to straightforward questions at any time without waiting on someone's availability.

For training purposes, Gemini can generate practice scenarios: "Create a realistic customer support scenario where the customer is frustrated about a billing error. Include the customer's emotional state, the actual problem, and what a good resolution looks like. I will practice responding before seeing the ideal response."

Knowledge Management

Every organization has knowledge trapped in documents, email threads, Slack messages, and the heads of long-tenured employees. Gemini's long context window makes it well suited for knowledge extraction and organization.

"Here are the last six months of our product team's decision documents. Create a searchable summary organized by topic area. For each decision, note the date, the decision made, the key reasons, and any dissenting views."

This turns scattered documentation into structured knowledge that new team members can actually navigate.

Gemini in Google Workspace for Business

For organizations using Google Workspace, Gemini's native integration creates a seamless experience across the tools teams already use daily.

Gemini in Gmail

Gemini in Gmail drafts replies, summarizes long email threads, and helps manage your inbox. The "Help me write" feature lets you describe what you want to say and generates a draft within the composer. For long threads with many participants, Gemini summarizes the key points and current status, saving you from scrolling through dozens of messages.

Gemini in Google Docs

In Docs, Gemini drafts, edits, and formats. Ask it to write a first draft from a prompt, refine existing text, or reorganize a document's structure. For collaborative documents, the first draft arrives faster, and the team's editing time goes to substance rather than structure.

Gemini in Google Sheets

In Sheets, Gemini creates formulas, generates pivot tables, and builds charts from your data. "Create a formula that calculates the running average of column B, grouped by the values in column A" is the kind of request that previously meant a documentation search or a call to the most spreadsheet-savvy person on the team.

Gemini in Google Slides

In Slides, Gemini generates slide content, suggests layouts, and creates images. Speaker notes generation is particularly useful — paste your talking points and Gemini produces structured speaker notes for each slide.

Gemini in Google Meet

During and after meetings, Gemini in Google Meet provides real-time transcription and generates meeting summaries. The automatic summary captures key discussion points, decisions, and action items — no one has to take notes manually.

Security, Privacy, and Compliance

Business adoption of AI tools requires addressing legitimate concerns about data security and regulatory compliance.

Data Handling

When using Gemini through Google Workspace for business (with a paid Workspace plan), your data is governed by Google's enterprise data protection commitments. Your prompts and data are not used to train Google's models. This is a critical distinction from the free consumer version, documented in Google's Workspace data processing terms.

For organizations in regulated industries, understand the data residency and processing implications. Google provides detailed documentation on where data is processed and stored, and enterprise plans include additional controls.

Access Controls

Google Workspace administrators can control Gemini access at the organizational unit level. This means you can:

- Enable Gemini for some departments and not others
- Restrict which Gemini features are available (for example, allowing text generation but not image generation)
- Set policies for how Gemini interacts with organizational data
- Monitor usage through admin reports

Compliance Considerations

If your organization is subject to specific regulations — HIPAA, GDPR, SOC 2, FedRAMP — evaluate Gemini's compliance certifications against your requirements. Google Workspace holds numerous compliance certifications, and Gemini features within Workspace inherit many of these protections. Specific certifications and scope can change, so verify current status against Google's compliance documentation.

For sensitive data, establish clear guidelines about what can and cannot be shared with AI tools. Even with enterprise-grade protections, avoid putting highly sensitive information — trade secrets, unreleased financial data, personal health information — into any AI system unless you have confirmed the specific deployment meets your compliance requirements.

Building an AI-Forward Culture

Technology adoption succeeds or fails based on culture, not features. Here is how to build an environment where Gemini actually gets used effectively.

Start with Champions

Identify people on each team who are naturally curious about AI tools. Give them early access, time to experiment, and a mandate to share what they learn. Champions become peer teachers, which is far more effective than top-down mandates.

Focus on Pain Points

Do not start with the most impressive AI capabilities. Start with the most annoying, time-consuming tasks your teams face. If sales spends three hours every week preparing call summaries, start there. Quick wins build momentum and credibility.

Create Psychological Safety

People need to feel safe experimenting and failing with new tools. If the first person to use Gemini makes a mistake and gets criticized, adoption stalls. Celebrate experimentation, share failures as learning, and make clear that learning to use AI effectively is part of professional development.

Measure Impact

Track time saved, output quality, and user satisfaction. Not everything needs to be quantified, but concrete metrics help justify continued investment and surface which applications deliver the most value.

Establish Guidelines, Not Rules

Rigid rules about AI use tend to be either too restrictive (stifling valuable applications) or too permissive (creating risk). Instead, establish principles: use AI to augment your expertise, always verify critical information, do not share confidential data without approval, and be transparent about AI involvement when it matters.

Common Business Use Cases by Department

Marketing: Content ideation, first drafts of blog posts and social media content, competitive messaging analysis, audience persona development, A/B test copy generation.

Sales: Prospect research, call preparation briefs, proposal customization, objection handling scripts, CRM data analysis, follow-up email drafting.

Human Resources: Job description writing, interview question development, policy documentation, employee FAQ creation, training material development.

Finance: Data analysis and visualization, report generation, budget scenario modeling, vendor comparison analysis, regulatory change summaries.

Operations: Process documentation, SOP creation, incident post-mortem drafting, vendor communication, project status reporting.

Legal: Contract review and comparison, policy drafting, compliance checklist creation, research summaries (with appropriate human verification).

Each department has its own high-value applications. The common thread: Gemini is most valuable for tasks that are important but time-consuming, require clear communication, or involve synthesizing information from multiple sources.

Getting Started: A 30-Day Adoption Plan

Week 1: Choose three recurring tasks where Gemini could save time. Use it for those tasks daily. Note what works and what does not.

Week 2: Refine your prompts based on the first week's experience. Share your best prompts with your immediate team. Invite them to try the same tasks.

Week 3: Expand to new use cases based on what your team has discovered. Create a shared document for team prompts and tips.

Week 4: Review the month's experience. Quantify time saved if possible. Identify the next set of use cases to tackle. Share learnings with leadership or adjacent teams.

This incremental approach avoids the common pitfall: announcing a grand AI initiative that generates excitement but no lasting behavior change. Small, practical wins compound into real transformation.

The organizations that get the most from Gemini are not the ones with the most sophisticated AI strategy. They are the ones where individual contributors have figured out how to save thirty minutes a day on tedious work — and shared those techniques with their teammates.

Chapter 23: Gemini for Developers

If you write code for a living — or even as a serious hobby — Gemini offers a toolkit that touches nearly every part of your workflow. From an IDE assistant that autocompletes and explains code, to a full API for building AI-powered applications, to deep integration with Google's cloud and Firebase platforms, Gemini's developer story is broad and genuinely useful.

This chapter covers the four pillars of Gemini's developer ecosystem: Gemini Code Assist for IDE-level help, the Gemini API through Google AI Studio and Vertex AI, Firebase integration for app development, and an honest comparison with the other major AI coding tools.

Gemini Code Assist: AI in Your IDE

Gemini Code Assist is Google's IDE integration, bringing Gemini directly into your development environment. It is available for VS Code, JetBrains IDEs (IntelliJ, PyCharm, WebStorm, and others), and Cloud Shell Editor. If you work in one of these environments, Code Assist slots into your daily workflow without changing how you work.

What Code Assist Does

Inline code completion. As you type, Code Assist suggests completions that go well beyond simple autocomplete. It understands your file's context, project structure, and the patterns you are following, and can suggest entire function implementations, not just the next token.

Chat-based assistance. A chat panel within your IDE lets you ask questions about your codebase, request explanations of unfamiliar code, and get help with specific tasks. "How does the authentication middleware in this project work?" or "Write a unit test for this function" — Code Assist handles these well because it has your project context.

Code transformation. Select a block of code and ask Code Assist to refactor it, add error handling, convert it to a different pattern, or optimize it. "Rewrite this callback-based function using async/await" is a one-step operation.

Code explanation. When you are working in an unfamiliar codebase — which is most of the time, honestly — highlight a section and ask "Explain what this code does." Code Assist returns a natural-language walkthrough that is often more helpful than reading the code line by line, especially for complex logic.

Commit message generation. Code Assist analyzes your staged changes and generates a descriptive commit message. Small feature, surprising amount of friction saved in daily work.

Getting the Most from Code Assist

Code Assist performs best when you give it context. Patterns that produce better results:

Write clear comments before implementing. A comment describing what a function should do becomes a specification for the suggestion. A comment like `// Parse the CSV file, validate each row against the schema, and return an array of valid records with a separate array of errors` gives Code Assist a clear target.

Keep related files open. Code Assist considers your open files as context. If you are writing a service that depends on a data model, having the model file open helps Code Assist understand the types and structures it should work with.

Use chat for complex tasks, inline completion for flow. Inline suggestions are best for maintaining your coding flow — accept or reject as you type. For involved tasks (writing tests, debugging, refactoring), use the chat panel where you can provide detailed instructions and review output before applying it.

Review everything. This cannot be overstated. Code Assist generates plausible-looking code that may have subtle bugs, security issues, or architectural problems. Treat every suggestion as a draft from a junior developer — potentially useful, definitely needs review.

Code Assist for Enterprise

Gemini Code Assist Enterprise is the upgraded tier for organizational use. The key addition is code customization — connecting Code Assist to your organization's private repositories so suggestions reflect your codebase's patterns, internal libraries, and coding conventions.

This is significant. A generic coding assistant suggests generic patterns. One customized with your internal code suggests patterns that match your team's actual practices, use your internal APIs correctly, and follow your style guides. For large engineering organizations, this dramatically increases the relevance and acceptance rate of suggestions.

Enterprise also includes integration with Google Cloud's security and administration tools, centralized license management, and usage analytics.

The Gemini API: Building AI-Powered Applications

If Code Assist is about using Gemini while you code, the Gemini API is about building Gemini into what you code. The API gives you programmatic access to the full range of Gemini models, letting you build applications that generate text, analyze images, process audio and video, and reason through complex problems.

Google AI Studio: The Starting Point

Google AI Studio is the fastest way to start working with the Gemini API. It is a web-based tool where you experiment with prompts, test different models and parameters, and — crucially — generate API keys and export working code.

The workflow is straightforward:

1. Open Google AI Studio in your browser
2. Select a Gemini model (3 Pro for maximum capability, 3 Flash for speed and cost efficiency, or 3.1 Flash-Lite for the cheapest, fastest option)
3. Write and test your prompt
4. Adjust parameters like temperature (creativity vs. consistency) and maximum output length
5. Click "Get code" to export a working code snippet in Python, JavaScript, Kotlin, Swift, Go, or REST

The export feature is what makes AI Studio genuinely useful as a development tool rather than just a playground. You go from experiment to working code in minutes.

Google AI Studio is best for prototyping, personal projects, startups, and applications where you want the simplest possible path to a working integration.

Vertex AI: Production-Grade AI

Vertex AI is Google Cloud's comprehensive AI platform — where you go when your application needs enterprise-grade infrastructure. The Gemini API on Vertex AI offers the same models and capabilities as Google AI Studio, with the additional layers production applications require.

Key differences from Google AI Studio:

- **IAM-based authentication** instead of API keys, integrating with Google Cloud's identity management
- **VPC Service Controls** for network-level security
- **Regional endpoints** for data residency requirements
- **Higher rate limits and quotas** for production traffic
- **SLAs** for uptime and latency
- **Integration with Google Cloud's monitoring, logging, and operations tools**
- **Model Garden** access to additional models alongside Gemini
- **Grounding with Google Search** for applications that need real-time information

If you are building an application that will serve real users at scale, Vertex AI is the right platform. The added complexity is justified by the operational capabilities you gain.

Core API Capabilities

The Gemini API exposes several capabilities that you can combine in your applications:

Text generation. The foundational capability — send a prompt, get a response. Useful for chatbots, content generation, summarization, translation, and any text-in-text-out application.

Multimodal input. Send images, audio, video, or PDFs alongside text. Gemini can describe images, transcribe audio, analyze video content, and extract information from documents. A single API call can process a mix of modalities.

Structured output. As covered in Chapter 20, you can configure the API to return JSON matching a specific schema. This is essential for applications where the model's output feeds into downstream processing.

Function calling. One of the most powerful API features. You define a set of functions (with parameters and descriptions), and Gemini decides when and how to call them based on the conversation. This lets you build applications where Gemini looks up information in databases, calls external APIs, performs calculations, or triggers actions in your systems.

For example, you might define `get_weather(city)`, `search_products(query, category)`, and `create_order(product_id, quantity)`. When a user says "What is the weather in Tokyo and can you order two umbrellas?", Gemini recognizes it needs to call both functions and structures the appropriate parameters.

Context caching. For applications that repeatedly reference the same large context — a product catalog, a documentation set, a legal corpus — context caching lets you upload it once and reference it across requests. This significantly reduces latency and cost for context-heavy applications.

Embeddings. The API generates vector embeddings for text — essential for building semantic search, recommendation systems, and retrieval-augmented generation (RAG) applications.

A Practical API Example

Here is what a basic Gemini API integration looks like in Python using the Google Gen AI SDK:

```
from google import genai

client = genai.Client(api_key="YOUR_API_KEY")

response = client.models.generate_content(
    model="gemini-3-flash",
    contents="Explain how garbage collection works in Go, in three paragraphs."
)

print(response.text)
```

That is a complete, working example. Zero to AI-generated content in five lines. The SDK handles authentication, request formatting, and response parsing.

For a more realistic application with conversation history:

```
from google import genai
from google.genai import types

client = genai.Client(api_key="YOUR_API_KEY")

chat = client.chats.create(
    model="gemini-3-flash",
    config=types.GenerateContentConfig(
        system_instruction="You are a helpful coding assistant specializing in P
ython.",
        temperature=0.3,
    ),
)

## Multi-turn conversation
response = chat.send_message("How do I read a CSV file in Python?")
print(response.text)

response = chat.send_message("Now show me how to filter rows where the 'status'
column equals 'active'.")
print(response.text)
```

The SDK manages conversation state automatically. Each message includes the full history, so Gemini has context from previous turns.

Firebase Integration

Firebase and Gemini together form a powerful stack for AI-powered applications, particularly mobile and web apps. The Firebase Genkit framework and the Vertex AI in Firebase SDKs make adding Gemini capabilities to Firebase-based applications straightforward.

Vertex AI in Firebase SDKs

The Firebase client SDKs let you call the Gemini API directly from your mobile or web app. Available for Swift (iOS), Kotlin (Android), Flutter, and JavaScript (web), these SDKs handle authentication through Firebase Auth and provide a client-side interface to Gemini.

Particularly useful for apps where you want AI features without building and maintaining a separate backend API layer. The Firebase SDK manages authentication, rate limiting, and abuse prevention through Firebase App Check.

Firebase Genkit

Genkit is an open-source framework from Firebase designed for building AI-powered features. It provides abstractions for common AI patterns:

- **Flows:** Composable, observable functions that orchestrate AI operations
- **Retrievers:** Integrations with vector databases for RAG applications
- **Evaluators:** Tools for testing and scoring AI output quality
- **Plugins:** Pre-built integrations with Gemini and other models

Genkit is available for Node.js and Go and runs anywhere — not just on Firebase or Google Cloud. Especially useful for complex AI features involving multiple steps, data retrieval, and quality evaluation.

Cloud Functions with Gemini

For server-side AI processing, Firebase Cloud Functions are a natural integration point. Write a Cloud Function that receives a request, calls the Gemini API, processes the result, and returns it to the client. The pattern keeps your API keys server-side and lets you add business logic around the AI call.

```
const { onCall } = require("firebase-functions/v2/https");
const { GoogleGenAI } = require("@google/genai");

const ai = new GoogleGenAI({ apiKey: process.env.GEMINI_API_KEY });

exports.summarize = onCall(async (request) => {
  const response = await ai.models.generateContent({
    model: "gemini-3-flash",
    contents: `Summarize this text in three bullet points: ${request.data.text}`,
  });
  return { summary: response.text };
});
```

Clean, scalable, and keeps the AI integration behind your own API layer where you can add caching, logging, and access control.

Comparison with Other AI Coding Tools

You have choices. Gemini is not the only AI tool for developers, and an informed decision requires understanding how it compares to the alternatives. An honest assessment as of May 2026:

Gemini vs. GitHub Copilot

GitHub Copilot, powered by OpenAI's models, was the first widely adopted AI coding assistant and remains one of the most popular.

Where Gemini Code Assist leads: - Context window — Gemini's million-token context means it can consider far more of your codebase when making suggestions - Google Cloud integration — if you are in the Google ecosystem, Code Assist connects natively to your infrastructure - Multimodal capabilities — you can share screenshots of UIs, architecture diagrams, or error messages alongside code - Enterprise code customization — training on your organization's private repositories

Where Copilot leads: - GitHub integration depth — Copilot's native integration with GitHub (pull request summaries, issue triage, code review) is natural and polished - Ecosystem maturity — Copilot has been in the market longer and has a larger community sharing tips and workflows - Agent mode — Copilot's agentic capabilities for multi-file tasks are mature

Verdict: Deeply embedded in the GitHub ecosystem? Copilot has home-field advantage. Working with Google Cloud or need extended context for large codebases? Code Assist is the stronger choice.

Gemini vs. Claude for Coding

Claude (from Anthropic) has earned a strong reputation among developers, particularly for code reasoning and long-context tasks.

Where Gemini leads: - Multimodal input — native handling of images, audio, and video alongside code - Google ecosystem integration — Workspace, Cloud, Firebase connectivity - Speed — Gemini 3 Flash is exceptionally fast for coding tasks where latency matters, and Gemini 3.1 Flash-Lite goes faster still for high-volume API workloads - Cost — Flash pricing is competitive for high-volume API usage

Where Claude leads: - Extended thinking for complex reasoning tasks — Claude's reasoning capabilities are highly regarded - Claude Code as a terminal-based agentic coding tool - Artifact generation for self-contained code outputs

Verdict: Both are excellent for coding. Gemini wins on ecosystem breadth and multimodal input. Claude is often preferred for deep reasoning about complex code. Many developers use both, choosing based on the specific task.

Gemini vs. ChatGPT for Coding

ChatGPT with GPT-5.4 (and GPT-5.4 Thinking) is a general-purpose AI that many developers use for coding tasks.

Where Gemini leads: - Context window size — significantly larger than ChatGPT's standard context - Native integration with Google development tools - Multimodal capabilities, especially for video and audio processing - API pricing at the Flash tier

Where ChatGPT leads: - Plugin and integration ecosystem breadth - Canvas feature for iterative code editing - Name recognition and community size - OpenAI's broader partnership ecosystem

Verdict: For pure coding tasks, Gemini 3 Pro is competitive with GPT-5.4. Gemini's advantage is context size and Google integration. ChatGPT's advantage is ecosystem breadth and familiarity.

The Practical Approach

Most professional developers in 2026 use more than one AI tool. The tools have different strengths, and switching based on task is a legitimate and effective strategy. Gemini Code Assist for inline IDE suggestions during daily work. The Gemini API for building AI features into your applications. Another tool when its strengths fit the job better.

The important thing is not brand loyalty — it is knowing each tool's strengths and choosing accordingly.

Best Practices for Developers Using Gemini

Always review generated code. AI-generated code can contain bugs, security vulnerabilities, deprecated API usage, and logic errors. The more critical the code, the more carefully you should review it.

Use AI for the first draft, not the final product. Let Gemini generate the boilerplate, the test scaffolding, the initial implementation. Then review, refactor, and refine with your domain knowledge.

Write good prompts for good code. The prompting fundamentals from Chapter 18 apply directly to code generation. Specify the language, framework, error handling approach, naming conventions, and constraints. "Write a Python function" is vague. "Write a Python 3.12 function using type hints that accepts a list of dictionaries and returns a pandas DataFrame, handling missing keys gracefully with default values" is specific.

Test AI-generated code thoroughly. Write tests for code Gemini produces — or better, write the tests first and have Gemini write code that passes them. Test-driven development pairs naturally with AI code generation.

Keep security front of mind. Do not paste secrets, API keys, or credentials into prompts. Review generated code for security issues — SQL injection, XSS vulnerabilities, improper authentication checks. AI models can generate code that works but is not secure.

Learn from the code, do not just use it. When Gemini suggests an approach you have not seen before, take a moment to understand it. AI coding tools are excellent learning accelerators if you engage with the code rather than accepting it blindly.

Getting Started

If you have not yet integrated Gemini into your workflow, here is the quickest path to value:

1. Install the Gemini Code Assist extension in your IDE. Use it for a week of normal development. Notice where it helps and where it does not.
2. Open Google AI Studio. Experiment with the Gemini API using a small project or prototype. Export code and build something simple.

3. If you work with Firebase, explore the Vertex AI in Firebase SDKs. Add a simple AI feature to an existing project — even just a summarization endpoint.
4. After two weeks, evaluate. Where is Gemini saving time? Where is it not helpful? Double down on what works; drop what does not.

The developers who get the most from AI tools are not the ones who use them for everything — they are the ones who know exactly when to use them and when to rely on their own expertise.

Chapter 24: Gemini for Creators and Freelancers

If you make things for a living — writing, design, video, music, photography, illustration, consulting, or any of the hundred other forms creative and freelance work takes — Gemini changes the economics of your day. Not by replacing your creative judgment, but by handling the work that surrounds it. The administrative overhead, client communication, research, first drafts, content repurposing, invoicing follow-ups — that is where AI gives independent creators and freelancers their time back.

This chapter is for people who work independently or in small teams and need to be productive across every part of their business. You are not just the creator — you are also the marketer, the project manager, the accountant, and the customer support team. Gemini can be a force multiplier across all of those roles.

The Freelancer's AI Advantage

Large companies have teams. Dedicated writers for marketing copy, analysts for market research, coordinators for project management, accountants for invoicing. As a freelancer or independent creator, you do all of it yourself. Every hour spent on administration is an hour not spent on the work your clients actually pay for.

This is where Gemini's value is most tangible. Not in replacing your core skill — the thing that makes clients hire you — but in accelerating everything else. When you can draft a proposal in ten minutes instead of an hour, respond to a client email in two minutes instead of fifteen, and repurpose a blog post into five social posts in five minutes instead of forty-five, the economics of your workday fundamentally change.

The math is straightforward. If Gemini saves ninety minutes a day on non-creative tasks, that is seven and a half hours a week. An extra billable day. Or an extra day for marketing. Or an extra day for rest, which freelancers notoriously neglect.

Content Creation and Repurposing

First Drafts and Ideation

The blank page is the creator's oldest enemy. Gemini does not write your final content — that requires your voice, your perspective, your expertise — but it obliterates the blank page problem.

"I need to write a blog post about pricing strategies for freelance designers. Give me five different angles I could take, each with a working title and a three-sentence summary of the argument."

From those five options, you pick the angle that resonates. Then: "I am going with angle three — the counterintuitive case for raising your prices during a recession. Create a detailed outline with five sections, including the key points and evidence I should include in each section."

Now you have a roadmap. Writing is no longer staring at a blank page — it is filling a structure with your knowledge and voice. Some creators write faster from an outline than from scratch. Others use Gemini's outline as a thinking tool and then write their own way. Either approach beats starting from nothing.

Content Repurposing

One piece of content should never live in just one place. A single long-form article can become social media posts, an email newsletter, a podcast script, a slide deck, and a video outline. But the reformatting is tedious, which is why most creators do not do it consistently.

Gemini makes repurposing systematic:

"Here is my 2,000-word blog post about color theory in brand design. Create the following from this content:

1. Five Twitter/X posts, each highlighting a different key point, under 280 characters each
2. A LinkedIn post (200 to 300 words) that frames the core argument for a business audience
3. An Instagram caption (150 words) with a more casual, visual-oriented angle

4. Three email newsletter subject lines that would make someone click through to read the full post
5. A 60-second video script summarizing the main points for a Reels or TikTok format"

One prompt, five platforms covered. You will still review and adjust each piece — your LinkedIn voice is different from your Instagram voice — but the heavy lifting is done.

Writing in Your Voice

A common fear is that AI-assisted content will sound generic. This is a legitimate concern, and the solution is to train Gemini on your voice.

Paste three to five examples of your best writing and instruct: "Analyze the writing style of these samples. Note the sentence structure, vocabulary level, use of humor, paragraph length, and any distinctive patterns. Then write a style guide that captures this voice."

Save that style guide. When you ask Gemini to draft content, include it: "Using the style guide below, write a first draft of [topic]. Match the tone and style as closely as possible."

The output will not be indistinguishable from your writing, but it will land much closer than a default response. And because you are editing rather than writing from scratch, the final version carries your authentic voice with a fraction of the time investment.

SEO and Content Strategy

Gemini helps with the strategic side of content creation, not just the writing.

"I run a freelance UX design business. My target clients are SaaS startups with 20 to 100 employees. Suggest 20 blog post topics that would attract this audience through organic search. For each topic, include a suggested title, the primary keyword to target, and the search intent (informational, commercial, or transactional)."

"Review this blog post for SEO. Does the title include the primary keyword naturally? Are the headings structured logically? Is the keyword density appropriate without being forced? Suggest specific improvements."

This does not replace a dedicated SEO strategy, but for freelancers doing their own content marketing, it provides expert-level guidance without expert-level costs.

Client Communication

Proposals and Pitches

Proposals are one of the most time-intensive parts of freelancing, and Gemini cuts that time dramatically.

"I am a freelance video producer pitching a brand video project to a direct-to-consumer skincare company. The project scope is a 90-second hero video for their website plus three 15-second social cuts. My estimated budget is $12,000 to $15,000. Write a professional proposal that covers the project overview, creative approach, timeline (four weeks), deliverables, and pricing. Tone should be confident and creative but not overly casual."

Customize the output with your specific creative vision, adjust pricing to match your actual rates, and you have a polished proposal in a fraction of the usual time.

For ongoing client work, build a proposal template prompt you customize for each new project. The more you refine the template, the less editing each proposal needs.

Difficult Client Conversations

Every freelancer eventually faces a difficult client situation — scope creep, late payments, unrealistic expectations, requested revisions that fundamentally change the project. These conversations require careful wording.

"A client has requested a fourth round of revisions on a logo project. My contract includes two rounds. I need to respond professionally, reminding them of the contract terms while offering the option to purchase additional revision rounds. I want to be firm but not damage the relationship."

Gemini drafts the message. You adjust tone based on what you know about the client — a long-term partner worth accommodating, or a one-time project where you need to hold the line? The draft gives you a starting point that is professional and clear, which is exactly what you need when you are emotionally involved.

Testimonial and Case Study Requests

Social proof is essential for freelancers, but asking clients for testimonials feels awkward, and most clients procrastinate because they do not know what to say.

"Draft a friendly email asking my client [name] for a testimonial about the website redesign project we just completed. Make it easy for them by including three specific questions they could answer: What was the project goal? What was it like working with me? What results have they seen? Keep it casual and short."

You can also use Gemini to turn raw client feedback into polished case studies: "Here are the key facts about a project I completed and the client's feedback email. Write a 300-word case study with sections for Challenge, Solution, and Results."

Business Operations

Invoicing and Financial Communication

"Draft a polite but firm follow-up email for an invoice that is 15 days past due. This is my first follow-up. Reference invoice number 2026-042, the amount of $3,500, and the original due date of March 15. Include the payment link and offer to discuss if there are any questions about the invoice."

For financial planning: "Here are my monthly revenue and expense figures for the last 12 months. Calculate my average monthly profit, identify any seasonal patterns, and project my revenue for the next quarter assuming current trends continue."

Contract and Legal Language

Freelancers often work with contracts they did not write. Gemini helps you understand them.

"Review this freelance services agreement. In plain language, explain the key terms regarding: intellectual property ownership, payment terms, cancellation policy, liability, and non-compete clauses. Flag anything that seems unusual or potentially unfavorable to the contractor."

This does not replace legal advice for high-stakes situations, but for everyday contracts, it provides clarity that might otherwise cost a billable hour from a lawyer.

Project Management

When you are juggling multiple clients and projects, Gemini helps you stay organized.

"I have three active projects: a website redesign due April 15 (currently in the design phase), a brand identity project due April 30 (currently in the discovery phase), and an ongoing content retainer with weekly deliverables. Create a weekly schedule that allocates my time across these projects, reserving Tuesday mornings for administrative tasks and Friday afternoons for business development."

"Review my project notes for the website redesign and create a status update I can send to the client. Include what was completed this week, what is planned for next week, and any decisions that need their input."

Creative Applications

Visual Content with Gemini

Gemini's multimodal capabilities extend to image generation and visual analysis. For creators, this opens several practical applications.

Mood boards and concept development. Describe the visual direction for a project and ask Gemini to generate concept images. These are not final deliverables — they are thinking tools for exploring directions and communicating vision to clients.

Image analysis for reference. Upload reference images and ask Gemini to analyze them: "What makes the composition of this photograph effective? Break down the use of color, leading lines, and negative space." This kind of analysis accelerates your creative development.

Alt text and image descriptions. For web content, accessibility matters. "Write alt text for each of these product images — descriptive enough for screen readers but concise enough for web use."

Video and Audio Content

If you create video or audio content, Gemini's multimodal capabilities are directly useful.

Script writing. "Write a script for a five-minute YouTube video about how freelance photographers should price their work. Open with a hook, include three main pricing strategies, and end with a call to action. Conversational tone, as if talking to a friend."

Show notes and descriptions. "Here is the transcript of my latest podcast episode. Write show notes that include a brief summary, timestamps for key topics, and links mentioned in the episode. Also write a YouTube description and three social media promotional posts."

Video analysis. Upload a clip and ask Gemini to analyze your presentation style, pacing, or content structure. Invaluable feedback for creators without a production team to give them notes.

Copywriting and Marketing

Freelance creators have to market themselves, and marketing copy is a distinct skill from the creative work itself.

Website copy. "Write the hero section copy for my freelance illustration portfolio website. I specialize in editorial illustration for tech publications. My style is colorful, conceptual, and slightly whimsical. The copy should appeal to art directors at tech magazines and blogs."

Email marketing. "Write a three-email welcome sequence for new subscribers to my newsletter about freelance design. Email 1: introduce myself and what they can expect. Email 2: share my best piece of content with context about why it matters. Email 3: soft pitch my course on design pricing."

Social media bios. "Write five variations of a professional bio for my social media profiles. I am a freelance motion designer with eight years of experience, working primarily with SaaS companies. Keep each version under 160 characters."

Scaling Without Hiring

One of Gemini's most compelling propositions for freelancers is the ability to handle more work without hiring. This is not about replacing human collaboration — there are tasks that genuinely need another person. But for many tasks, what you actually need is more hours in the day, and Gemini provides that.

Research assistance. Before Gemini, researching a new client's industry might take two hours. Now you can get a comprehensive briefing in minutes: "I am meeting with a potential client in the commercial real estate industry. Give me a briefing on the current state of the commercial real estate market, the major challenges companies in this space face, and the key industry terminology I should know."

Translation and localization. Working with international clients? Gemini's translation capabilities let you communicate in their language without hiring a translator for routine correspondence.

Administrative automation. Meeting scheduling follow-ups, thank-you notes, contract summaries, expense categorization — the cumulative time cost of these small tasks is enormous. Gemini handles each quickly.

The effect compounds. When you reclaim ten to fifteen hours per week from administrative and preparatory work, you can take on more clients, invest more time in each project, or build the parts of your business — marketing, networking, skill development — that get neglected in delivery mode.

Ethical Considerations for Creators

Using AI in creative work raises questions that are worth thinking through honestly.

Transparency with clients. Should you tell clients you use AI tools? It depends on context. If AI helps you write emails and manage projects, no disclosure is typically needed — those are your business tools. If AI is generating content the client will publish under their name, disclosure is appropriate. If AI is contributing to the creative output itself — generating images, writing copy, producing music — be transparent about its role and let the client decide what they are comfortable with.

Intellectual property. The legal landscape around AI-generated content is still evolving. Know the current status in your jurisdiction. For client work, clarify in your contracts who owns what, and whether AI-generated elements have any implications for intellectual property claims.

Maintaining your edge. The skills that make you valuable as a creator — your taste, your judgment, your unique perspective — are not things AI can replicate. But they atrophy if you stop exercising them. Use AI to handle the work that does not require your creative judgment, and invest the time you save in deepening the skills that do.

Pricing in the AI era. As AI makes certain tasks faster, clients may expect lower prices. Resist the urge to race to the bottom. You are not selling time — you are selling outcomes. Delivering a better result in less time because you use AI well is your competitive advantage, not a reason to charge less.

Building Your AI-Enhanced Workflow

The freelancers and creators who get the most from Gemini integrate it systematically rather than using it sporadically. Here is how to build that habit.

Identify your top ten recurring tasks. List the tasks you do every week that are not directly billable creative work. Client emails, proposals, invoicing, social media, research, scheduling, reporting. These are your automation candidates.

Build a prompt for each one. Spend an afternoon writing and testing prompts for each task. Save them where you can grab them quickly.

Spend the first ten minutes of every project with Gemini. Before starting a new project: get a briefing on the client's industry, brainstorm creative directions, outline your approach. A small investment that makes the actual creative work faster and better.

Review and refine monthly. What is working? What is not? Which prompts need updating? Which new tasks could benefit from AI assistance? A monthly review keeps your workflow evolving.

The goal is not to automate your creativity. It is to automate everything around your creativity, so you can spend more of your finite time and energy on the work that only you can do.

Part VII: Safety, Ethics, and Limitations

"An expert is a person who has made all the mistakes that can be made in a very narrow field."

— Niels Bohr

Chapter 25: What Gemini Gets Wrong

Every AI model has blind spots, and Gemini is no exception. Google has built one of the most capable AI systems on the planet — one that reasons across text, images, video, and code in ways that would have seemed impossible just a few years ago. But capability is not reliability. Gemini will occasionally produce answers that are wrong, biased, incomplete, or simply made up.

This chapter is not here to discourage you from using Gemini — quite the opposite. The more clearly you understand where Gemini stumbles, the more effectively you can use it. Knowing what to watch for turns you from a passive consumer of AI output into a critical user who catches problems before they matter.

Here are the major categories of errors, why they happen, and — most importantly — what to do about them.

Hallucinations: When Gemini Makes Things Up

The most widely discussed failure mode in AI is hallucination — the tendency for a language model to generate information that sounds confident and plausible but is entirely fabricated. Gemini hallucinates. So does ChatGPT. So does Claude. This is not a bug unique to any one system; it is a fundamental characteristic of how large language models work.

Hallucinations happen because Gemini does not "know" facts the way you do. It predicts the most statistically likely next sequence of words based on patterns learned during training. Most of the time those predictions align with reality. Sometimes they do not.

Here is what hallucination looks like in practice:

- **Fabricated citations.** Ask Gemini for sources on a topic, and it returns author names, journal titles, and publication years that do not exist. The formatting looks perfect. The content is fiction.
- **Invented statistics.** Ask for data on market trends, and Gemini produces specific percentages and dollar figures it generated rather than retrieved.

- **False biographical details.** Ask about a public figure, and Gemini blends real facts with fabricated ones — a correct birthdate paired with a university they never attended.
- **Confident nonsense.** Ask a technical question, and Gemini delivers an answer with the same authoritative tone it uses for things it gets right.

Why Gemini Hallucinates

Several factors make hallucination more or less likely:

- **Obscure topics.** The less training data Gemini has seen on a subject, the more likely it fills gaps with plausible-sounding fabrications.
- **Specific numbers and dates.** Gemini is particularly unreliable on precise figures, especially when those figures were not prominently represented in training data.
- **Recent events.** Gemini's training data has a cutoff. For events near or after that cutoff, the model may blend real information with speculation.
- **Questions that assume a false premise.** Ask "When did Microsoft acquire Google?" and Gemini may try to answer rather than challenge the premise.

How to Protect Yourself

The single most effective defense against hallucination is **Google Search grounding**. When Gemini grounds its response in live search results, you get citations you can click and verify. If an answer matters, have Gemini search for it rather than answer from memory.

Beyond that:

- **Verify critical facts independently.** Never trust a single AI for medical, legal, financial, or safety-critical information.
- **Ask Gemini to flag its uncertainty.** A prompt like "Answer this and tell me which parts you are most and least confident about" can surface useful hedges.
- **Be skeptical of specificity.** The more specific a claim (exact percentages, precise dates, full citations), the more carefully you should verify it.

- **Use the "Double-check" feature.** Gemini offers a built-in option to verify its response against Google Search results. Use it.

Knowledge Limitations

Gemini's knowledge has boundaries, and understanding them helps you work within them effectively.

The Training Cutoff

Like all large language models, Gemini was trained on a snapshot of information. It does not continuously learn from your conversations or the wider internet in real time. Google Search grounding bridges this gap for many queries, but Gemini's "native" knowledge — what it can answer without searching — has a fixed horizon.

Gemini may not know about:

- Very recent events, product launches, or policy changes
- New scientific findings published after the training cutoff
- Updated statistics, prices, or regulations
- Recently deceased or newly prominent public figures

Depth vs. Breadth

Gemini's training data skews toward content that is well-represented on the English-language internet. This creates predictable gaps:

- **Niche professional domains.** Gemini knows a lot about popular programming languages but less about obscure industrial protocols. It can discuss well-known legal principles but may falter on jurisdiction-specific case law.
- **Non-English content.** Gemini supports many languages, but its depth of knowledge is unevenly distributed. Topics discussed primarily in languages other than English may get shallower treatment.
- **Local and regional knowledge.** Gemini handles well-documented global topics better than local businesses, municipal regulations, or regional customs.

- **Rapidly evolving fields.** AI itself, cryptocurrency, and emerging medical treatments change faster than training cycles can keep up.

Working Around Knowledge Gaps

- **Use extensions.** Google Search, Maps, Flights, and other extensions give Gemini access to live data its training alone cannot provide.
- **Provide context yourself.** Working in a specialized domain? Paste relevant documents or data into the conversation. Gemini's million-token context window makes this practical in ways earlier models could not match.
- **Cross-reference with specialized tools.** For medical questions, consult medical databases. For legal questions, consult legal resources. Gemini is a generalist, not a domain-specific expert system.

Image Generation Issues and Biases

Gemini's image generation capabilities, powered by the Imagen 4 model family, are impressive but imperfect. The issues fall into several categories.

Representation and Diversity Biases

Google has made significant efforts to ensure Gemini generates diverse and representative images. Sometimes these efforts overshoot. In early 2024, Gemini generated historically inaccurate images — depicting people of various ethnicities in contexts where that diversity was anachronistic (such as diverse Nazi-era German soldiers). Google temporarily paused image generation of people to address this.

The underlying challenge is real: training data reflects historical biases, and correcting for them without introducing new inaccuracies is genuinely difficult. As of May 2026, Google has refined its approach, but be aware that:

- Generated images of people may not always match the demographic specifics you have in mind
- Historical scenes may include creative liberties
- Stereotypical representations can still surface, particularly for occupations and social roles

Anatomical and Physical Errors

Like all current image generation models, the Imagen 4 family can produce images with:

- Extra or missing fingers
- Distorted hands and limbs
- Inconsistent lighting or shadows
- Text rendered incorrectly within images
- Facial features that look subtly wrong upon close inspection

These errors have improved dramatically over earlier models, but have not been eliminated. If you are generating images for professional use, inspect them carefully.

Content Restrictions

Gemini refuses to generate certain categories of images, including:

- Realistic depictions of identifiable public figures
- Violent or graphic content
- Sexually explicit material
- Content that could be used for deception or misinformation

These restrictions are deliberate policy choices by Google. If your image generation request is declined, it usually triggered one of these guardrails — sometimes appropriately, sometimes not. Rephrasing to clarify your intent can help in borderline cases.

SynthID Watermarking

Every image Gemini generates is watermarked with SynthID, a digital watermark embedded at the pixel level — invisible to the human eye but detectable by software. This is Google's approach to AI-generated image provenance. You cannot remove the watermark, and you should know it exists if you are using generated images in any context.

Math and Reasoning Limitations

Gemini is not a calculator, and it is not a theorem prover. It is a language model that can reason about math and logic — sometimes brilliantly, sometimes not.

Where Gemini Struggles with Math

- **Multi-step arithmetic.** Gemini solves many math problems correctly, but as steps increase, the probability of error in any single step compounds. A ten-step calculation is far more likely to contain an error than a two-step one.
- **Large numbers.** Gemini sometimes makes errors with very large or very small numbers, losing precision in ways a calculator never would.
- **Word problems with tricky setups.** Problems designed to be counterintuitive or carry misleading surface features can trip Gemini up. It may latch onto the obvious (but wrong) interpretation.
- **Symbolic math.** Gemini handles basic algebra and calculus, but complex symbolic manipulation — simplifying large expressions, solving systems of equations — is where dedicated tools like Wolfram Alpha are more reliable.

Where Gemini Struggles with Reasoning

- **Logic puzzles.** Classic logic puzzles, especially those requiring you to track multiple constraints simultaneously, can produce wrong answers. Gemini may reach a plausible-sounding conclusion that violates one of the stated constraints.
- **Spatial reasoning.** Tasks requiring visualization of three-dimensional arrangements or tracking positions and movements can be challenging.
- **Counting.** This sounds absurd, but language models — including Gemini — can struggle with simple counting tasks, like "How many times does the letter 'r' appear in the word 'strawberry'?" The model processes tokens, not individual characters.
- **Multi-step deduction.** Long chains of if-then reasoning are fragile. Each step carries some probability of error, and those probabilities multiply.

Deep Think Helps — But Does Not Eliminate Errors

Gemini 3 Pro's Deep Think – and the dedicated Gemini 3 Deep Think mode – significantly improves performance on complex reasoning. By spending more time reasoning through a problem before producing a response, Deep Think catches errors standard mode misses. But it is not infallible. Deep Think is better at math and reasoning than standard Gemini, not perfect at either.

What to Do

- **Use Gemini for reasoning about math, not for computing.** Have Gemini explain how to solve a problem, then verify the actual computation with a calculator or spreadsheet.
- **Break complex problems into steps.** Have Gemini work through one step at a time, and verify each before moving to the next.
- **Enable Deep Think for complex reasoning.** If you have access to Google AI Pro, use Deep Think for math-heavy or logic-heavy tasks.
- **Cross-check with specialized tools.** Google Sheets, Python, Wolfram Alpha, and purpose-built calculators beat any language model at computation.

Outdated or Incorrect Procedural Knowledge

Gemini sometimes provides outdated instructions for tasks that have changed over time. Software interfaces change, menu items move, APIs get updated, processes evolve. Gemini's training data captures a snapshot, and that snapshot ages.

Common areas where this surfaces:

- **Software tutorials.** Gemini may describe menu locations or settings that have since moved or been renamed.
- **API documentation.** Code examples may reference deprecated endpoints or outdated syntax.
- **Policy and regulatory information.** Rules change. What was true when training data was compiled may not be true today.
- **Pricing and plan details.** Product pricing changes frequently. Verify cost answers against current sources.

The fix is straightforward: for any procedural task, verify against the official, current documentation. Use Gemini to understand concepts and approaches, but confirm specifics.

How to Spot Errors

Developing an instinct for when Gemini might be wrong is one of the most valuable skills you can build. Patterns to watch for:

- **Excessive confidence without hedging.** When Gemini states something as absolute fact without any qualification, that is not a sign of accuracy — it is just how language models talk. Real experts hedge; Gemini often does not.
- **Suspiciously perfect answers.** If an answer is exactly what you wanted to hear, be more skeptical, not less. Gemini is trained to be helpful, and that can mean telling you what you want rather than what is true.
- **Details that are hard to verify.** If Gemini cites a study you cannot find, a quote that does not appear in any search results, or a statistic with no source, treat it as unverified until proven otherwise.
- **Answers to questions you already know are tricky.** If a topic is contentious or nuanced and Gemini hands you a simple, clean answer, it may be oversimplifying.
- **Inconsistency across responses.** Ask the same question twice in different conversations. If you get significantly different answers, at least one is likely wrong.

Building a Verification Habit

The goal is not to distrust everything Gemini says. The goal is appropriate calibration — trusting Gemini more for things it does well and less for things it does not. A simple framework:

High trust (verify occasionally): - General explanations of well-established topics - Writing assistance (drafts, edits, formatting) - Brainstorming and ideation - Code structure and approach suggestions

Medium trust (verify regularly): - Specific facts and claims - Technical details and procedures - Summaries of documents you have provided - Code that compiles and runs

Low trust (always verify): - Medical, legal, or financial advice - Citations and sources - Statistics and precise figures - Recent events near the training cutoff - Anything you plan to publish or act on with significant consequences

Gemini is an extraordinarily powerful tool. The difference between a powerful tool used well and one used carelessly is the person holding it. Now that you know where the edges are, you are better equipped to stay well within them.

Chapter 26: Privacy, Security, and Safe Use

When you use Gemini, you are having a conversation with a Google product. That sentence deserves a moment. Google is one of the largest data companies in human history, and understanding how your Gemini interactions fit into Google's broader data ecosystem is essential to using the tool responsibly and protecting yourself.

This is not an alarmist take on privacy. Google has built legitimate privacy controls into Gemini, and many are quite good. But privacy does not happen by default — it happens because you understand what is being collected, what controls exist, and how to configure them for your comfort level.

What Google Collects When You Use Gemini

Start with the basics. When you have a conversation with Gemini, Google may collect:

- **Your prompts.** Every message you type or speak to Gemini.
- **Gemini's responses.** The full text of what Gemini says back to you.
- **Attached files.** Images, documents, or other files you upload during a conversation.
- **Metadata.** Your IP address, device type, browser, language settings, and the time and date of your interactions.
- **Feedback signals.** If you rate a response (thumbs up, thumbs down) or report it, that feedback is collected.
- **Location data.** If you have location services enabled, Gemini may use your approximate location to provide more relevant answers.

This collection serves several purposes: improving Gemini's models, maintaining service quality, enforcing safety policies, and — depending on your settings — personalizing your experience.

The Critical Distinction: Stored vs. Used for Training

Google draws a line between data stored for your account and data used to improve Gemini's models. These are not the same thing, and the distinction matters.

When Gemini Activity is on (covered in a moment), your conversations are saved to your Google account and may be reviewed by human reviewers to improve the product. When Gemini Activity is off, your conversations are still processed by Google's servers to generate responses, but they are not saved to your account history and are not used for model improvement — though Google may retain them for up to 72 hours for safety and abuse prevention.

A meaningful difference. If you are discussing sensitive topics, turning off Gemini Activity gives you a substantially different privacy posture than leaving it on.

Google Activity Controls

Google provides specific controls for how your Gemini data is handled. Here is how to find and configure them.

Gemini Apps Activity

This is the primary control. Navigate to your Google Account settings, then to "Data & privacy," then to "Gemini Apps Activity" (or go directly to myactivity.google.com).

When Gemini Apps Activity is **on:** - Your conversations are saved to your Google account - You can view, search, and delete past conversations - Your data may be used to improve Gemini (with human review possible) - Conversations are retained for up to 18 months by default (you can change this to 3 or 36 months)

When Gemini Apps Activity is **off:** - New conversations are not saved to your account history - Your data is not used to improve Gemini models - Google may still retain conversations for up to 72 hours for safety purposes - You lose the ability to see your conversation history

What the Retention Period Means

When you set a retention period (3, 18, or 36 months), Google automatically deletes conversations older than the chosen window. "Deletes" in Google's systems means the data is removed from your activity page and queued for deletion from Google's servers — a process that can take additional time to complete across all backup systems.

How to Delete Specific Conversations

You can delete individual conversations from your Gemini history at any time:

1. Open Gemini and look at your conversation history in the sidebar
2. Click the three-dot menu on any conversation
3. Select "Delete"
4. Confirm the deletion

You can also bulk-delete from myactivity.google.com by selecting a date range or wiping everything.

Auto-Delete Settings

Google lets you configure automatic deletion of your Gemini activity on a rolling basis. Choose to auto-delete data older than 3, 18, or 36 months. If privacy is a priority, 3 months is the most aggressive option available.

Workspace Data Protections

If you use Gemini through Google Workspace (the business and enterprise version), the privacy picture changes significantly — and generally for the better.

The Workspace Data Promise

Google has made explicit commitments about Workspace data:

- **Your organization's data is not used to train Gemini's foundation models.** This is a firm commitment for Workspace customers. The content of your emails, documents, and conversations processed by Gemini in Workspace stays within your organization's data boundary.
- **Admin controls.** Your organization's IT administrator controls whether Gemini features are enabled, who has access to them, and what data Gemini can access.

- **Data Processing Agreements.** Business and Enterprise Workspace customers operate under Google's Cloud Data Processing Addendum, which provides contractual privacy protections that go beyond what consumer users receive.
- **Regional data storage.** For organizations with data residency requirements, Google offers controls for where data is stored and processed.

What This Means in Practice

If your company uses Google Workspace with Gemini, content you process through Workspace-integrated Gemini features (Gemini in Gmail, Docs, Sheets) is protected by your organization's terms with Google, not by consumer privacy settings. Generally stronger protection.

One nuance: if you also use the consumer Gemini app (gemini.google.com) with your personal Google account, those conversations operate under consumer privacy terms, not Workspace terms. Keep work conversations in Workspace-integrated tools, not the consumer app.

Admin Controls for Organizations

If you are an IT administrator, you have granular control over Gemini in your organization:

- Enable or disable Gemini features per user or organizational unit
- Control which Gemini features are available (chat, Workspace integrations, image generation)
- Set data sharing and retention policies
- Monitor usage through admin reports
- Configure data loss prevention (DLP) rules that apply to Gemini interactions

Sensitive Information Guidelines

Knowing the technical details of data collection is one thing. Knowing what to share and what to keep out is another.

What You Should Never Share with Gemini

Categories of information that should never go into any AI system, including Gemini:

- **Passwords and authentication credentials.** Never paste passwords, API keys, secret tokens, or similar credentials into a Gemini conversation.
- **Social Security numbers, national ID numbers, or government identifiers.** High-value targets for identity theft — keep them out of any AI.
- **Credit card numbers or full bank account details.** Gemini has no legitimate need for your financial account numbers.
- **Medical records with identifying information.** Ask Gemini general health questions, but do not paste in medical records that include your name, date of birth, or other identifying details.
- **Confidential business information (in the consumer app).** Using the free consumer version? Do not paste proprietary business data, trade secrets, or confidential client information. Use Workspace-integrated Gemini for business work.
- **Other people's private information.** Do not share personal data about other individuals without their consent.

A Practical Test

Before sharing information with Gemini, ask yourself: "Would I be comfortable if a Google employee read this?" Because under certain settings, a human reviewer at Google might. If the answer is no, do not share it — or turn off Gemini Apps Activity first.

Using Gemini at Work

Many employers are developing AI usage policies. Before using Gemini for work, check whether your organization has one. Common restrictions:

- No sharing customer data with consumer AI tools
- No uploading proprietary code or intellectual property
- No using AI for decisions that require human review (HR, legal, compliance)

- Required disclosure when AI is used to produce work output

No AI policy yet? That does not mean anything goes. Use common sense: treat the consumer Gemini app like a public space, and do not share anything there you would not post on a public forum.

Children and Family Safety

Google has specific policies about children and Gemini, and they are worth understanding if you are a parent or educator.

Age Requirements

In most countries, the minimum age to use Gemini is 13 (or the equivalent age in jurisdictions that set a higher floor). The notable exception: in the European Economic Area, Switzerland, and the United Kingdom, the minimum age remains 18. In schools that use Google Workspace for Education, students aged 13 and over can also access Gemini through their school accounts. Children under 13 can be granted access by a parent through Family Link with supervisory controls in place.

For teen accounts, additional safeguards apply:

- Content filters are more restrictive
- Certain features may be limited or unavailable
- Gemini Activity settings may have different defaults
- Image generation of people may be restricted

Supervised Accounts and Family Link

For families using Google Family Link, parents can manage their child's access to Gemini through supervised account settings. Family Link is the primary mechanism for granting Gemini access to children under 13 with parental oversight, and it gives parents ongoing control over:

- Whether the child has access to Gemini at all
- Activity and history settings
- Content restrictions and feature limits

Practical Advice for Parents

Even with safeguards in place, no AI content filter is perfect. Practical guidance:

- **Talk to your children about AI.** Help them understand that Gemini is a tool, not an authority. It can be wrong, and it does not replace learning.
- **Set expectations about schoolwork.** Be clear about when Gemini is appropriate for homework and when it is not. (Chapter 21 covers academic integrity in detail, with further ethical discussion in Chapter 27.)
- **Monitor early usage.** When your child first starts using Gemini, check in regularly on what they are using it for and what kinds of responses they get.
- **Explain that conversations are not private.** Children should understand that what they type into Gemini is processed by Google and may be reviewed by people. They should never share personal information, location details, or anything they would not tell a stranger.

Using Gemini on Public or Shared Devices

If you use Gemini on a shared computer, public library terminal, or any device not exclusively yours:

- **Sign out when you are done.** Your Gemini conversations are tied to your Google account; staying signed in gives the next user access to your conversation history.
- **Use incognito or private browsing.** This prevents session data from being stored on the device.
- **Do not save passwords on shared devices.** Applies to your Google account generally, not just Gemini.
- **Watch screen visibility.** In public spaces, people can read your screen. Do not discuss sensitive topics with Gemini where others can see.

Data Breaches and Security Considerations

No system is immune to security incidents. Google has one of the most sophisticated security infrastructures in the world, but it is worth thinking about what happens if something goes wrong.

- **Google's security track record.** Google invests billions in security and has a strong track record, but no company is immune to breaches. The data you share with Gemini lives in Google's infrastructure and is subject to the same protections — and risks — as the rest of your Google account.
- **Two-factor authentication.** Enable 2FA on your Google account. The single most effective thing you can do to protect your Gemini data (and all your Google data).
- **Review account activity regularly.** Check your Google account's security page (myaccount.google.com/security) periodically for unauthorized access.
- **Prompt injection and adversarial attacks.** As AI systems get more integrated into workflows, there is a growing category of attacks where malicious content in documents, emails, or web pages manipulates AI behavior. Google actively works to prevent them, but be cautious about asking Gemini to process content from untrusted sources.

Your Privacy Checklist

A quick summary of actions to take to use Gemini with a privacy posture you are comfortable with:

1. **Review your Gemini Apps Activity settings** and decide whether you want conversations saved
2. **Set an auto-delete period** if you keep activity on (3 months is the most privacy-protective option)
3. **Enable two-factor authentication** on your Google account
4. **Establish personal rules** about what categories of information you will and will not share with Gemini
5. **Use Workspace-integrated Gemini** for business content, not the consumer app
6. **Check your employer's AI policy** before using Gemini for work
7. **Review and configure teen account settings** if your children use Gemini
8. **Periodically review and delete** your Gemini conversation history

Privacy is not a one-time configuration. It is an ongoing practice. Google's controls are solid, but they only work if you use them. Take fifteen minutes to review your settings now, and revisit every few months as Google updates Gemini's features and policies.

Chapter 27: The Ethics of AI Assistance

You have spent the last 26 chapters learning what Gemini can do. This chapter asks a different question: what *should* you do with it?

AI ethics is not an abstract philosophical exercise. It is a set of practical decisions you make every time you open Gemini. Should you use it to write a school essay? Should you disclose that an email was drafted by AI? Can you use a Gemini-generated image commercially? Is it acceptable to automate tasks someone else gets paid to do?

These are not hypothetical questions. They are decisions real people face every day, and there are no universally agreed-upon answers. This chapter offers a framework for thinking through them — along with practical guidance for the situations most Gemini users encounter.

Academic Integrity

This is the ethical question that generates the most heat, so address it directly.

The Core Tension

AI tools like Gemini can write essays, solve math problems, generate code, summarize readings, and answer exam questions. Students have access. The question is not whether students will use them — they already are. The question is where to draw the line between legitimate use and academic dishonesty.

Where Most Institutions Draw the Line

Academic integrity policies are evolving rapidly, but a general consensus is emerging:

- **Submitting AI-generated work as your own is cheating.** If your professor asks you to write an essay and you have Gemini write it, then put your name on it — that is plagiarism by most institutional definitions, even though you did not copy from another human.

- **Using AI as a study tool is generally acceptable.** Asking Gemini to explain a concept, quiz you, or help you understand a reading is similar to using a textbook or a tutor.
- **Using AI for brainstorming and outlining is a gray area.** Some instructors welcome it; others do not. The key is transparency.
- **Using AI for editing and proofreading is usually acceptable** but varies by assignment and institution.

Practical Guidelines for Students

If you are a student, here is a practical framework:

1. **Read your institution's AI policy.** Many schools have published specific guidelines. Follow them.
2. **When in doubt, ask your instructor.** A quick email — "Is it okay if I use Gemini to brainstorm ideas for this paper?" — can save you from an integrity violation.
3. **Disclose your use.** If you used AI anywhere in your work, say so. Many instructors now ask for or accept AI disclosures.
4. **Learn the material.** Using Gemini to avoid learning defeats the purpose of education. Use it to learn more effectively, not to bypass learning entirely.
5. **AI detectors exist — and are unreliable.** Tools that claim to detect AI-generated text produce both false positives and false negatives at significant rates. Do not rely on "not getting caught" as a strategy; rely on honest use.

Practical Guidelines for Educators

If you are an instructor:

1. **Set clear expectations.** Students cannot follow rules they do not know. State your AI policy explicitly in your syllabus.
2. **Design AI-resistant assessments when appropriate.** Assignments requiring personal reflection, connection to in-class discussion, or analysis of very recent events are harder for AI to complete convincingly.

3. **Consider allowing and teaching responsible AI use.** Students who learn to use AI effectively and ethically now will be better prepared for workplaces where these tools are standard.
4. **Do not rely solely on AI detection tools.** They are not reliable enough to serve as the basis for academic integrity charges.

Disclosure: When Should You Say "AI Helped"?

Beyond academia, the disclosure question comes up constantly. When should you tell people that Gemini assisted with something?

Professional Context

There is no universal legal requirement to disclose AI use in most professional contexts (as of May 2026), but norms are developing quickly:

- **Job applications.** If a posting asks for a writing sample and you have Gemini write it, you are misrepresenting your abilities. Using Gemini to polish your own draft is closer to using a spell-checker — but norms vary by industry.
- **Client deliverables.** If a client is paying for your expertise and you use Gemini to generate significant portions of the work, disclosure is ethically appropriate. Many clients are fine with it; what they are not fine with is being deceived.
- **Published content.** If you are writing articles, blog posts, or books, many publications now have AI disclosure policies. Even when they do not, transparency builds trust.
- **Internal work.** Using Gemini to draft emails, prepare meeting notes, or analyze data is increasingly normal and generally does not require disclosure — unless your organization's policy says otherwise.

A Simple Rule of Thumb

If someone would be surprised or feel deceived to learn that AI assisted with your work, you should probably disclose. If AI assistance is in the same category as a search engine or a word processor — a tool that helped you work more efficiently rather than replacing your judgment — disclosure is less critical.

How to Disclose

When disclosure is appropriate, keep it simple and matter-of-fact:

- "I used Gemini to help draft this document, which I then reviewed and edited."
- "This initial analysis was generated with AI assistance and verified against primary sources."
- "AI was used in the brainstorming phase of this project."

No need to be apologetic. AI assistance is a tool, and using tools well is a skill.

Copyright and AI-Generated Content

Copyright law has been catching up to AI, and the landscape as of May 2026 is clearer than it was a year ago — though specific cases continue to work their way through the courts. What you need to know:

Text Generated by Gemini

In January 2025, the U.S. Copyright Office published Part 2 of its AI report, focused on copyrightability. Two holdings from that guidance are central:

- **Prompts alone do not provide sufficient human control to make AI output copyrightable.** Pure prompt-driven works — where a person types instructions and accepts whatever the model produces — are not eligible for copyright protection.
- **Copyright is available when a human contribution is perceptible in the AI output, or when a human creatively arranges, modifies, or selects from AI-generated material.** Edits, curation, structural choices, and creative arrangements that reflect a person's authorship can support a copyright in the resulting work.

The Copyright Office concluded that existing law is sufficient to handle these questions and did not call for new legislation. In practical terms:

- If you have Gemini write an essay from scratch and submit it unchanged, the text is unlikely to be copyrightable.

- If you use Gemini as part of your creative process — providing direction, editing the output, restructuring it, weaving it together with your own writing — the resulting work may well be copyrightable based on your human contribution.
- Courts are still applying this framework to specific facts, and gray areas persist around how much editing is "enough."

Other countries are taking varying approaches, and international law in this area remains fragmented.

Images Generated by Gemini

AI-generated images face the same framework, with some additional wrinkles:

- **Google's Terms of Service.** Google's terms give you the right to use images generated by Gemini, but read the current terms carefully — they have evolved over time and may include restrictions on commercial use.
- **Copyright protection.** Following the same logic as text, purely AI-generated images with no meaningful human creative input are unlikely to be copyrightable in the United States. If you heavily direct, select, and arrange AI-generated images — or modify them with your own creative input — the resulting work may receive protection. The 2025 Copyright Office guidance applies here too: prompts alone are not enough; perceptible human authorship or creative arrangement is.
- **Training data concerns.** Gemini's image generation model (Imagen) was trained on a vast dataset of images, some created by human artists. Whether that training constitutes copyright infringement is the subject of ongoing litigation. It does not directly affect your right to use the images you generate, but it is part of the broader legal landscape.
- **SynthID watermarking.** All Gemini-generated images carry an invisible SynthID watermark. Software can detect it, and platforms that implement AI content detection may treat these images differently.

Practical Guidance on Copyright

- **Do not assume AI output is copyrightable.** If copyright protection matters to you, make substantial creative contributions beyond writing prompts.

- **Read Google's current terms of service.** The terms governing use of Gemini-generated content can change. Check before using AI content commercially.
- **Add your own creative work.** The more you edit, modify, arrange, and build upon AI output, the stronger your claim to the resulting work.
- **Be cautious with commercial use of generated images.** Google generally permits commercial use, but the legal landscape is evolving.
- **Keep records of your creative process.** If you ever need to demonstrate human creative input in a work that includes AI-generated elements, documentation will be valuable.

Job Displacement and Economic Impact

The elephant in the room. AI tools like Gemini can do some tasks people currently get paid to do. What does that mean for jobs?

The Honest Answer

Nobody knows the full impact yet. Predictions range from utopian (AI frees everyone to do more creative work) to dystopian (massive unemployment). The reality will likely be somewhere in the middle, varying enormously by industry, role, and geography.

What we can say with reasonable confidence:

- **Some tasks will be automated.** Basic writing, simple data analysis, routine customer service, and other repetitive cognitive tasks are already being augmented or replaced by AI tools.
- **Some jobs will change significantly.** Roles in writing, design, programming, research, and analysis are being reshaped. The skills that matter are shifting from "can you do this task?" to "can you direct AI to do this task, verify the output, and add value beyond what AI provides?"
- **New roles are emerging.** AI prompt engineering, AI policy, AI ethics, AI training, and AI integration are creating new categories of work.
- **The transition will be uneven.** Some industries and regions will be hit sooner and harder than others.

What This Means for You

- **Learn AI tools.** You are already doing it by reading this book. The people most at risk from AI displacement are those who refuse to engage with these tools at all.
- **Focus on what AI cannot do well.** Relationship building, physical presence, ethical judgment, creative vision, emotional intelligence, and deep domain expertise are all areas where humans remain essential.
- **Stay adaptable.** Specific tools and capabilities will change rapidly. The meta-skill of learning new tools quickly is more valuable than mastery of any single AI platform.
- **Advocate for responsible transition.** If you are in a position of leadership, consider how AI adoption affects the people in your organization. Rapid automation without retraining or transition support creates real human cost.

The Ethics of Using AI to Do Someone Else's Job

If you use Gemini to do work your company used to pay a freelancer to do, is that ethical? A genuine question without a clean answer. Some perspectives:

- Using better tools to work more efficiently is how economies have always evolved.
- There is a difference between gradually adopting more efficient tools and abruptly eliminating roles without transition support.
- If you are getting hired as a human and secretly having AI do the work, you are being deceptive — to the person paying you and to the people who lost the opportunity.

Responsible Use Principles

Drawing from the themes of this chapter, a set of principles for responsible AI use you can adapt to your own context:

1. Be Honest

If someone asks whether AI was involved in your work, tell the truth. If a situation calls for disclosure, disclose. Deception undermines trust — not just in you, but in the broader adoption of AI tools.

2. Verify Before You Trust

Gemini is a tool, not an oracle. Verify important claims. Do not pass AI output to others as fact. You are responsible for the accuracy of what you share, regardless of where it originated.

3. Protect Privacy

Do not share other people's personal information with Gemini. Do not use AI to generate content about real individuals without their knowledge or consent. Respect the privacy boundaries discussed in Chapter 26.

4. Respect Intellectual Property

Do not use AI to circumvent copyright, reproduce copyrighted material, or create works designed to be confused with the work of specific creators. When in doubt, create something original rather than imitative.

5. Use AI to Augment, Not Replace, Your Judgment

AI can inform your decisions, but it should not make them for you — especially decisions with significant consequences for other people. Medical diagnoses, legal advice, hiring decisions, and similar high-stakes judgments require human oversight.

6. Consider the Broader Impact

When you use AI, you are participating in a technology that affects society at large. Consider whether your use contributes to a world you want to live in. You do not need to agonize over every prompt — but you should occasionally think about the bigger picture.

7. Stay Informed

AI capabilities, laws, norms, and best practices are changing rapidly. What is acceptable today may not be tomorrow, and vice versa. Stay current with developments in AI ethics and policy.

The Bigger Picture

We are in the early years of a profound technological shift. AI tools like Gemini are becoming embedded in how we work, learn, create, and communicate. The choices we make now — individually and collectively — will shape how this technology develops and who benefits.

The fact that you are reading a chapter on AI ethics suggests you care about getting it right. That matters. The most dangerous AI users are not the ones who think about ethics and sometimes get it wrong — they are the ones who never think about it at all.

Use Gemini. Use it boldly and creatively. But use it honestly, thoughtfully, and with awareness that the words and images it generates go out into a world of real people with real consequences.

Epilogue

You know Gemini now. Not just the surface — the marketing bullets and the flashy demo — but the real thing: how it works, where it excels, where it stumbles, and how to get the most out of it for the work and life that matter to you. That puts you ahead of the vast majority of people who use AI every day without ever learning to use it well.

If you want to go further, *Gemini: The Advanced Guide*, the next book in this series, covers advanced techniques and workflows in the same depth. It picks up where this book leaves off and takes you into expert-level prompting, API integration, and workflows that push Gemini to its limits.

For everyone — power users too — the most important thing to take from this book is not any single feature, prompt technique, or Google Workspace integration. It is a way of thinking. The specific capabilities of Gemini will change. Models will get faster, smarter, more capable. Features will be added, renamed, and occasionally removed. The interface you see today will not be the interface you see in a year. The Google ecosystem will keep expanding, and Gemini's role within it will keep growing. That is the nature of a technology moving this quickly.

What will not change are the principles: communicate clearly, verify what matters, understand the tool's limitations, and keep your own judgment. The people who get the most from AI are not the ones who memorize every feature — they are the ones who develop good instincts for when to trust, when to verify, and when to push back. Those instincts transfer across tools, across updates, and across whatever comes next.

Google has built something genuinely impressive with Gemini — an assistant that lives inside the ecosystem hundreds of millions of people already depend on, one that can see, hear, read, and reason across nearly any kind of content you throw at it. But the assistant is only as useful as the person using it. An AI that makes you a better thinker is worth far more than one that simply makes you faster. Gemini, at its best, does both.

You have the knowledge now. Go put it to work.

Part VIII: Reference

"Science is what we understand well enough to explain to a computer. Art is everything else we do."

— Donald Knuth

Appendix A: Keyboard Shortcuts and Interface Tips

This appendix is your quick reference for navigating Gemini efficiently. Whether you are on the web interface at gemini.google.com, the mobile app, or Gemini inside Google Workspace, these tips will help you work faster.

Web Interface Shortcuts (gemini.google.com)

Gemini's web interface supports several keyboard shortcuts that save time once they are muscle memory.

Conversation Shortcuts

Action	Shortcut
New conversation	Ctrl + Shift + O (Windows/Linux) / Cmd + Shift + O (Mac)
Focus on input field	/ (when not already typing)
Submit prompt	Enter
New line without submitting	Shift + Enter
Stop generating	Esc or click the stop button
Copy last response	Click the copy icon on the response

Navigation Shortcuts

Action	Shortcut
Toggle sidebar	Click the hamburger menu (top left)
Scroll through conversations	Use sidebar scroll
Switch between conversations	Click conversation in sidebar
Return to home screen	Click the Gemini logo

Text Formatting in Prompts

Gemini recognizes basic formatting cues in your prompts:

- Use line breaks (`Shift + Enter`) to structure complex prompts with separate sections
- Use numbered lists in your prompts to request numbered output
- Use bullet points to organize multiple questions or requirements
- Enclose text in quotation marks to indicate exact text you want Gemini to reference

Invoking Extensions with @

Direct Gemini to a specific Extension by typing @ followed by the Extension name. For example:

- `@Google Maps How far is it from here to the airport?`
- `@YouTube Find a tutorial on sourdough bread`
- `@Google Flights Flights from LAX to JFK next Friday`

This is useful when your query could be handled by multiple Extensions and you want a specific one. You can also combine @ invocations with regular text in a single prompt.

Response Interaction

Every Gemini response comes with a set of interaction options. Knowing them saves time.

Response Actions

- **Copy** — Copies the full response text to your clipboard. The copy icon appears when you hover over or tap a response.
- **Share** — Creates a shareable link to the conversation (or a portion of it). Useful for collaborating with others.
- **Export to Docs** — Sends the response directly to a new Google Doc. This is one of the fastest ways to move AI-generated content into an editable document.
- **Export to Gmail** — Drops the response into a Gmail draft. Particularly useful when Gemini has helped you draft an email.

- **Modify response** — Offers options to make the response shorter, longer, simpler, more casual, or more professional. This is faster than writing a follow-up prompt asking for adjustments.
- **Show drafts** — Gemini often generates multiple draft responses. Click "Show drafts" or use the arrow buttons to view alternative versions.
- **Thumbs up / Thumbs down** — Rate responses to help improve Gemini. Thumbs down also lets you provide specific feedback about what went wrong.
- **Double-check with Google** — Highlights claims in the response that Gemini can verify against Google Search. Green highlights indicate supported claims; orange highlights indicate claims that could not be verified.

Regenerate and Edit

- **Regenerate response** — Click the regenerate icon to get a fresh response to the same prompt. Useful when the first response misses the mark.
- **Edit your prompt** — Hover over your own message and click the edit (pencil) icon to modify your prompt and regenerate. This is much faster than retyping.

Prompt Input Tips

Multiline Prompts

For complex prompts, use `Shift + Enter` to create line breaks. Structured prompts produce better results. Compare:

Single line: "Write a marketing email for a product launch include a subject line and call to action make it professional but friendly"

Structured (using Shift + Enter):

```
Write a marketing email for a product launch.

Product: Wireless noise-canceling headphones, $149
Audience: Tech-savvy professionals, ages 25-45
Tone: Professional but friendly
Include:
```

```
- Subject line
- Three key benefits
- Call to action with urgency
Length: 200-250 words
```

The structured version will produce significantly better results.

File Uploads

- Click the + icon or the attachment button to upload files
- Drag and drop files directly into the chat window
- Supported file types include images (JPEG, PNG, GIF, WebP), PDFs, text files, and code files
- For Google AI Pro users (and above), you can upload multiple files in a single conversation
- When uploading images, you can add a text prompt alongside the image to direct Gemini's analysis

Voice Input

- Click the microphone icon to dictate your prompt
- Gemini will transcribe your speech and submit it as a text prompt
- On mobile, voice input is especially convenient for longer prompts
- You can switch between voice and text input freely within a conversation

Mobile App Tips (Android and iOS)

Android-Specific Tips

- **Invoke Gemini from anywhere** by long-pressing the home button or saying "Hey Google" (if configured)
- **Overlay mode** — Gemini can appear as an overlay on top of other apps, letting you ask questions about what is on your screen
- **Share to Gemini** — Use Android's share sheet to send text, images, or links directly to Gemini from other apps
- **Widget** — Add the Gemini widget to your home screen for quick access

iOS-Specific Tips

- **Gemini app** — Available as a standalone app from the App Store

- **Gemini in the Google app** — Also accessible through the Google app
- **Share extension** — Share content to Gemini from other apps using the iOS share sheet
- **Live Activities** — When Gemini is processing a long request, progress may appear in Dynamic Island or Live Activities on supported devices

Mobile Gesture Tips

- Swipe left on a response to see alternative drafts
- Long-press on text in a response to select and copy specific portions
- Pull down to refresh a conversation
- Swipe right from the left edge to open the conversation sidebar

Google Workspace Integration Tips

Gemini in Gmail

- Look for the Gemini icon (sparkle) when composing an email
- Use "Help me write" to generate a draft from a brief description
- Select existing text and use Gemini to refine, formalize, or elaborate
- In your inbox, use Gemini to summarize long email threads

Gemini in Google Docs

- Access Gemini via the Gemini icon in the toolbar or by typing @ and selecting Gemini
- Use "Help me write" for new content generation
- Select existing text and right-click for Gemini-powered editing options
- Ask Gemini to summarize the entire document or specific sections

Gemini in Google Sheets

- Use Gemini to generate formulas from natural language descriptions
- Ask Gemini to create tables from unstructured data
- Use "Help me organize" to structure data
- Generate charts and visualizations with natural language requests

Gemini in Google Slides

- Generate entire slide decks from a topic or outline
- Create individual slides with specific content
- Generate speaker notes for existing slides
- Ask Gemini to suggest images or design improvements

Gemini in Google Meet

- Enable Gemini note-taking during meetings
- Get AI-generated meeting summaries after calls
- Use Gemini to translate conversations in real time (supported languages)
- Review action items extracted by Gemini from meeting transcripts

Browser Tips

Chrome Integration

- Gemini can be accessed directly from Chrome's address bar on supported configurations
- The Gemini side panel in Chrome lets you ask questions about the page you are viewing
- Right-click on selected text to send it to Gemini for explanation or analysis

Tab Management

- Keep a Gemini tab pinned in your browser for quick access
- Use `Ctrl + T` (or `Cmd + T`) to open a new tab, then type gemini.google.com
- Bookmark gemini.google.com to your favorites bar for one-click access

Settings Worth Configuring

These settings are easy to overlook but meaningfully improve your experience:

- **Response language** — Set your preferred language for Gemini's responses in Settings

- **Extensions** — Enable the extensions you use (Google Workspace, Maps, YouTube, Flights/Hotels) in Settings > Extensions
- **Dark mode** — Toggle dark mode in Settings or follow your system theme to reduce eye strain
- **Gemini Apps Activity** — Configure your privacy settings (see Chapter 26)
- **Response style** — Some Gemini configurations allow you to set a default response style preference

Power User Habits

After working with Gemini for a while, these habits make you noticeably more efficient:

1. **Start prompts with the verb.** "Summarize," "Write," "Explain," "Compare," "List" — leading with the action gets better results.
2. **Use edit, do not retype.** When a response is close but not right, edit your original prompt rather than writing a new one from scratch.
3. **Check alternative drafts.** Gemini often generates multiple versions. The first one shown is not always the best.
4. **Export immediately.** If a response is good, export it to Docs or copy it right away. Do not assume you will come back for it later.
5. **Use the modify buttons.** "Shorter," "Longer," "Simpler," "More professional" — these one-click modifications are faster than writing a follow-up prompt.
6. **Organize your conversations.** Rename conversations in the sidebar to make them findable later. A conversation called "Q3 Marketing Plan" is far more useful than "New conversation."

Appendix B: Prompt Template Library

This appendix provides 77 ready-to-use prompt templates organized by category. Copy them directly into Gemini and customize the bracketed placeholders for your specific needs. These templates incorporate the prompting principles covered in Chapter 18.

Writing and Content Creation

1. Professional Email

```
Write a professional email to [recipient/role] about [topic].
Tone: [formal/friendly/urgent]
Key points to include:
- [Point 1]
- [Point 2]
- [Point 3]
Length: [short/medium/long]
```

2. Blog Post

```
Write a blog post about [topic].
Target audience: [describe audience]
Tone: [informative/conversational/persuasive]
Include: an engaging introduction, [number] main sections with subheadings, and
a conclusion with a call to action.
Length: approximately [word count] words.
```

3. Social Media Post

```
Write a [platform: LinkedIn/Twitter/Instagram/Facebook] post about [topic].
Goal: [inform/engage/promote/inspire]
Tone: [professional/casual/enthusiastic]
Include: [hashtags/call to action/question for engagement]
Length: [character/word limit]
```

4. Product Description

```
Write a product description for [product name].
Product type: [category]
```

```
Key features: [list 3-5 features]
Target customer: [describe ideal customer]
Tone: [luxurious/practical/technical/playful]
Length: [word count] words.
Include a compelling headline.
```

5. Press Release

```
Write a press release announcing [event/product/news].
Company: [company name]
Date: [date]
Location: [city, state]
Key details:
- [Detail 1]
- [Detail 2]
- [Detail 3]
Include a quote from [person, title].
Follow standard press release format with headline, dateline, body, and boilerpl
ate.
```

6. Cover Letter

```
Write a cover letter for [job title] at [company name].
My relevant experience: [brief summary]
Key qualifications from the job posting:
- [Qualification 1]
- [Qualification 2]
- [Qualification 3]
Tone: professional, confident, enthusiastic.
Length: approximately 300 words.
```

7. Thank You Note

```
Write a [professional/personal] thank you note to [recipient] for [reason].
Tone: [warm/formal/heartfelt]
Include a specific detail: [something memorable from the interaction]
Length: [3-5 sentences / 1-2 paragraphs]
```

8. Newsletter

```
Write a [weekly/monthly] newsletter for [audience/subscribers].
Topic: [main theme]
Sections to include:
- [Section 1]
- [Section 2]
```

```
- [Section 3]
Tone: [informative/friendly/professional]
Include a subject line and preview text.
```

Research and Analysis

9. Topic Summary

```
Summarize [topic] in [number] paragraphs.
Audience: [expert/general/student]
Cover: key concepts, current state, and major debates or developments.
Cite sources where possible using Google Search.
```

10. Comparison Analysis

```
Compare [Option A] and [Option B] across the following criteria:
- [Criterion 1]
- [Criterion 2]
- [Criterion 3]
- [Criterion 4]
Format: table with a summary paragraph.
Audience: [describe who this is for]
```

11. Pros and Cons List

```
Create a detailed pros and cons analysis of [topic/decision/product].
Context: [why this decision matters]
Consider: cost, time, quality, risk, and [any other relevant factors].
Format: two-column list with brief explanations for each point.
Conclude with a balanced recommendation.
```

12. Literature Review

```
Provide an overview of current research and thinking on [topic].
Cover:
- Key theories and frameworks
- Major findings from recent studies
- Areas of consensus and debate
- Gaps in current knowledge
Audience: [undergraduate/graduate/professional]
Use Google Search to find recent sources.
```

13. Market Research Brief

```
Provide a market research overview for [industry/product category].
Cover:
- Market size and growth trends
- Key players and market share
- Target demographics
- Emerging trends and opportunities
- Potential challenges
Use Google Search for current data. Note where figures are estimates.
```

14. SWOT Analysis

```
Create a SWOT analysis for [company/product/project].
Context: [brief description of the situation]

Format as four sections:
- Strengths (internal, positive)
- Weaknesses (internal, negative)
- Opportunities (external, positive)
- Threats (external, negative)

Include 4-6 points per section with brief explanations.
```

Business and Professional

15. Meeting Agenda

```
Create a meeting agenda for [meeting purpose].
Attendees: [list roles or names]
Duration: [time]
Include:
- Welcome and introductions ([minutes])
- [Topic 1] ([minutes])
- [Topic 2] ([minutes])
- [Topic 3] ([minutes])
- Action items and next steps ([minutes])
Format with time allocations and discussion owners.
```

16. Project Proposal

```
Write a project proposal for [project name].
Objective: [what the project will achieve]
Background: [why this project is needed]
Include:
- Executive summary
- Scope and deliverables
- Timeline with milestones
- Budget estimate
- Risks and mitigation strategies
- Success metrics
Length: [1-2 pages / 3-5 pages]
```

17. Performance Review Self-Assessment

```
Help me write a self-assessment for my performance review.
My role: [job title]
Review period: [timeframe]
Key accomplishments:
- [Accomplishment 1]
- [Accomplishment 2]
- [Accomplishment 3]
Areas I have grown: [describe]
Goals for next period: [describe]
Tone: confident but not boastful, specific and results-oriented.
```

18. Business Email Follow-Up

```
Write a follow-up email after [meeting/call/proposal].
Context: [what was discussed]
Key takeaways:
- [Takeaway 1]
- [Takeaway 2]
Next steps: [what needs to happen]
Tone: professional, action-oriented.
Length: brief (under 200 words).
```

19. Standard Operating Procedure

```
Write a standard operating procedure (SOP) for [process name].
Purpose: [why this process exists]
Scope: [who this applies to]
Steps: [list the major steps, and I will ask you to expand each one]
Include: prerequisites, step-by-step instructions, quality checks, and troublesh
```

```
ooting tips.
Format: numbered steps with sub-steps where needed.
```

20. Presentation Outline

```
Create a presentation outline for [topic].
Audience: [who will be watching]
Duration: [time limit]
Goal: [inform/persuade/train]
Include:
- Title slide concept
- [Number] content slides with key points and talking notes
- Data/evidence to include
- Conclusion and call to action
Format: slide-by-slide with bullet points and speaker notes.
```

Education and Learning

21. Concept Explanation

```
Explain [concept] as if I am a [beginner/intermediate/advanced learner].
Use [an analogy/a real-world example/step-by-step breakdown].
Then give me 3 questions to test my understanding.
```

22. Study Guide

```
Create a study guide for [subject/exam/topic].
Cover these topics:
- [Topic 1]
- [Topic 2]
- [Topic 3]
For each topic, include:
- Key concepts and definitions
- Important formulas or frameworks
- Common exam questions
- Memory aids or mnemonics
```

23. Practice Quiz

```
Create a [number]-question quiz on [topic].
Difficulty: [easy/medium/hard]
Question types: [multiple choice/short answer/true-false/mixed]
```

```
Include an answer key with explanations at the end.
Target level: [high school/undergraduate/graduate/professional]
```

24. Lesson Plan

```
Create a lesson plan for teaching [topic] to [audience/grade level].
Duration: [class length]
Learning objectives:
- Students will be able to [objective 1]
- Students will be able to [objective 2]
Include:
- Warm-up activity ([minutes])
- Direct instruction ([minutes])
- Guided practice ([minutes])
- Independent practice ([minutes])
- Assessment and wrap-up ([minutes])
Materials needed: [list any required materials]
```

25. Book Summary

```
Summarize the book "[title]" by [author].
Include:
- Main thesis/argument (2-3 sentences)
- Key ideas from each major section (bullet points)
- Notable quotes or concepts
- Strengths and weaknesses
- Who should read this book and why
Length: [500/1000/1500] words.
```

26. Research Paper Outline

```
Create a detailed outline for a research paper on [topic].
Thesis: [your thesis statement]
Required sections: introduction, literature review, [methodology if applicable],
 analysis, conclusion.
For each section, suggest:
- Key arguments or points
- Types of evidence to include
- Potential counterarguments to address
Academic level: [undergraduate/graduate]
Citation style: [APA/MLA/Chicago]
```

Creative and Personal

27. Short Story Premise

```
Generate [number] short story premises based on these parameters:
Genre: [genre]
Setting: [time period and location]
Themes: [list themes]
For each premise, include: a one-paragraph synopsis, the main character, and the
 central conflict.
```

28. Recipe Creation

```
Create a recipe for [dish or type of food].
Dietary restrictions: [any restrictions]
Skill level: [beginner/intermediate/advanced]
Prep time limit: [time]
Servings: [number]
Include: ingredient list with quantities, step-by-step instructions, and tips fo
r best results.
```

29. Travel Itinerary

```
Create a [number]-day travel itinerary for [destination].
Travel dates: [dates or season]
Budget: [budget level]
Interests: [list interests: history, food, nature, nightlife, etc.]
Include:
- Daily schedule with morning, afternoon, and evening activities
- Restaurant recommendations for each day
- Transportation tips between locations
- Estimated costs
- Insider tips
```

30. Gift Ideas

```
Suggest [number] gift ideas for [recipient description].
Occasion: [birthday/holiday/thank you/other]
Budget: [price range]
Their interests: [list interests]
They already have: [items to avoid duplicating]
For each suggestion, include: what it is, why it fits, and where to find it.
```

31. Workout Plan

```
Create a [number]-week workout plan for [goal: weight loss/muscle building/gener
al fitness/flexibility].
Experience level: [beginner/intermediate/advanced]
Available equipment: [list equipment or "no equipment"]
Time per session: [minutes]
Days per week: [number]
Include: warm-up, exercises with sets and reps, rest periods, and cool-down.
Note any modifications for different fitness levels.
```

32. Meal Plan

```
Create a [number]-day meal plan.
Dietary preferences: [vegetarian/vegan/keto/Mediterranean/no restrictions]
Calories per day: [target or "not tracking"]
Allergies or restrictions: [list any]
Cooking skill: [minimal/moderate/advanced]
Include: breakfast, lunch, dinner, and [number] snacks.
Add a consolidated grocery list at the end.
```

Technical and Development

33. Code Explanation

```
Explain the following code:

[paste code]

Cover:
- What this code does (overall purpose)
- How it works (line by line or section by section)
- Any potential issues or improvements
Audience: [beginner/intermediate/advanced] developer
```

34. Code Generation

```
Write [programming language] code that [description of what the code should do].
Requirements:
- [Requirement 1]
- [Requirement 2]
- [Requirement 3]
```

```
Include: comments explaining key sections, error handling, and example usage.
Follow [language-specific style guide or conventions].
```

35. Bug Fix

```
I have a bug in my [programming language] code. Here is the code:

[paste code]

Expected behavior: [what should happen]
Actual behavior: [what is happening]
Error message (if any): [paste error]

Identify the bug, explain why it occurs, and provide the corrected code.
```

36. Code Review

```
Review the following code for:
- Bugs or logical errors
- Performance issues
- Security vulnerabilities
- Code style and readability
- Best practices

[paste code]

Provide specific suggestions with explanations.
```

37. API Documentation

```
Write API documentation for the following endpoint:
Endpoint: [method] [URL]
Purpose: [what it does]
Parameters: [list parameters]
Authentication: [type]
Include: description, request example, response example (success and error), and
 usage notes.
Format: standard REST API documentation.
```

38. Database Query

```
Write a [SQL/NoSQL] query to [description of what data to retrieve or modify].
Database structure:
- Table/Collection: [name], fields: [list fields]
- Table/Collection: [name], fields: [list fields]
```

```
Requirements: [any filters, sorting, grouping, or joins needed]
Explain the query logic.
```

Data and Analysis

39. Data Interpretation

```
Analyze the following data and provide insights:

[paste data or describe the dataset]

Specifically:
- What are the key trends?
- Are there any anomalies or outliers?
- What conclusions can be drawn?
- What additional data would help deepen the analysis?
Present findings in [bullet points/narrative/executive summary] format.
```

40. Survey Questions

```
Create a [number]-question survey about [topic].
Purpose: [what you want to learn]
Target respondents: [describe audience]
Include a mix of:
- Multiple choice questions
- Likert scale questions (strongly agree to strongly disagree)
- Open-ended questions
Keep questions neutral and unbiased.
Estimated completion time: [minutes].
```

41. Financial Analysis

```
Help me analyze the following financial data:

[paste data or describe scenario]

Calculate and explain:
- [Metric 1: e.g., profit margin]
- [Metric 2: e.g., year-over-year growth]
- [Metric 3: e.g., break-even point]
Present findings in a format suitable for [audience: management/investors/team].
Note: verify all calculations independently.
```

42. Report Summary

```
Summarize the following report/document:

[paste text or describe document]

Provide:
- Executive summary (3-5 sentences)
- Key findings (bullet points)
- Data highlights
- Recommendations or conclusions
- Questions that the report leaves unanswered
Length: [word count]
```

Communication and Interpersonal

43. Difficult Conversation Script

```
Help me prepare for a difficult conversation about [topic].
The situation: [describe the context]
My goal: [what outcome I want]
The other person's likely perspective: [what they might think or feel]

Provide:
- Opening statement
- Key points to make
- How to respond to likely pushback
- How to find common ground
- Closing / next steps
Tone: [firm but respectful/empathetic/direct]
```

44. Apology Message

```
Help me write an apology to [recipient] for [what happened].
Context: [additional details]
What I want to communicate:
- Acknowledgment of what went wrong
- Acceptance of responsibility
- What I plan to do differently
Tone: [sincere/professional/personal]
Length: [brief/detailed]
```

45. Negotiation Preparation

```
Help me prepare to negotiate [what you are negotiating].
My position: [what I want]
Their likely position: [what they want]
My leverage: [strengths in my position]
Their leverage: [strengths in their position]

Provide:
- Opening position
- Target outcome
- Walk-away point
- Key arguments to make
- Likely counterarguments and responses
- Potential compromises
```

46. Feedback Delivery

```
Help me give constructive feedback to [person/role] about [behavior or performan
ce issue].
Specific examples: [describe 1-2 examples]
Impact of the behavior: [how it affects the team/work/outcomes]
Desired change: [what I want to see instead]

Write the feedback using the SBI framework (Situation, Behavior, Impact).
Tone: supportive and growth-oriented.
```

Planning and Strategy

47. Goal Setting

```
Help me set SMART goals for [area: career/fitness/learning/financial/personal].
Current situation: [where I am now]
Where I want to be: [desired outcome]
Timeline: [when I want to achieve this]

Create [number] goals that are Specific, Measurable, Achievable, Relevant, and T
ime-bound.
For each goal, include 2-3 action steps.
```

48. Decision Framework

```
Help me decide between [Option A] and [Option B] (and [Option C] if applicable).
Context: [why this decision matters]
My priorities:
1. [Priority 1]
2. [Priority 2]
3. [Priority 3]

Analyze each option against my priorities.
Identify risks and unknowns for each option.
Suggest what additional information would help me decide.
Recommend the best option with reasoning.
```

49. Project Timeline

```
Create a project timeline for [project name].
Start date: [date]
Target completion: [date]
Major phases:
- [Phase 1]: [brief description]
- [Phase 2]: [brief description]
- [Phase 3]: [brief description]
Dependencies: [any tasks that must complete before others can start]
Format: Gantt-style text representation or detailed timeline with milestones.
```

50. Risk Assessment

```
Identify and assess risks for [project/decision/initiative].
Context: [describe the situation]

For each risk, provide:
- Description of the risk
- Likelihood (high/medium/low)
- Impact (high/medium/low)
- Mitigation strategy
- Contingency plan

Organize from highest to lowest priority.
```

Marketing and Sales

51. Marketing Strategy

```
Create a marketing strategy outline for [product/service/company].
Target audience: [describe]
Budget: [range or "limited"/"moderate"/"substantial"]
Timeline: [duration]
Goals: [awareness/leads/sales/retention]

Include:
- Target audience personas
- Key messaging and value propositions
- Recommended channels
- Content calendar outline
- KPIs to track
```

52. Ad Copy

```
Write [number] variations of ad copy for [product/service].
Platform: [Google Ads/Facebook/Instagram/LinkedIn]
Target audience: [describe]
Goal: [clicks/conversions/awareness]
Include:
- Headline (within platform character limits)
- Body text
- Call to action
Tone: [urgent/friendly/professional/playful]
```

53. Customer Persona

```
Create a detailed customer persona for [product/service].
Industry: [industry]
Include:
- Name, age, job title, income
- Goals and motivations
- Pain points and frustrations
- How they discover products like ours
- Decision-making process
- Objections they might have
- Preferred communication channels
```

54. Sales Email Sequence

```
Create a [number]-email sales sequence for [product/service].
Target: [describe the ideal customer]
Trigger: [what initiates the sequence: sign-up, download, inquiry]

For each email, include:
- Subject line
- Body (150-250 words)
- Call to action
- Timing (days after trigger)
- Goal of this specific email in the sequence
```

Editing and Refinement

55. Proofread and Edit

```
Proofread and edit the following text for:
- Grammar and punctuation errors
- Clarity and readability
- Tone consistency
- Redundancy
- Word choice

[paste text]

Provide the corrected version and a summary of changes made.
```

56. Tone Adjustment

```
Rewrite the following text in a [more formal/more casual/more empathetic/more au
thoritative/more concise] tone:

[paste text]

Preserve the original meaning and key information.
```

57. Simplification

```
Rewrite the following text at a [6th grade/8th grade/10th grade/general adult] r
eading level:
```

```
[paste text]

Simplify vocabulary and sentence structure while preserving accuracy.
Explain any technical terms that cannot be simplified.
```

58. Translation with Context

```
Translate the following text from [source language] to [target language]:

[paste text]

Maintain the original tone and intent.
Where direct translation would lose meaning, adapt for the target culture.
Flag any idioms or phrases where the translation involved significant interpreta
tion.
```

Image and Visual

59. Image Generation

```
Generate an image of [detailed description].
Style: [photograph/illustration/watercolor/digital art/3D render]
Mood: [bright/moody/professional/whimsical]
Color palette: [describe colors]
Composition: [close-up/wide shot/aerial view/etc.]
Do not include any text in the image.
```

60. Image Analysis

```
Analyze this image and tell me:
- What is depicted (describe in detail)
- The composition and visual elements
- The mood or tone
- Any text visible in the image
- [Any specific question about the image]

[upload image]
```

61. Design Brief

```
Create a design brief for [project type: logo/website/brochure/social media grap
hics].
Brand: [brand name]
```

```
Brand values: [list 3-5 values]
Target audience: [describe]
Competitors: [list 2-3 competitors for reference]
Include: style direction, color suggestions, typography recommendations, mood/in
spiration notes, and specific deliverables needed.
```

Personal Development

62. Habit Building Plan

```
Help me build a habit of [desired habit].
Current routine: [describe your typical day]
Obstacles I anticipate: [list barriers]
Motivation: [why this matters to me]

Create a 30-day plan using habit stacking and progressive difficulty.
Include: daily actions, weekly milestones, and strategies for handling setbacks.
```

63. Skills Gap Analysis

```
I want to [career goal or skill objective].
My current skills: [list current skills and proficiency levels]
The target role/skill set requires: [list required skills]

Identify:
- Skills I already have that transfer
- Skills I need to develop
- Recommended learning resources for each gap
- Suggested timeline for development
- Quick wins I can achieve in the first 30 days
```

64. Journal Prompt Generator

```
Generate [number] reflective journal prompts focused on [theme: gratitude/growth
/relationships/career/creativity/self-awareness].
Mix of:
- Quick prompts (can answer in 2-3 sentences)
- Deep prompts (require 10-15 minutes of reflection)
- Action-oriented prompts (lead to a concrete next step)
```

Home and Practical

65. Home Repair Guidance

```
How do I [describe the repair or project]?
Current situation: [describe what is happening]
My skill level: [beginner/some experience/experienced]
Tools I have: [list available tools]

Provide:
- Step-by-step instructions
- Materials needed (with quantities)
- Safety precautions
- When to call a professional instead
- Estimated time and difficulty
```

66. Budget Planning

```
Help me create a [monthly/annual] budget.
Income: [amount and sources]
Fixed expenses:
- [Expense 1]: [amount]
- [Expense 2]: [amount]
Financial goals: [list goals]

Create a budget using the [50/30/20 / zero-based / envelope] method.
Identify areas where I might reduce spending.
Note: this is for planning purposes only, not financial advice.
```

67. Event Planning Checklist

```
Create a planning checklist for [event type: wedding/birthday party/corporate ev
ent/graduation].
Date: [date]
Guest count: [number]
Budget: [amount]
Venue: [type or specific venue]

Include:
- Timeline of tasks (12 months out to day-of)
- Budget breakdown by category
- Vendor checklist
- Day-of schedule
- Contingency plans
```

68. Moving Checklist

```
Create a comprehensive moving checklist for moving from [current location type]
to [new location type].
Move date: [date]
Distance: [local/long-distance/international]
Special considerations: [pets/children/home office/etc.]

Organize by timeline:
- 8 weeks before
- 4 weeks before
- 2 weeks before
- 1 week before
- Moving day
- First week in new home
```

Specialized Templates

69. Job Interview Preparation

```
Help me prepare for an interview for [job title] at [company].
Job description highlights: [paste key requirements]
My relevant experience: [brief summary]

Provide:
- 10 likely interview questions with suggested answers
- 5 questions I should ask the interviewer
- Key talking points about my experience
- Common pitfalls to avoid for this type of role
- Research I should do about the company
```

70. Legal Document Summary

```
Summarize the following legal document in plain language:

[paste document text]

Explain:
- What this document is and its purpose
- Key obligations for each party
- Important dates or deadlines
- Potential risks or concerns
```

```
- Terms that are unusual or worth questioning

Note: this is for understanding only, not legal advice. Consult an attorney for
legal decisions.
```

71. Product Launch Plan

```
Create a product launch plan for [product name].
Launch date: [date]
Product description: [brief description]
Target market: [describe]
Budget: [range]

Include:
- Pre-launch activities (8 weeks out)
- Launch week activities
- Post-launch follow-up (4 weeks after)
- Marketing channels and tactics
- Success metrics and KPIs
- Potential risks and contingencies
```

72. Customer Service Response

```
Write a customer service response to the following complaint:

[describe or paste the complaint]

Tone: [empathetic/professional/solution-focused]
Company policy on this issue: [describe relevant policy]
What I can offer: [list available remedies]

Include: acknowledgment of the issue, apology where appropriate, proposed soluti
on, and next steps.
```

73. Contract Summary and Questions

```
Review this contract and identify:

[paste contract text or key sections]

- Key terms and obligations
- Payment terms and conditions
- Termination clauses
- Liability and indemnification
- Any unusual or potentially problematic clauses
```

- Questions I should ask before signing

Note: this is informational only. Consult a lawyer before signing contracts.

74. Onboarding Plan

```
Create an onboarding plan for a new [job title] joining our [team/department].
Start date: [date]
Team size: [number]
Key tools they will use: [list tools]
Their main responsibilities: [list responsibilities]

Include:
- Day 1 schedule
- Week 1 goals and activities
- 30-day milestones
- 60-day milestones
- 90-day evaluation criteria
- Key people to meet and their roles
```

75. Competitive Analysis

```
Create a competitive analysis of [your company/product] vs. [competitor 1] and
[competitor 2].
Industry: [industry]
Key comparison areas:
- [Area 1: e.g., pricing]
- [Area 2: e.g., features]
- [Area 3: e.g., market position]
- [Area 4: e.g., customer satisfaction]

Format: comparison table with narrative analysis.
Use Google Search for current information.
Identify our competitive advantages and vulnerabilities.
```

76. Content Calendar

```
Create a [1-month/3-month] content calendar for [brand/business/personal brand].
Platforms: [list platforms]
Posting frequency: [times per week per platform]
Content pillars:
- [Pillar 1: e.g., educational]
- [Pillar 2: e.g., behind the scenes]
- [Pillar 3: e.g., promotional]
- [Pillar 4: e.g., user-generated/community]
```

```
Format: weekly grid with post type, platform, topic, and caption notes.
Include key dates and holidays relevant to [industry].
```

77. Troubleshooting Guide

```
Create a troubleshooting guide for [product/system/process].
Common issues users face:
- [Issue 1]
- [Issue 2]
- [Issue 3]

For each issue, provide:
- Symptoms
- Likely cause
- Step-by-step resolution
- When to escalate
Format: searchable FAQ style.
```

Tips for Using These Templates

1. **Customize the placeholders.** The more specific your inputs, the better Gemini's output. Do not leave placeholders as "[describe]" — fill them in with real details.
2. **Iterate.** Use these templates as starting points. After Gemini responds, refine with follow-up prompts: "Make it shorter," "Add more detail to section 2," "Change the tone to be more formal."
3. **Combine templates.** You can merge elements from multiple templates. Need a blog post with a comparison analysis? Combine templates 2 and 10.
4. **Save your customized versions.** When you find a template that works well for your recurring needs, save your customized version with your specific defaults filled in. Create a Gem (Chapter 14) for templates you use frequently.
5. **Adjust the length and depth.** Add "Length: [word count]" or "Depth: [overview/detailed/comprehensive]" to any template to control the output size.

Appendix C: Troubleshooting Common Issues

This appendix covers the problems Gemini users hit most often, along with practical fixes. If something is not working the way you expect, start here.

Gemini Will Not Respond or Is Very Slow

Symptoms: Gemini shows a loading indicator indefinitely, responds with an error message, or takes much longer than usual to generate a response.

Likely causes and fixes:

- **Server load.** Gemini's servers can hit high demand, especially after major announcements or during peak hours. Wait a few minutes and try again.
- **Internet connection.** Check your connection by loading another website. An unstable connection can cause Gemini to time out mid-response.
- **Browser issues.** Clear your cache and cookies, or try a different browser. Gemini works best in Chrome but supports other modern browsers.
- **VPN or proxy interference.** Some VPNs and corporate proxies interfere with Gemini. Disable your VPN temporarily to test.
- **Long or complex prompts.** Extremely long prompts or heavy processing (like analyzing a large uploaded file) take longer. This is normal.
- **Regional availability.** Gemini is not available in every country. Traveling or using a VPN that routes through an unsupported region can cause access issues.

If the problem persists: Check Google's service status at status.google.com. If Gemini is in an outage, the issue is on Google's end and you have to wait.

"I'm Not Able to Help with That" or Content Refusals

Symptoms: Gemini declines to answer your question or generate content, citing safety guidelines.

Why this happens: Gemini has safety filters that block certain content categories: explicit material, dangerous instructions, content that could facilitate harm, and content about real individuals in certain contexts.

What to do:

- **Rephrase your request.** Legitimate requests sometimes trip overly broad filters. Rephrase to make your intent clearer. Instead of "How do I hack into..." try "How do I recover access to my own account if I am locked out of..."
- **Provide context about your purpose.** "I am a teacher creating educational materials about..." or "I am a fiction writer working on a scene that involves..." helps Gemini recognize that your request is legitimate.
- **Try a different angle.** If Gemini will not discuss a topic directly, it may discuss it from an educational, historical, or analytical perspective.
- **Accept the limitation.** Some categories are firm restrictions no rephrasing will overcome. Gemini will not generate explicit content, detailed instructions for weapons or drugs, or content designed to harass specific individuals.
- **Check for temporary restrictions.** During sensitive events (elections, natural disasters), Google sometimes restricts certain topics for a period.

Image Generation Fails or Produces Unexpected Results

Symptoms: Gemini refuses to generate an image, generates something very different from what you described, or produces images with obvious errors.

Common issues and solutions:

- **Request declined.** Gemini will not generate realistic images of identifiable public figures, violent content, explicit content, or certain other categories. If your request involves a real person, try an illustration or cartoon style, or describe the type of person without naming anyone.

- **Results do not match description.** Be more specific. Instead of "a dog in a park," try "a golden retriever puppy sitting on green grass in a sunlit park, photorealistic style, close-up shot." More detail produces better results.
- **Text in images is garbled.** AI image models struggle with rendering text. If you need text in an image, generate the image without text and add it afterward in an image editor.
- **Hands and fingers look wrong.** A known limitation of current image generation. If hands matter, generate multiple versions and pick the best, or specify "hands not visible" in your prompt.
- **Style is inconsistent.** Name the style you want: "digital illustration," "oil painting," "watercolor," "3D render," "photorealistic photograph." Without a style, Gemini will pick one.
- **Image generation is unavailable.** Google occasionally pauses or restricts image generation while addressing issues. Check Google's announcement channels for updates.

Gemini Gives Incorrect or Outdated Information

Symptoms: Gemini provides facts, statistics, or instructions that you know (or discover) are wrong.

What to do:

- **Use the Double-check feature.** Click "Double-check with Google" on any response. Gemini highlights claims and shows you whether Google Search supports them.
- **Enable Google Search grounding.** For factual questions, ask Gemini to search the web rather than answer from training. Phrases like "search for the latest..." or "look this up..." trigger search-grounded responses.
- **Verify independently.** For important decisions, verify Gemini's claims against authoritative sources. See Chapter 25 for a framework on when to trust and when to verify.

- **Report the error.** Use the thumbs-down button on incorrect responses and add specific feedback. This helps Google improve the model.
- **Provide the correction.** Tell Gemini "That is incorrect. The actual answer is..." and it will incorporate the correction into the ongoing conversation.

Conversations Disappear or Cannot Be Found

Symptoms: You cannot find a previous conversation, or your conversation history appears empty.

Possible causes:

- **Gemini Apps Activity is turned off.** With Gemini Apps Activity disabled in your Google Account, conversations are not saved to history. You will only see the current session.
- **Auto-delete is configured.** If you set auto-delete to 3 months, conversations older than that are removed automatically.
- **You manually deleted conversations.** Deleted conversations cannot be recovered.
- **You are signed into a different Google account.** Conversations are tied to the account you used. Make sure you are signed into the right one.
- **Browser storage issues.** Clear your cache and reload Gemini. Cached data sometimes prevents the sidebar from loading properly.

Prevention: If conversation history matters to you, keep Gemini Apps Activity on and set the auto-delete period to a duration that works for your needs.

File Uploads Fail

Symptoms: Gemini refuses to accept a file, shows an upload error, or does not seem to process the uploaded file.

Troubleshooting steps:

- **Check file size.** There are limits on upload size. If your file is very large, compress it or split it into smaller parts.
- **Check file format.** Gemini supports common formats (JPEG, PNG, PDF, TXT, and many more) but not every format. Convert to a widely supported one.
- **Try a different browser.** Upload issues are sometimes browser-specific. Chrome is typically most reliable.
- **Check your Gemini plan.** Some upload capabilities (multiple files, very large files) require Google AI Pro (or above). Verify that your plan supports what you are trying to do.
- **Re-upload.** Uploads sometimes fail due to a network hiccup. Try the same file again.
- **Paste the text instead.** If a file refuses to upload, copy and paste the text content directly into the conversation.

Extensions Are Not Working

Symptoms: Gemini does not pull data from Google Extensions (Flights, Maps, YouTube, Workspace) when you expect it to.

Troubleshooting:

- **Check that Extensions are enabled.** Go to Settings > Extensions in Gemini and verify the ones you want are toggled on.
- **Be explicit.** Instead of "find flights to Paris," try "use Google Flights to find flights from New York to Paris in June 2026." Naming the Extension helps.
- **Grant the right permissions.** Some Extensions need access to your Google account data (Gmail, Drive). Check that you have granted them.
- **Workspace Extensions require Workspace.** Gemini Extensions for Gmail, Docs, Drive, and other Workspace apps require an active Google Workspace account with Gemini enabled by your administrator.
- **Some Extensions are regional.** Not all Extensions are available in every region.

Gemini Forgets Earlier Context in a Conversation

Symptoms: Gemini seems to forget instructions or context you provided earlier in the same conversation.

Why this happens: Gemini has a very large context window (over 1 million tokens for Gemini 3 Pro), but extremely long conversations can deprioritize context. Details from early in the conversation may get less attention as it grows.

What to do:

- **Restate important context.** If Gemini has forgotten a key instruction, restate it: "Remember, I asked you to write in a formal academic tone."
- **Start a new conversation for new topics.** If you are switching to an unrelated topic, start fresh rather than continuing.
- **Use Gems for recurring instructions.** If you keep giving Gemini the same instructions (tone, format, persona), create a Gem (Chapter 14) that includes them by default.
- **Put critical instructions first.** Framing instructions are most effective at the start of your prompt, not buried in the middle or at the end.

Gemini Responses Are Too Long, Too Short, or Poorly Formatted

Symptoms: Gemini gives you a five-paragraph essay when you wanted a one-sentence answer, or a brief reply when you wanted a detailed analysis.

How to fix it:

- **Specify length.** Add "in 2–3 sentences," "in approximately 500 words," "as a brief bullet list," or "in a detailed 1,000-word analysis."
- **Specify format.** Ask for "a numbered list," "a table with columns for X, Y, and Z," "a single paragraph," or whatever format you need.

- **Use the Modify buttons.** After a response, use "Shorter," "Longer," or "Simpler" to adjust in one click.
- **Give an example.** If you want a specific format, show what you are looking for.

Cannot Access Google AI Pro Features

Symptoms: Features like Deep Think, Gems, Deep Research, or image generation are not available to you.

Check these things:

- **Verify your subscription.** Premium features require a Google AI Pro subscription (or AI Ultra, or a Workspace plan with Gemini included). Check your status at one.google.com.
- **Check model selection.** Some features only run on specific models. Make sure you have the right one selected (e.g., Gemini 3 Pro for Deep Think).
- **Age and account restrictions.** Some features are unavailable on teen accounts or accounts managed by organizations.
- **Regional availability.** Not every feature launches worldwide at once. A feature available in the United States may not be in your region yet.
- **Feature rollout timing.** Google rolls out new features gradually. A just-announced feature may not have reached your account yet.

Gemini Gives Different Answers to the Same Question

Symptoms: You ask the same question twice and get noticeably different responses.

Why this is normal: Gemini's responses have built-in randomness (called "temperature"). This is by design — it keeps Gemini from sounding robotic and allows varied, creative responses. The trade-off is that identical input does not always produce identical output.

What to do if you need consistency:

- **Save good responses immediately.** If Gemini gives you something you like, copy or export it right away.
- **Be more specific.** The more constrained your prompt, the less room for variation. Specific requirements, formats, and constraints narrow the range of outputs.
- **Use Gems.** A Gem with specific instructions helps maintain consistency across conversations.
- **Check alternative drafts.** Gemini often produces multiple drafts per response. Check them all before regenerating.

Account or Sign-In Problems

Symptoms: You cannot sign into Gemini, get authentication errors, or are redirected unexpectedly.

Steps to resolve:

1. Make sure you are signed into a Google account at accounts.google.com
2. Ensure your Google account is in good standing (not suspended or restricted)
3. Clear your browser cookies for google.com and gemini.google.com
4. Try signing in through an incognito/private browser window
5. Disable browser extensions that might interfere (ad blockers, privacy extensions)
6. If you have multiple Google accounts, ensure you are using the correct one
7. Check that Gemini is available in your country

For Workspace users: Contact your IT administrator. They may need to enable Gemini for your account or org unit.

When to Contact Google Support

If none of the above solutions resolve your issue:

- Visit the Google Gemini Help Center
- Post in the Google Gemini community forums
- For Workspace customers, use your organization's Google Workspace support channel
- For billing issues related to Google AI Pro, AI Plus, or AI Ultra, contact Google One support

When reporting an issue, include what you were trying to do, what happened instead, your browser and device, and any error messages. Screenshots help.

Appendix D: Glossary of AI Terms

This glossary defines the key terms you will encounter when using Gemini and reading about AI more broadly. Terms are listed alphabetically.

AI (Artificial Intelligence) The broad field of computer science focused on creating systems that can perform tasks typically requiring human intelligence, such as understanding language, recognizing images, making decisions, and generating content.

AI Hallucination When an AI model generates information that is factually incorrect, fabricated, or unsupported by its training data, despite presenting it with apparent confidence. See Chapter 25 for a detailed discussion.

AI Safety The research and practice of ensuring AI systems behave in ways that are beneficial and do not cause unintended harm. Includes alignment, robustness, and content filtering.

Alignment The process of ensuring an AI model's behavior matches the intentions and values of its designers and users. A well-aligned model follows instructions accurately, avoids harmful outputs, and behaves predictably.

API (Application Programming Interface) A set of protocols and tools that allow software applications to communicate with each other. The Gemini API lets developers integrate Gemini's capabilities into their own applications.

Audio Overviews (NotebookLM) A NotebookLM feature that generates podcast-style audio discussions about your uploaded documents. Two AI-generated hosts discuss and explain the content of your sources in a conversational format.

Bard Google's original conversational AI product, launched in March 2023. Bard was rebranded as Gemini in February 2024 when it was upgraded to run on the Gemini family of models.

Canvas A collaborative content creation feature in Gemini that provides a side-by-side workspace for writing and editing documents or code. Similar in concept to ChatGPT's Canvas and Claude's Artifacts.

Chain of Thought A prompting technique where the AI is asked to show its reasoning step by step rather than jumping directly to an answer. This often improves accuracy on complex problems.

Chatbot A software application designed to simulate conversation with human users. Gemini is a chatbot, though its capabilities extend well beyond simple scripted responses.

Context Window The maximum amount of text (measured in tokens) that an AI model can process in a single conversation. Gemini 3 Pro has a context window of over 1 million tokens, meaning it can process extremely long documents, codebases, or conversation histories.

Deep Research A Google AI Pro feature that performs multi-step web research on your behalf. Gemini creates a research plan, searches multiple sources, synthesizes findings, and produces a comprehensive report with citations.

Deep Think (Extended Reasoning) A mode available in Gemini 3 Pro that allows the model to spend more time reasoning through complex problems before producing a response. Particularly useful for math, logic, coding, and analysis tasks. A dedicated Gemini 3 Deep Think mode (Feb 2026) extends this further for the hardest problems.

Diffusion Model A type of generative AI model used for image generation. The model learns to create images by gradually removing noise from random patterns. The Imagen 4 family, which powers Gemini's image generation, is built on diffusion-style techniques.

Embedding A numerical representation of text, images, or other data in a high-dimensional space, where similar items are positioned close together. Embeddings are used in search, recommendation systems, and AI applications.

Extensions Connections that allow Gemini to interact with Google services and third-party tools in real time. Examples include Google Flights, Google Maps, YouTube, and Google Workspace extensions.

Few-Shot Prompting A technique where you provide several examples of the desired input-output pattern in your prompt, helping the AI understand exactly what you want. Compare with zero-shot prompting (no examples) and one-shot prompting (one example).

Fine-Tuning The process of further training an AI model on a specific dataset to improve its performance on particular tasks. Fine-tuning adapts a general-purpose model for specialized use cases.

Foundation Model A large AI model trained on broad data that can be adapted for many different tasks. Gemini's models are foundation models — they are not built for a single purpose but can handle writing, analysis, coding, image understanding, and more.

Gemini Google's family of multimodal AI models and the consumer product built on them. "Gemini" refers to both the models (Gemini 3 Pro, Gemini 3 Flash, Gemini 3.1 Flash-Lite, etc.) and the conversational interface at gemini.google.com.

Gemini Apps Activity A Google Account setting that controls whether your conversations with Gemini are saved to your account history and used to improve Gemini models. See Chapter 26.

Gemini Live A real-time voice conversation feature available in the Gemini mobile app for Google AI Pro subscribers (and above). Gemini Live enables natural, back-and-forth spoken conversations with Gemini, supporting interruptions and fluid dialogue. Ideal for hands-free brainstorming, language practice, and conversational tasks. See Chapter 12 for details.

Gems Custom Gemini assistants that you create with specific instructions, personas, and behaviors. Similar to ChatGPT's Custom GPTs. Gems maintain their configured personality and instructions across conversations.

Generative AI (GenAI) AI systems that can create new content — text, images, audio, video, code — rather than simply analyzing or classifying existing content. Gemini is a generative AI system.

Google AI Plus The entry-level paid consumer tier of Gemini ($7.99–$9.99/month depending on region, as of May 2026). Sits below Google AI Pro and gives users higher rate limits, expanded Deep Research, and limited Pro-class model access compared to the Free tier.

Google AI Pro The mainstream paid consumer tier of Gemini ($19.99/month as of May 2026), the successor to "Gemini Advanced" / "Google One AI Premium" after Google's May 2025 rename. Provides access to the flagship model, larger context windows, Deep Think, Deep Research, Gems, Workspace integration, 2 TB of Google One storage, and other premium features. Sits between Google AI Plus (entry-level) and Google AI Ultra (top tier) in the consumer ladder.

Google AI Studio A free, web-based tool for developers to experiment with and prototype using Google's Gemini models. Provides an interface for testing prompts, adjusting parameters, and generating API keys.

Google AI Ultra The top-tier paid consumer tier of Gemini ($249.99/month as of May 2026). Provides the highest usage limits across Gemini, image and video generation, and Deep Research, plus priority access to new and experimental models.

Google DeepMind The AI research lab within Google, formed by merging Google Brain and DeepMind in April 2023. Google DeepMind develops the Gemini models and other advanced AI research.

Google One AI Premium The previous name of the subscription plan that bundled Gemini Advanced with 2 TB of Google One storage. Renamed to Google AI Pro at Google I/O 2025; same $19.99/month price.

Grounding The process of connecting an AI model's responses to verifiable external sources, such as Google Search results or specific documents. Grounding reduces hallucination by anchoring responses to real data.

Guardrails Safety mechanisms built into AI systems to prevent harmful, inappropriate, or undesired outputs. Gemini's guardrails include content filters, safety classifiers, and policy enforcement.

Imagen Google's image generation model family. The Imagen 4 family (launched May 20, 2025) powers Gemini's image generation as of May 2026, with three variants: Imagen 4 (standard), Imagen 4 Fast (lower latency), and Imagen 4 Ultra (highest quality). Outputs include up to 2K resolution and a SynthID watermark.

Inference The process of an AI model generating a response to an input. When you send a prompt to Gemini and receive a response, the response generation is the "inference" step.

Knowledge Cutoff The date beyond which an AI model has no training data. Events, publications, and changes that occurred after the knowledge cutoff are not part of the model's "native" knowledge. Google Search grounding helps bridge this gap.

Large Language Model (LLM) An AI model trained on vast amounts of text data to understand and generate human language. Gemini's text capabilities are powered by a large language model, though Gemini is technically a multimodal model that handles more than just language.

Latency The time delay between sending a prompt and receiving a response. Lower latency means faster responses. Gemini 3 Flash is designed for lower latency than Gemini 3 Pro, and Gemini 3.1 Flash-Lite goes lower still.

Multimodal The ability to process and generate multiple types of data — text, images, audio, video, and code — within a single model. Gemini is natively multimodal, meaning it was designed from the ground up to handle different modalities, not retrofitted.

Natural Language Processing (NLP) The branch of AI focused on enabling computers to understand, interpret, and generate human language. NLP underpins Gemini's ability to understand your prompts and produce natural-sounding responses.

NotebookLM A Google AI product designed for working with your own documents. You upload sources (PDFs, Google Docs, websites, YouTube videos), and NotebookLM lets you ask questions about them, generate summaries, and create Audio Overviews.

Parameter In AI, a parameter is a value within the model that is learned during training. The number of parameters is often used as a rough indicator of model capability. Larger models generally have more parameters.

Prompt The text, image, or other input you provide to Gemini to elicit a response. The quality of your prompt significantly affects the quality of Gemini's output.

Prompt Engineering The practice of crafting prompts to achieve specific, high-quality outputs from AI models. Covered extensively in Chapters 18–20.

RAG (Retrieval-Augmented Generation) A technique where an AI model retrieves relevant information from external sources before generating a response. Gemini's Google Search grounding is a form of RAG.

Responsible AI Google's framework of principles and practices for developing and deploying AI in ways that are safe, fair, and beneficial. Includes fairness, safety, privacy, accountability, and transparency.

Safety Filters Automated systems that review AI inputs and outputs for harmful content and block or modify them when they violate policies.

SynthID Google DeepMind's technology for watermarking AI-generated content. SynthID embeds an invisible, machine-detectable watermark in images (and potentially other media) generated by Google's AI tools, including Gemini's image generation.

System Prompt / System Instructions Instructions provided to an AI model that define its behavior, persona, or constraints for a conversation. In Gemini, Gems use system instructions to customize behavior.

Temperature A parameter that controls the randomness of an AI model's output. Lower temperature produces more predictable, conservative responses. Higher temperature produces more varied, creative responses. In the Gemini API, you can adjust temperature; in the consumer interface, it is set automatically.

Token The basic unit of text that AI models process. A token is roughly equivalent to three-quarters of a word in English. "Artificial intelligence" is two words but might be three tokens. Context windows and pricing are typically measured in tokens.

Transformer The neural network architecture that underlies most modern large language models, including Gemini. Introduced in a 2017 Google research paper ("Attention Is All You Need"), the Transformer architecture enables models to process relationships between words across long sequences of text.

Vertex AI Google Cloud's machine learning platform, which provides enterprise access to Gemini models along with tools for training, deploying, and managing AI applications. Vertex AI is for developers and organizations, not consumer use.

Zero-Shot Prompting Asking an AI model to perform a task without providing any examples — relying solely on the model's training to understand what is being asked. Most everyday Gemini prompts are zero-shot.

Appendix E: What's New in 2025–2026

AI moves fast. This appendix chronicles the major developments in the Gemini ecosystem from the Bard-to-Gemini rebrand through May 2026 — the timeline of how the product you are using today came to be.

The Bard-to-Gemini Rebrand (February 2024)

On February 8, 2024, Google renamed Bard to Gemini. This was not just cosmetic. The rebrand coincided with upgrading the underlying model from Google's older PaLM architecture to the new Gemini model family. The consumer product at bard.google.com moved to gemini.google.com, and Google began positioning Gemini as its flagship AI product across the ecosystem.

At the same time, Google launched a dedicated Gemini mobile app for Android and integrated Gemini into the Google app on iOS. The rebrand signaled that Google was unifying its AI strategy under a single name — moving past the perception that Bard was a "me too" ChatGPT competitor and toward a differentiated, Google-integrated assistant.

Gemini 1.5 Pro and the Million-Token Context Window (February 2024)

Alongside the rebrand, Google announced Gemini 1.5 Pro with a context window of up to 1 million tokens — far beyond any competing model at the time. Not just a numbers game: a million tokens meant you could upload entire books, large codebases, or hours of video and have Gemini process them in a single conversation.

Gemini 1.5 Pro also introduced a Mixture of Experts (MoE) architecture, routing different parts of a query to specialized sub-networks. The result was faster and cheaper to run than a dense model of comparable capability.

The practical impact was immediate: Gemini could handle tasks that required large amounts of context, from summarizing lengthy research papers to analyzing complex multi-file code projects.

Gemini 1.5 Flash (May 2024)

Google introduced Gemini 1.5 Flash as a lighter, faster model for everyday tasks where speed and cost mattered more than maximum capability. Flash shared the architecture of 1.5 Pro but was tuned for lower latency and higher throughput.

Flash became the default for many Gemini interactions, reserving Pro for the work that demanded it. This two-tier approach — a fast everyday model and a powerful model for complex work — became a core part of Google's Gemini strategy.

Gems: Custom Gemini Assistants (Mid-2024)

In mid-2024, Google launched Gems — custom Gemini assistants you create with specific instructions, personality traits, and behaviors. Gems are Gemini's answer to ChatGPT's Custom GPTs. You define what the Gem should do, how it should respond, and what role it should play, and it carries those traits across conversations.

Gems made Gemini significantly more useful for recurring tasks. Instead of re-explaining your preferences every new conversation, you could build a Gem that already understood your context. A writing Gem matching your tone, a coding Gem following your team's conventions, a tutoring Gem set at the right level — one-time setup instead of per-conversation overhead.

Imagen 3 and Native Image Generation (Mid-2024)

Google upgraded Gemini's image generation to Imagen 3, a more capable model that produced higher-quality, more photorealistic images with better prompt adherence. Imagen 3 improved on its predecessors in several ways:

- Better understanding of complex, multi-element prompts
- More photorealistic output when photorealism was requested
- Improved text rendering within images (though still imperfect)

- Better handling of diverse representation without the over-correction issues that had plagued earlier versions
- SynthID watermarking embedded in every generated image

Image generation became native to the conversation — you could ask for images mid-dialogue instead of switching to a separate tool.

Imagen 4 (May 20, 2025)

Google launched the Imagen 4 family, a substantial step up from Imagen 3. Imagen 4 ships in three variants:

- **Imagen 4** — the standard model
- **Imagen 4 Fast** — a low-latency variant for rapid iteration
- **Imagen 4 Ultra** — a higher-quality variant for prompts where every detail matters

Imagen 4 produces images at up to 2K resolution with substantially improved text rendering, sharper detail, and faster generation. It became the default for image generation in Gemini and across Google Workspace apps.

The Subscription Rename: Google AI Pro and Friends (May 2025 onward)

At Google I/O 2025, Google reorganized its consumer AI subscriptions. "Gemini Advanced" / "Google One AI Premium" was renamed to **Google AI Pro** at the same $19.99/month price. Google added a new flagship tier above it, **Google AI Ultra** at $249.99/month, for power users who push AI tools hard. In the months that followed, Google introduced a third consumer tier below Pro: **Google AI Plus** ($7.99–$9.99/month depending on region) for users who wanted more than the Free tier without committing to Pro pricing. Workspace plans (Business Starter/Standard/Plus, Enterprise) continued to bundle Gemini for organizational customers.

NotebookLM Audio Overviews (Late 2024)

NotebookLM, Google's document-based AI research tool, introduced Audio Overviews — AI-generated podcast-style discussions about your uploaded sources. Upload documents, click a button, and NotebookLM produces a multi-minute audio conversation between two AI hosts who discuss, explain, and debate the content.

Audio Overviews went viral. The quality of the discussions surprised users, and the feature became one of Google's most talked-about AI demos. It showed what was possible when AI generation moved beyond text and images into synthesized audio.

NotebookLM is a separate product from Gemini, but the two share underlying technology and are increasingly integrated into Google's broader AI ecosystem.

Gemini 2.0 Flash (December 2024)

In December 2024, Google launched Gemini 2.0 Flash, opening the Gemini 2.0 generation. The 2.0 Flash model brought several advances:

- **Multimodal output.** 2.0 Flash could generate text and images natively and produce synthesized speech — a true multimodal input/output model.
- **Improved agentic capabilities.** The model was better at acting on behalf of users — navigating websites, executing multi-step tasks, and interacting with tools and APIs.
- **Faster performance.** True to the Flash philosophy, 2.0 Flash was noticeably faster than its predecessor.

Google positioned Gemini 2.0 as the foundation for its "agentic AI" vision — AI that does not just answer questions but accomplishes tasks.

Deep Research (Early 2025)

Deep Research launched as a Gemini Advanced feature that performs multi-step web research autonomously. Rather than a single search-grounded response, Deep Research:

1. Analyzes your research question
2. Creates a research plan
3. Conducts multiple web searches across different angles
4. Reads and synthesizes information from many sources
5. Produces a comprehensive, cited report

The result is a document that would take a human researcher hours to compile, produced in minutes. Deep Research was a real step toward agentic AI — Gemini was not just answering a question but executing a multi-step workflow.

For students, professionals, and researchers, Deep Research quickly became one of Gemini's most valued features. It bridged the gap between "ask a question, get an answer" and "here is a fully researched briefing."

Gemini 2.5 Pro (March 2025)

Gemini 2.5 Pro arrived as Google's most capable model to date, with a headline feature: native "thinking." The model was designed to reason through problems step by step before responding, the way a person might work through a complex problem on paper before giving a final answer.

Key improvements in 2.5 Pro:

- **Extended reasoning (Deep Think).** The model could spend much more time thinking through complex problems, dramatically improving performance on math, science, coding, and multi-step analysis.
- **Improved coding ability.** 2.5 Pro topped several coding benchmarks, demonstrating strong performance across many languages and task types.
- **Better instruction following.** Notably more precise on complex, multi-part instructions.
- **1 million+ token context window.** Kept the massive context window of its predecessors while using it more effectively.

Gemini 2.5 Pro established Google as a serious contender for the most capable AI model, competing directly with OpenAI's frontier models and Anthropic's Claude.

Gemini 2.5 Flash (May 2025)

Following the pattern, Google released Gemini 2.5 Flash as the fast, efficient counterpart to 2.5 Pro. Flash 2.5 brought reasoning improvements to the everyday tier:

- Thinking capabilities at a fraction of the cost and latency of 2.5 Pro
- Strong performance on common tasks like writing, summarization, and code generation

- The new default model for most Gemini interactions

The gap between Flash and Pro narrowed with each generation. For most everyday tasks, Flash 2.5 was more than capable, and many users only reached for Pro on particularly complex reasoning or analysis.

Canvas: Collaborative Content Creation (2025)

Canvas brought a side-by-side editing workspace to Gemini — a persistent panel alongside the conversation for iteratively refining documents and code. Instead of getting a response, copying it elsewhere, editing it, and pasting it back, you could work on content directly within Gemini.

Canvas followed similar features in ChatGPT and Claude, but Google's implementation tied into the Workspace ecosystem. You could start a document in Canvas and export directly to Google Docs, or begin a coding project and keep refining it in place.

Google Workspace Integration Expansion (2024–2026)

Across 2024 and into 2025–2026, Google steadily expanded Gemini's integration across Google Workspace:

- **Gmail.** Gemini gained the ability to draft emails, summarize threads, suggest responses, and search across your inbox contextually.
- **Google Docs.** "Help me write" evolved into a capable drafting and editing assistant that could understand and modify entire documents.
- **Google Sheets.** Gemini added natural-language formula generation, data analysis, chart creation, and the ability to answer questions about your spreadsheet data.
- **Google Slides.** Gemini could generate entire presentations from a topic or outline, build individual slides, and suggest design improvements.
- **Google Meet.** AI-powered meeting summaries, note-taking, and real-time translations.
- **Google Drive.** Gemini could search and summarize across your Drive files, pulling context from multiple documents.

Workspace integration was Google's biggest competitive advantage over standalone AI tools. Because Gemini could see your actual emails, documents, and data (with appropriate permissions), it could provide contextually relevant assistance that no external tool could match.

Gemini Code Assist Expansion (2025)

Google expanded Gemini Code Assist, its AI coding assistant for developers, with deeper IDE integration and stronger code generation. Code Assist became available in VS Code, JetBrains IDEs, and Cloud Workstations, providing:

- Inline code completion
- Multi-file context awareness
- Code explanation and documentation generation
- Bug detection and fix suggestions
- Test generation

For developers, Code Assist became a legitimate competitor to GitHub Copilot and other AI coding tools.

Gemini 3 Pro (November 18, 2025)

Google launched Gemini 3 Pro on November 18, 2025, opening the 3-era of Gemini models. Gemini 3 Pro raised the bar across the board: stronger reasoning, more reliable instruction-following, and improved performance on coding and multimodal benchmarks. It retained the 1M+ token context window introduced in earlier generations and brought tighter integration with the rest of Google's stack.

Gemini 3 Flash (December 2025)

Google followed quickly with Gemini 3 Flash, the fast, cost-efficient sibling to 3 Pro. Flash 3 became the new default in the Gemini app, replacing 2.5 Flash. The 3-era pattern echoed earlier generations: a flagship Pro model for the hardest tasks, a Flash model that handles the vast majority of everyday work, and a continuing narrowing of the quality gap between the two.

Gemini 3 Deep Think and Gemini 3.1 Pro Preview (February 2026)

In February 2026, Google introduced **Gemini 3 Deep Think** – a dedicated extended-reasoning mode that takes Deep Think substantially further, allocating more compute to reasoning before producing an answer. It targets the hardest math, logic, coding, and analytical problems, where accuracy matters more than speed.

The same month, Google shipped a **Gemini 3.1 Pro preview** (February 19, 2026), iterating on 3 Pro with refinements to reasoning quality and instruction-following.

Gemini 3.1 Flash-Lite (March 3, 2026)

Google released **Gemini 3.1 Flash-Lite** on March 3, 2026 – the most efficient and lowest-latency model in the 3-era lineup. Flash-Lite targets high-volume, latency-sensitive workloads, particularly through the API: chatbots, content moderation, classification, and similar tasks where cost and speed dominate.

U.S. Copyright Office, Part 2 (January 2025)

In January 2025, the U.S. Copyright Office published Part 2 of its AI report. The headline holdings: prompts alone do not provide sufficient human control to make AI output copyrightable, but works are protectable when human authorship is perceptible in the output or when a human creatively arranges or modifies AI-generated material. The Office concluded that existing law was sufficient and did not call for new legislation. We discuss this guidance and its practical implications in Chapter 27.

Timeline Summary

Date	Milestone
Feb 2024	Bard rebrands to Gemini; Gemini 1.5 Pro launches with 1M token context
May 2024	Gemini 1.5 Flash launches

Date	Milestone
Mid-2024	Gems (custom assistants) launch; Imagen 3 powers image generation
Late 2024	NotebookLM Audio Overviews launch
Dec 2024	Gemini 2.0 Flash launches with multimodal output
Jan 2025	U.S. Copyright Office publishes Part 2 of its AI report
Early 2025	Deep Research launches for Gemini Advanced
Mar 2025	Gemini 2.5 Pro launches with Deep Think (extended reasoning)
May 2025	Imagen 4 family launches (May 20); Gemini 2.5 Flash launches; Gemini Advanced renamed to Google AI Pro at I/O; Google AI Ultra introduced
2025	Canvas launches; Workspace integration continues expanding; Google AI Plus introduced as entry-level paid tier
Nov 2025	Gemini 3 Pro launches (Nov 18)
Dec 2025	Gemini 3 Flash launches; becomes default in the Gemini app
Feb 2026	Gemini 3 Deep Think mode launches; Gemini 3.1 Pro preview ships (Feb 19)
Mar 2026	Gemini 3.1 Flash-Lite launches (Mar 3)
2024–2026	Continuous expansion of Gemini across Google Workspace, Android, and Google Cloud

Looking Ahead

Google has signaled that the trajectory will continue: more capable models, deeper integration into Google products, stronger agentic capabilities, an expanding ecosystem of tools and APIs. The pace shows no signs of slowing.

For updates beyond what this appendix covers, check The Keyword (blog.google), the Google DeepMind blog (deepmind.google), and the resources in Appendix F.

Appendix F: Resources and Further Reading

This appendix collects the most useful resources for staying current with Gemini, deepening your AI knowledge, and finding the broader community.

Official Google AI Resources

Gemini - Gemini web interface: gemini.google.com - Gemini Help Center: support.google.com/gemini - Gemini release notes and updates: blog.google/technology/ai

Google DeepMind - Google DeepMind blog: deepmind.google/blog - Research publications: deepmind.google/research

NotebookLM - NotebookLM: notebooklm.google.com - NotebookLM Help Center: support.google.com/notebooklm

Developer Resources - Google AI Studio: aistudio.google.com - Gemini API documentation: ai.google.dev - Vertex AI: cloud.google.com/vertex-ai - Google Cloud AI blog: cloud.google.com/blog/products/ai-machine-learning

Google Workspace and Gemini - Gemini for Google Workspace: workspace.google.com/solutions/ai - Workspace admin help for Gemini: support.google.com/a/answer/13623588 - Google Workspace Updates blog: workspaceupdates.googleblog.com

Privacy and Safety - Google AI Principles: ai.google/responsibility/principles - Google Privacy Policy: policies.google.com/privacy - Google Account Activity Controls: myactivity.google.com - SynthID information: deepmind.google/technologies/synthid

---

Community and Forums

Google Communities - Google Gemini Community Forum: Accessible through the Google Help Center. A good place to ask questions, report issues, and see what other users are running into. - Google Workspace Community: For questions about Gemini in Workspace products.

Reddit - r/Bard (now largely focused on Gemini): Active community discussing Gemini features, tips, and issues. - r/artificial: Broader AI discussion that frequently covers Gemini developments. - r/GoogleGeminiAI: Dedicated Gemini discussion community.

YouTube - Google's official YouTube channels post Gemini tutorials and feature announcements. - Search "Gemini AI tutorial" for community-created walkthroughs and tips.

X (Twitter) - Follow @Google, @GoogleAI, and @GoogleDeepMind for official announcements. - The AI community on X is active and often surfaces Gemini tips, tricks, and news before they appear elsewhere.

Newsletters and Blogs Worth Following

Staying current with AI requires good information sources. These newsletters and blogs consistently deliver:

- **The Keyword (Google's official blog)** — First-party announcements about Gemini and all Google products.
- **The Verge AI section** — Accessible technology journalism covering AI developments including Gemini.
- **Ars Technica AI coverage** — Technically detailed reporting on AI models and capabilities.
- **Ben's Bites** — Popular daily AI newsletter that covers major developments across all AI platforms.
- **The Neuron** — Daily AI newsletter with concise summaries of the most important developments.
- **TLDR AI** — Brief, daily roundup of AI news, papers, and tools.

- **Import AI** — Weekly newsletter focused on AI research and policy, written by Jack Clark (co-founder of Anthropic).
- **One Useful Thing** — Ethan Mollick's Substack on practical AI use, especially in education and work.

Books for Deeper Learning

If this book sparked an interest in understanding AI more deeply, these titles are excellent next steps:

Understanding AI Concepts - *Co-Intelligence: Living and Working with AI* by Ethan Mollick — Practical, thoughtful guidance on integrating AI into work and life. - *The Alignment Problem* by Brian Christian — A deep dive into the challenges of making AI systems behave as intended.

AI History and Context - *Genius Makers* by Cade Metz — The story of the people and companies (including Google/DeepMind) who built modern AI. - *The Coming Wave* by Mustafa Suleyman — Written by a DeepMind co-founder, this explores where AI and other technologies are heading.

Technical Understanding (Accessible) - *AI 2041* by Kai-Fu Lee and Chen Qiufan — Science fiction stories paired with technical explanations of the AI concepts involved.

Companion Titles from Finnoybu Press

This book is part of a series of definitive AI guides from Finnoybu Press. If you use other AI platforms alongside Gemini, these companion titles offer the same comprehensive, practical coverage:

ChatGPT: The Definitive Guide (2026 Edition) The complete guide to OpenAI's ChatGPT — from first conversations through Custom GPTs, the GPT Store, DALL-E image generation, Advanced Voice Mode, and professional workflows. If you use both Gemini and ChatGPT, this book helps you understand where each tool excels.

ChatGPT: The Power User Guide (2026 Edition) For users who already know the basics and want to push ChatGPT to its limits. Advanced prompting, API integration, automation, Custom GPTs development, and expert-level workflows.

Claude: The Definitive Guide (2026 Edition) The complete guide to Anthropic's Claude — covering Claude's unique strengths in analysis, writing, and reasoning, along with Artifacts, Projects, and the full range of Claude's capabilities.

Claude Code: The Power User Guide (2026 Edition) A deep dive into Claude's coding capabilities and the Claude Code CLI — for developers and technical users who want to maximize Claude's potential for software development.

Gemini: The Advanced Guide (2026 Edition) Advanced techniques and workflows for experienced Gemini users — API integration, advanced prompting strategies, automation, and expert-level workflows that push Gemini to its limits.

All Finnoybu Press titles are available wherever books are sold. Visit our website for the latest catalog and updates.

Publisher Information

Finnoybu Press - Website: press.finnoybu.org - Email: press@finnoybu.org

For corrections, suggestions, or feedback on this book, write to press@finnoybu.org. We read every message and fold reader feedback into future editions.

A Note on Links and Resources

The AI landscape changes fast. Websites reorganize, products rebrand, URLs shift. If a link here no longer works, search for the resource name directly — the content likely still exists at a new URL.

This appendix reflects resources available as of May 2026. For current links and additional resources found after publication, check the companion page for this book at press.finnoybu.org.

www.ingramcontent.com/pod-product-compliance
Lightning Source LLC
LaVergne TN
LVHW060024210926
848481LV00013B/3783